The Study of Religious Experience

THE STUDY OF RELIGIOUS EXPERIENCE

Approaches and Methodologies

Edited by Bettina E. Schmidt

SHEFFIELD UK   BRISTOL CT

Published by Equinox Publishing Ltd.

UK: Office 415, The Workstation, 15 Paternoster Row, Sheffield S1 2BX
USA: ISD, 70 Enterprise Drive, Bristol, CT 06010

www.equinoxpub.com

First published 2016

ISBN   978 1 78179 256 8   (hardback)
       978 1 78179 257 5   (paperback)

British Library Cataloguing-in-Publication Data

A catalogue record for this book is available from the British Library.

Library of Congress Cataloging-in-Publication Data

Names: Schmidt, Bettina E., editor.
Title: The study of religious experience : approaches and methodologies /
   edited by Bettina E. Schmidt.
Description: Bristol, CT : Equinox Publishng Ltd, 2016. | Includes bibliographical
   references and index.
Identifiers: LCCN 2015042028 (print) | LCCN 2016016974 (ebook) |
ISBN 9781781792568 (hb) | ISBN 9781781792575 (pb) | ISBN 9781781794180
(e-PDF) | ISBN 9781781794197 (e-epub)
Subjects: LCSH: Experience (Religion)
Classification: LCC BL53 .S773 2016 (print) | LCC BL53 (ebook) | DDC
   204/.207--dc23
LC record available at https://lccn.loc.gov/2015042028

Typeset by CA Typesetting Ltd, Sheffield, UK

Printed and bound in the UK by Lightning Source UK Ltd, Milton Keynes and
Lightning Source Inc, La Vergne, TN

Contents

Section Three:
Theological and Philosophical Approaches
to the Study of Religious Experience

Section Four:
Reflections on Types of Religious Experience

Foreword

It is often said but not always put into practice, that the definition and academic study of religious and spiritual experiences needs, indeed more than that, *demands* both a variety of approaches and that they be inter-disciplinary. This variety needs to take into account a range of cultural, spiritual, and religious traditions, as well as the many different academic methods that might be and have been used to study them. The term 'academic' needs to be emphasized because Alister Hardy's intention was to set up a Unit (now Centre) for the academic study of what he called 'the spiritual nature of man'.

The introduction to this volume acknowledges the heritage of the Religious Experience Research Centre that Hardy founded, but in the context of the critical history of academic approaches both before and since his time is therefore in itself a very useful initial survey of these. But the book takes the issues and their discussion even further. It includes actual examples of approaches from anthropology; philosophy, the study of religions (which is in itself polymethodic), theology, biblical studies, and history.

The three sections deal with anthropological approaches, methodological challenges, and different forms and variations of religious experience. Each of the chapters within these sections not only emphasises a different methodological approach but looks at a different culture, religion, or theme as appropriate and focuses on the experiences of ordinary people. The range in further detail is impressive. Ethnography is used to approach the study of the paranormal, out of ethnology and neurophenomenology comes a cross-cultural examination of the universality of religious experience, fieldwork done in the Valley of the Dawn in Brazil considers the way that experience is embodied, and cultural-linguistic challenges in relation to texts dealing with near death and out of the body experiences provides a challenge to the theory that experience is culturally-linguistically generated. There is then a chapter arguing for the term 'religious experience' being deictic; that is, its meaning is dependent on the context. This is followed by three chapters dealing with the many faces of religious experience in the internet's cyberspace and in a religionless spirituality expressed in music. The three authors of the final section look at different issues in the study of religious experience in Christianity from theological perspectives, recent New Testament scholarship, and a re-evaluation of some philosophical positions.

This brief overview indicates the depth and originality of this collection of essays and with them the continuing value of the rigorous academic study of religious experience now thriving under Bettina E. Schmidt's direction at the University of Wales Trinity Saint David, Lampeter. It is a rich and welcome addition to the literature that has something for anyone with a serious interest in this area of investigation.

Peggy Morgan
Mansfield College, University of Oxford
RERC Director 1996–2002

Acknowledgements

I wish to thank the Alister Hardy Trust for its ongoing support of the Religious Experience Research Centre (RERC), Lampeter. I also want to thank everyone involved in the RERC at the University of Wales Trinity Saint David in Lampeter and in particular, Jean Matthews, Thomas Pitchford, and my colleagues in the Faculty of Humanities and Performing Arts, who contribute willingly to the RERC Lampeter and support our activities.

Bettina E. Schmidt

Introduction

Bettina E. Schmidt

Sir Alister Hardy, a renowned scientist, approached the complex field of religious and spiritual experience from a similar disciplined and scientific manner with which he approached natural science. However, he soon reached the boundaries of science and religion (Hardy 1966: 9-10). In *The Divine Flame* he explained his approach to religion as a naturalist and aimed to conduct a systematic study of the religious phenomenon. His first step was therefore to gather data by asking people from the public to send him accounts of first-hand experiences with spiritual or religious powers. While the response from adverts in religious magazines was weak, he received an overwhelming response after adverts containing the so-called Hardy Question (Have you ever been aware of or influenced by a presence or power, whether you call it God or not, which is different from your everyday self?) appeared in newspapers such as the Guardian, Observer, Times and Daily Mail. People approached him with personal accounts of experiences that they sometimes had never before shared with others (Rankin 2008: 3). Encouraged by the massive response, Hardy established in 1969 the Religious Experience Research Centre (RERC) that has been since then at the forefront of the academic study of religious experiences.[1]

The RERC archive, which is now located at the University of Wales Trinity Saint David, contains more than 6000 accounts with personal descriptions of a religious or spiritual experience, and the number is growing every year. While most of the accounts are the responses to the Hardy Question sent to the RERC by people of various faiths (or not) in the UK, the archive now also contains collections of accounts of Near-Death Experiences (NDE), Afterlife experiences, experiences with angels, and experiences of people outside the UK (e.g., China and India). Among the accounts at the RERC are experiences from ordinary people of different beliefs and commitments, including agnostics. Common is the subjective nature of the experience that often took place in solitude. One of the first accounts describes, for instance, the uplifting experience the person felt in a hotel room in London in 1948 (RERC 000001[2]). Another refers to an experience in the West Indies, during a walk through the hills of St Kitts:

> As I sat on a low wall opposite a beautiful tree covered with pink blossom[s], thrown into relief by the high hill behind it, I was suddenly made aware of my surroundings in a manner difficult to describe in words. The tree became vibrant, 'real' (in the sense that the 'burning bush' did to Moses in the O.T.) and I was transported into what I can only term 'reality', and was filled with a great surge of joy (i.e., like C.S. Lewis's 'Surprised by Joy'). This was fundamental and I was 'caught up into it' and was a part of it. I felt a great sense of awe and reverence, permeated by the presence of a power which was completely real and in which I had my part to play. I knew that all was well and that all things were working together for good. (RERC 000011)

This experience took place when the other members of the group had left and the experience had a rest. Its references to Christian texts such as the Bible and C. S. Lewis are not unusual for people growing up in Western societies and are quite often included in the accounts. Biblical references frequently serve as a means to make sense of the experiences, as people often did not discuss them with anyone for a long time after they took place. However, not all accounts are interpreted within a Christian framework; a common feature in most accounts is the sense of uniqueness of the experience, that it is not possible to repeat it, and that it changed one's perception and experience of life:

> I decided to climb to the top, have a rest and see what the view was like. I was in no positive mood at all—neither happy nor sad—just simply musing about people, events, the way one does. I judged it to be about noon (I didn't have my watch with me) and it was cloudless and very hot; so hot in fact that I had to keep shifting my position every minute or so because of the racks. I was idly looking at the snow-capped Pyrenees in the distance when suddenly the oddest feeling came over me. I can only describe it as a sort of harmonious peacefulness. I could not figure out why I was suddenly so happy. But I do remember saying to myself that everything, me, the mountains, the rocks I sat on, the trees is the distance, that everything was is its right place, and that there could be no other way than this. Coupled with this I was suddenly aware of how quiet it had become; previous to this there had been a lot of crickets and dragonflies buzzing around, but now nothing, as if they had been arrested in mid-flight. I then had the craziest notion of all; I felt that if I had a mind to, if I wanted to make the effort, I could actually reach out and touch the mountain tops thirty or forty miles away! I was so convinced of this that I had trouble talking myself out of it; the reason being that if I did reach out and touch the snow covered peaks I would somehow break the spell, the stillness of which I seemed to be the epicentre. This strange feeling must have lasted at least an hour or more because when I did eventually move, my jeans were too hot to touch and my shins were burnt but I had not noticed this at all. I must add lastly, that I had not been drinking or taking drugs of kind when this event occurred. The next day, naturally I returned to the same spot at the same time. The weather conditions were

similar, and nothing had changed. But although I stayed for nearly three hours (this time I had my watch with me), the experience mystical or otherwise, was not repeated. (RERC 004989)

The study of religious experience is still in its infancy, despite the vast amount of data at hand and some ground-breaking work on Near Death Experiences by Peter and Elisabeth Fenwick (1995) and Penny Santori (2008), among others. In addition to debating how to approach religious experience, scholars cannot even agree on a common definition. Hardy defined religious experience as 'a deep awareness of a benevolent non-physical power which appears to be partly or wholly beyond, and far greater than, the individual self' (Hardy 1979: 1). Such an experience can take place in solitude or as part of a communal ritual—either firmly linked to a specific religious tradition or not at all—that results in dramatic movements or is restricted to internal emotions. And here lies the problem. We can amass data of personal accounts, but in the end they remain subjective narratives of what *might* have happened.

The key problem with the study of religious experience is that the experience is felt internally even if it is manifests externally (e.g., in possession rituals). Religious experience is usually described as private and unavailable 'for empirical (that is, sensory) confirmation' even when later these accounts become 'very public and therefore available for empirical confirmation' (McCutcheon 2012: 8). For the theologian Rudolf Otto (1859–1937), the internal experience was the key to the understanding of religion. He described the idea of a pure religious experience as *mysterium tremendum et fascinans* and wrote in a letter: 'In whatever language they resound, these most exalted words that have ever come from human lips always grip one in the depths of the soul, with a mighty shudder exciting and calling into play the mystery of the other world latent therein' (in Turner and Mackenzie 1977: 4). Otto insisted that religious experience is unique compared with other forms of experiences and feelings and that we need specific tools for its understanding. Otto even disqualified scholars who never had such an experience from its study (see Otto 1917). However, his position is at odds with the academic need to explain and analyse all aspects of human experience and actions in an objective, scientific way. Consequently, Otto is widely disregarded by academia, although he is not the only one with such an essentialist approach to the study of religious experience. Ninian Smart, for instance, writes that 'religious experience involves some kind of "perception" of the invisible world, or involves a perception that some visible person or thing is a manifestation of the invisible world' (Smart 1984: 15). These perceptions of the invisible world are as subjective as Otto's experience of the *numinous*, for which empirical evidence is impossible to provide. While Otto can provide access to an understanding of the perspective of people experiencing it, the essentialist nature of his definition of religious experience makes it impossible to confirm the experience in a systematic or naturalistic manner.

Russell McCutcheon argues vehemently against the essentialist approach and writes that the assumption that religion cannot be explained only felt is not academic (2012: 11). He even disagrees with the assumption that religious experiences are internal and autonomous, disconnected by the mundane world. He insists that they are universally shared by others (2012: 9). Referring to Wittgenstein, McCutcheon writes:

> To put it another way, the ability to have an experience, much less to report that one has had one, may itself be evidence of one's prior participation in a certain sort of social world, one comprised of specific rules of other social worlds. What some might understand as the supposed immediacy of experience-present may actually be but an internalized residue of an earlier social world (its calculus), invented by others and that, through the actions of others, has been imprinted on us—or better put, *within* us. (McCutcheon 2012: 8)

The opposite positions that are represented here by Otto and McCutcheon are at the heart of any debate around the study of religious experience, and also reflected in this book.

Some scholars approach the topic of religious experience in a more descriptive way by categorizing types of religious experience (e.g., Franks-Davis 1989: 33-65). Stepping aside from any discussion of the essentialist nature of religious experience, some even decline any discussion about whether or not these experiences can be described as religious, even if experienced by agnostics or atheists. David Hay, for instance, decides to ignore his interviewees' refusals to categorize their experiences as religious and argues that 'it would be more correct to say that it is a type of experience which is commonly given a religious interpretation' (Hay 1982: 162-63). He overlooks the significance of the beliefs of the individuals who reported these experiences (Day 2011: 113). However, labelling something establishes a power relationship between the scholar and the person experiencing it—and this relationship is usually unequal.

Ann Taves (1999) even regards the interplay between experiencing religion and explaining experience as the central methodological problem in this field. She highlights that many of the labels used by academics of different disciplines (and in different historical periods) to describe and categorize the means of communication between the human and spiritual worlds are challenged by the actors themselves since they 'obscure the subjective experience of the native actor' (Taves 1999: 9). Her argument is to take the religious connotation out of the equation by moving away 'from single terms to more extended descriptive statements that identify common features' and are acceptable across disciplines and by the subjects themselves (Taves 1999: 8). Her approach to include in the interpretation the positions of people experiencing religion and of people explaining experience shows a new direction of the study of religious experience, beyond the debate of essentialism. Instead of disregarding the explanations of the people having experiences Taves urges scholars to include them. In her study of Anglo-American Protestants and ex-Protestants (1999) Taves even includes a third position, which she calls 'the mediating tradition' (1999: 348) because people experiencing these involuntary acts do not live in isolation from the surrounding discourses. She writes that 'the mediators believed that the way in which they accessed religion was scientific rather than simply a matter of faith and that the character of their methods legitimated the religious reality of that which they discovered as a result of their methods' (Taves 1999: 349).

Taves' threefold typology results accordingly in the understanding of religious experience in terms of skill development. Seemingly involuntary acts that include uncontrolled bodily movements, spontaneous vocalizations, unusual sensory experiences, and alterations of consciousness and/or memory—her definition of religions experience—are no longer disregarded as symptoms of mental weakness or an expression of false religion. In her later monograph, *Religious Experience Reconsidered* (2009), she consequently suggests describing the experiences labelled under 'religious experience' as 'experiences people consider special' within a broader field (Taves 2009: 12). Nonetheless, she does not expand her approach to all kinds of experiences as for instance, Timothy Fitzgerald criticises but remains 'within the already conventionally established contours of religious studies' (2010: 297). Fitzgerald would like Taves to expand her work outside the realm of religious studies and to include, for instance, the justice system or even the experiences of scientists such as Newton and Darwin. Their experiences can also be 'deemed special' as Fitzgerald argues.

Moreover, while Gotama Shakyamuni's insight about the emptiness of *dhammas* has been examined under the label of 'study of religious experience', no one has looked into Newton's insight about gravity: 'Why has this insight, and the consequent theorization of a path of carefully monitored empirical observation, been classified differently from the insights of Newton et al., that is as "religious" rather than "scientific"?' (Fitzgerald 2010: 299). Taves does not go this far, however, and insists on 'experiences deemed religious' (2009: 15).

Taves often refers in her work to William James and in particular his key book, *Varieties of Religious Experience*, published more than one hundred years ago and based on his Gifford Lectures in Edinburgh in 1901/1902. In this book he highlights the importance of personal experiences. He even argues that the type of person someone is determines the form of religious experience this person will experience. Most important, however, is that James sees religious experience not as something different from ordinary experiences or contradicting the laws of nature. Although he often refers to experiences of founders of religious traditions, he insists that the maintenance of religious traditions relies on a constant process of revalidation that happens when other members have further personal experiences, similar to the founder of the tradition. James argues that someone's beliefs and knowledge influences the experience and also the way someone relates to it; for instance, whether someone interprets the experience as demonic or divine depends on the context in which someone lives.

Another important factor is pre-existing belief systems, for instance whether specific elements (e.g., seeing a light in a near-death experience) are regarded as important and will be narrated, or as unimportant and soon forgotten. Hence, aspects that do not conform to the pre-existing belief system of the person experiencing it will be neglected in narratives about it. Following James, I argue (Schmidt 2016) that we need to understand the set of beliefs and values that provide the cultural framework in which the experience is embedded.

When transferring the study of religious experience to a totally different cultural context, such as China, the complexity of the problem with terminology becomes even more visible. Yen-zen Tsai, for instance, argues strongly that we cannot study religious experiences 'with an uncritical, universalist presupposition' (in Tsai and Kuan 2010: 9). He urges us to consider the contextual specificity whenever we study religious experiences.[3] Two of his project collaborators write that because of the Western bias in the discourse of religious experience, 'the analytical framework has to be culturally sensitive and aware of contextual meanings of "religious experience" when it is applied to various cultures and religions... Whether an experience is deemed religious depends upon the interpretation of the experience. It is finally judged by its cultural-linguistic community' (Tsai and Kuan 2010: 20). Consequently, religious experience is defined in the Taiwan research project as 'the experience of encountering alterity deemed religious, mystical, transcendental, extraordinary or anomalous' (Tsai and Kuan 2010: 22), an all-embracing and consequently vague definition.

Yet, 'having religiosity as a constituent of culture does not produce an equal concept of religious experience' (Dickie 2007: 9). We need to acknowledge not only the differences among religious traditions but also the internal differences of each group. It is important, as Maria Amelia Schmidt Dickie writes, to locate the study of experiences firmly inside a social scientific framework:

> From a strict Social Anthropology methodological and theoretical perspective, culture not only creates names but conditions their understanding. From this we assume that the meaning conveyed by the expression 'religious experience' will vary according to the culture in which the person addressed is immersed. (Dickie 2007: 6)

Dickie was concerned mainly with the understanding of the term 'religious experience' for her own research in Brazil. The problem was, 'There is a literal translation of the expression in Portuguese. However, it does not guarantee an adequate translation of its meaning' (Dickie 2007: 6). For this reason, she conducted a pilot study to test terminology.

While terminology has also been a problem with my own research on spirit possession in Brazil, where I had to discover first a term that embraced what the people involved in the practice felt, important at this point is Dickie's wider methodological position. In the tradition of Hardy (1966: 30), this volume embraces firmly the academic nature of the study of religious experience. Hardy argues that although it is not possible to study the emotional side of religious experience in the same scientific (here: quantitative and experimental) manner as the reaction of atoms and electrons, 'we can certainly use it for the systematic study of the *external evidence* of the behaviour of men and women who appear to be moved by such experience' (Hardy 1966: 33). And this is exactly the aim of this book, although in a wider manner that embraces not only the quantitative method but also qualitative, ethnographic, and hermeneutical approaches.

The authors represent a range of academic disciplines such as anthropology, philosophy, study of religions, theology, biblical studies, and history. Each chapter showcases a specific approach linked to original research undertaken by these renowned experts. A common aspect of these chapters is that the focus is on religious experience of ordinary people and not restricted to the experiences of religious leaders or founders of religious traditions. However, the method and approach each author presents differ.

Fiona Bowie opens the presentation with her historical and methodological reflections on the study of the paranormal. Beginning with the role of experience in the anthropological study of religion, Bowie presents an informative overview, from E. B. Tylor and Andrew Lang to the ontological turn in the 21st century. Her overview leads to the introduction of a form of cognitive, empathetic engagement that is based on openness to the other, critical awareness of one's own perspective, and reluctance to move too quickly to explanation. Bowie's ethnographic approach to the study of religious experience highlights the significance of experience and puts the interpretation of experience at the core of the academic enterprise.

Bowie's overview is followed by Michael Winkelman's chapter that discusses cross-cultural approaches within a biological framework. Winkelman begins with the ethnological approach and shows that it enables scholars to study the similarities in the reports of religious experience across people, time, and cultures. He then shifts to the neurophenomenological approach and argues that it establishes homologies of the structure and content of these experiences with brain functions and provides a basis for understanding the significance in relation to human nature. Hence, Winkelman's approach combines cognitive and biological understanding of religion. Both chapters together represent a spectrum of approaches within anthropology. While Bowie refers to the significance of ethnographic observations, Winkelman proposes a cross-cultural approach that demonstrates the universality of religious experiences. Each chapter shows the differences in the approaches to religious experience within anthropology by highlighting ethnography on the one side and universality on the other.

Bowie and Winkelman set the tone for the next chapters that present specific case studies linked to the study of religious experience but using different methods. Emily Pierini presents in her chapter the fieldwork method in the study of religious experience. Based on her ethnographic fieldwork in the Spiritualist Christian Order Vale do Amanhecer (Valley of the Dawn) in Brazil, Pierini addresses the question of researching a particular kind of religious experience that arises from phenomena of spirit mediumship. It discusses the implications of the ethnographic method, tackling particularly the engagement of the researcher's body in the field as a methodological tool for approaching a practice that is grounded in embodied forms of encounter with the sacred.

The following chapter by Gregory Shushan in this section discusses the cultural-linguistic challenges when studying Near-Death and Out-of-Body Experiences (NDEs and OBEs). Shushan argues that these experiences can be found around the world in a variety of texts. However, despite local phenomenological differences, there is an essential thematic and structural continuity to the accounts cross-culturally. His chapter challenges the thesis that religions are culturally unique and that all experience is culturally-linguistically generated.

The last chapter by me in this section presents a new framework for thinking of religious experience. Opposing a generalising perspective, I argue for provincialising religious experience. Instead of regarding religious experience as a universal category, I suggest seeing it as deictic term that allows the contextualisation of each experience.

The next section presents two different approaches to the study of religious experience. Robert Pope explores theology's ambivalence towards religious experience as a particular set of distinguishable experiences. While experiences have been crucial in Christian history, Pope argues that they have not been core in the formation of systematic theology. The other chapter in this section is by Tristan Nash, a philosopher of religion. He shows that traditional arguments focus upon the origin or the source of the religious experience as proof of or evidence for the existence of God. Alternative assessments highlight the value of what is revealed by the religious experience in terms of quality of the experience, its philosophical coherence, and its moral value for the subject of the experience. Nash, however, challenges these positions and argues for a third model in which a proof for God is offered not in terms of the source of the experience, but rather in terms of what is revealed by it.

The last section presents three areas of religious experience that are often overlooked in its study, despite their importance. While each chapter discusses very different mediums of religious experience—the internet, scriptures and music—each author widens the spectrum of religious experience. Instead of restricting religious experience to only private experiences narrated in personal accounts, these chapters show the dynamic nature of religious experience and its many faces. The first chapter in this section is by Catrin Williams and discusses the significance of religious experience in recent New Testament scholarship, with special focus on the Gospel of John. She examines in her chapter the challenges and opportunities posed by attempts to uncover the experiential dimensions of the beliefs and practices of early Christian communities.

The following chapter by June Boyce-Tillman looks at the link between spirituality and music. She examines in particular the development of the area of spirituality throughout the twentieth century. Embarking from Nietzsche's assertion of the death of God, Boyce-Tillman examines the place of religious experience in philosophies of the arts. She ends with offering the possibility of a religionless spirituality that is reflected in music.

The last chapter by Gary Bunt discusses religious experience in cyberspace. He reflects on the new technological developments of the 21st century and how they impact on religious experience. Even the most reluctant or technophobic agents of diverse forms of religious belief and expression in diverse cultures have found a place online. Bunt argues that as much as being an agent of change, religious expression on the internet may also engender conformity and tradition, especially within specific micro-areas of religious interests driven by notions of membership.

The chapters demonstrate the vast range of approaches to the study of religious and spiritual experience. Focusing on specific case studies, each chapter presents a unique way of study that is so difficult to define but continues to fascinate.

Short Biographical Note
Bettina E. Schmidt is a cultural anthropologist, professor of study of religions at the University of Wales Trinity Saint David, and Director of the Alister Hardy Religious Experience Research Centre in Lampeter.

Notes

1. The original name was 'Religious Experience Research Unit' although 'Unit' was changed later to 'Centre'.

2. All accounts referenced with a six-digit number following the acronym RERC are from the Archive of the Alister Hardy Religious Experience Research Centre, University of Wales Trinity Saint David, Lampeter, UK.

3. Consequently, *Religious Experience in Contemporary Taiwan,* a research project under the guidance of Yen-zen Tsai, uses the concept of religious experiences in a very broad way but embedded in Taiwanese culture and society.

Section One:
Anthropological Approaches to the Study of Religious Experience

How to Study Religious Experience: Historical and Methodological Reflections on the Study of the Paranormal

Fiona Bowie

The World Made Strange—Personal Encounters with Non-ordinary Reality

Imagine for a minute that you are lying in bed, perhaps dreaming, or with an intractable problem playing on your mind. You decide to get up, but as you glance down you see your somnambulant body still lying on the bed. If this is your first such experience, the chances are that the shock will wake you up and you—by which I mean the thinking, conscious bit of you—will suddenly return to your physical body. If you are a bit more adventurous, you might decide to explore your surroundings and take a look around the room or even float out of the window into the next room or down the stairs. If, on the other hand, you have been cultivating out-of-body travel, perhaps using some of the many recommended techniques,[1] you may seize the opportunity to venture further afield. You might choose to explore distant cities or to travel to other planes of consciousness. If this is a spontaneous experience, or even if you have been surreptitiously training for it, the chances are that you will not tell anyone. You may yourself wonder if you dreamt or imagined the whole experience, or fear the onset of some psychotic or neurological disorder. You probably won't categorize your experience as religious unless you met an angel or some other holy figure in your travels. It may, however, lead to some quite profound thoughts about the nature of consciousness. That is, if you don't put the whole episode down to over-indulgence at dinner the night before. If you are cultivating the experience of out-of-body travel or are particularly adept, you may also find that you can leave your body while fully awake. Children who suffer repeated abuse often learn to dissociate their consciousness from their physical bodies (Dalenberg et al. 2012). A sudden shock, such as an imminent collision or fall, may also momentarily shift one's conscious perspective outside the body.[2]

What if, on the other hand, you dream about a departed loved one? Maybe you spend some time together walking and talking. The person might seem to be physically present, so real and solid, a presence so vivid and comforting. Or you might be going about your daily business and become faintly or fully aware of the presence of someone you love, whether alive or dead. You might have been thinking about that person, or the sensation could come out of the blue. If you do not have a framework with which to make sense of such experiences, the chances are you keep them to yourself or only tell one or two trusted family members or friends. Erlendur Haraldsson, in a survey published in the *Journal of the Society for Psychical Research* in 1985, noted that 26 percent of those represented in the Human Values Survey in the UK thought that they had had contact with the dead. This rose to 41 percent in Iceland and is highest among widows and widowers (see also Haraldsson 2012). Such experiences are universal, although how they are interpreted and their cultural acceptance varies over time and from one culture to another. Typically, such encounters with the dead (or those physically distant but alive) are characterised by their long-lasting emotional impact. If the meeting takes place in a dream-state, it has an unusual clarity and unlike most dreams does not fade away as one awakens. These dream encounters can often be recalled in minute detail after many years. In some cases, evidential information is communicated by the departed loved-one, that is, information that can be subsequently verified, which was not known to the person in advance or communicated by some other normal means.

In her book *The Afterlife of Billy Fingers* (2013), American writer Annie Kagan describes several occasions in which her dead brother appears to communicate important information to her telepathically. Just as she was waking up one morning, three weeks after Billy's death, Kagan heard his unmistakable voice calling her name from above her. She thought she must be dreaming, but the voice insisted that she was not and that she should find the red notebook he had given her the year before and start writing. The voice seemed to come from outside rather than inside Kagan's head, and in subsequent conversations, Billy often gave his sister messages for people that meant little to her but were apposite and meaningful for the recipients. On one occasion, the voice said very insistently that she should find his car. Kagan did not know whether her brother even had a car, looked up at the ceiling, and asked Billy how she was supposed to find his car. The reply came that she should look in his cardholder. She opened the manila envelope she had been sent with her brother's belongings and pulled out a cardholder with a business card from a Mercedes dealer inside. She then heard Billy tell her to get the things from his car. She phoned the Mercedes dealer who confirmed that he did have the car, which Billy had written off by driving into a tree in Florida a week before his death. Billy had been living out of his car at the time, and it still had a box of his belongings that contained the remnants of his life, including his journals and photographs of happier times. The dealer promised to return the belongings to Kagan. While these incidents may not count as scientific proof, they were enough to convince Kagan that she was communicating with her dead brother and that the conversations were not just her imagination.

A strong emotional tie seems to increase the possibility of communication between the living and the dead. Frank Hives, an English political officer living in Nigeria in the early twentieth century, had spontaneous out-of-body experiences. On one occasion he found himself in a familiar churchyard in Hampshire, England, where his brother-in-law was the Rector. Hives's discarnate guide led him to a funeral service where, looking down on the coffin, he saw the name of his brother who, as far as Hives was aware, was settled and living in New Zealand. He tried speaking to people but they appeared not to see or hear him. On awaking in Nigeria, Hives was sure that his brother was dead. He wrote an account of his experience and got his fellow officers to witness it, then wrote to his sister in England for confirmation. His letter crossed with one from his sister, informing him of his brother's death and confirming the date and details that he had seen when out of his body (Hives 1931: 69-85).

Knowing of a death of someone emotionally close, either because of a dream or some other form of direct communication from the deceased, or through remote viewing or out-of-body travel, appears to be both common and universal. Hives had tried using his psychic powers for material advantage to determine the names of racehorse winners. He knew instinctively that he was laying himself open to lower forces or 'Tempters', and that the information did not come from his usual guide, termed 'the Doorkeeper' (Hives 1931: 109-28). His punishment came in the form of ill-health, poltergeist activity, and a battle between a figure of good and a figure of evil. The physicality of the incident was reminiscent of Jacob's fight with the angel in Genesis 32:22-32.

The Franciscan psychic, exorcist, out-of-body traveller, confessor and saint, Padre Pio (1887–1968), also did battle with evil spirits and 'the devil'. These appear to have been material rather than just psychological manifestations that left Padre Pio physically scarred. Padre Pio also had a reputation for bi-location, appearing as a solid apparition in a place far distant from his physical body, which remained in his monastic cell. While this may not be a common gift, the annals of the Society for Psychical Research and publications of the society's members indicate that it is not uncommon either, and there are often witnesses to such feats. One such case involved a Dr Tanous, who apparently had tea with a friend in Canada while asleep in New York, their conversation being overheard by the friend's wife from the next room (Auerbach 1986).

Telepathic communication, out-of-body travel, and encounters with guides or forces of good and evil stand in stark contrast to a narrowly materialist view of the universe. They involve the premise that the conscious observer or self can be seen as distinct from the physical body and is not an emergent property of the brain, although it is not wholly separate from it either. These experiences often have a physical element to them and indicate a blurring of boundaries rather than separation of material and immaterial realms. The challenge that faces us as social scientists and scholars of religion is how to study such experiences without getting bogged down in debates around verification or hung up on definitions of religion. The same or a similar experience may be termed religious by one person but not another, or in one context but not in others. I am concerned with experiences that have some element of 'non-ordinary consciousness', which have transpersonal elements and which appear to affirm that we are more than the sum of our physical bodies. All too often such experiences bring us back to the physical plane, pointing to the fact that they do not lie solely in the realms of imagination or dreams but act as portals between everyday and supra-normal consciousness. Extraordinary experiences can reveal the interpenetration of mind and matter, of material and immaterial aspects of existence. They involve the imagination and engage the emotions, expanding our sense of the possible, without entirely leaving the material world of facts and objects bounded by time and space.

Anthropological Explanations for the Nature and Origins of Religion

From its inception as a discipline, anthropology sought to ally itself with the natural sciences. In a paper published in 1888, Edward Burnett Tylor (1832–1917) set out to improve the anthropological method by means of statistical comparison in the orderly comparative manner established by Herbert Spencer. Tylor's concern was, as George Stocking observes, classically positivistic, seeking to put anthropology on the same footing as mathematics, physics, chemistry, and biology (Stocking 1996: 4). If anthropology had confined its remit to kinship terminology and laws of marriage and descent, all might have been well, at least for a while. Tylor's interests however, like those of the missionary scholars, travellers, colonial servants, and ethnographers who gathered the data on which he relied, encompassed beliefs and customs, myths and rituals. One of the founding fathers of the ethnographic method, Bronislaw Malinowski, writing in 1923, remained acutely aware of the challenge this posed to the nascent discipline. Like the Cambridge psychiatrist and anthropologist W. H. R. Rivers (1864–1922), Malinowski sought to integrate the material and cultural life of a people with individual psychic and religious elements, claiming,

After all, man is physically but one animal species among others, while his soul has been for a long time already in the keeping of another science—that of psychology. The unfortunate fact is that man has been created with a body and a soul as well, and this original sin, after having incessantly haunted the reflective mind through myth, religion, theology, and metaphysics, comes now to lay its curse on anthropology. Physical and cultural anthropology are divided by the deep rent between soul and body, mind and matter, which is no easier to bridge over in science than in the somewhat looser speculations which precede it. (Malinowski 1923: 314)

The ambition to encompass the whole of human social experience meant that anthropology was well placed to integrate different approaches to the individual and society. It drew on archaeology, history, mythology, culture, and individual psychology. Despite this, the commonest anthropological approach to the study of religion from the nineteenth century to the present involves steadfastly ignoring or even ridiculing any ontological claims, especially those of supposedly less civilized or non-Western peoples. The new generation of professional field-anthropologists at the beginning of the twentieth century, such as A. C. Haddon and Rivers, recognised that the systematic collection of ethnographic 'facts' was more important than the selective use of data haphazardly collected in order to fit some evolutionary criteria (Urry 1993: 5), but this did not make them any more sympathetic to the study of religious experience than their armchair-anthropology predecessors.

Tylor had built his career from the 1860s onwards on the theory of social or classical evolutionism. While acknowledging that there may be some diffusionary elements of culture and belief as well as historical interactions between peoples, the thrust of Tylor's scientific anthropology was based on the psychic unity of mankind. Following Spencer's social evolutionism and influenced by Charles Darwin's theories of natural evolution, Tylor argued that people pass through evolutionary stages regarding both social organisation and religious ideas. The concepts of 'survivals' and 'adhesions' (correlations) was central to Tylor's statistical, comparative method. Forms of animism, for instance, might survive in polytheistic and even monotheistic societies, but the direction of movement is one way. Tylor believed there is an inevitable evolution from primitive beliefs to rationality and science. When he came up with his minimal definition of religion as 'belief in spiritual beings' (1871), he assumed that such beliefs were rational but mistaken. A dream in which a deceased ancestor communicates with the dreamer, for instance, leads to a belief in the survival of spirits and the existence of a soul or *anima* (giving rise to the term 'animism' as a description of the earliest form of religion). If human beings had souls, as ancient peoples might have reasoned, other animals and even inanimate objects such as rocks, waterfalls, 'fetishes' (manufactured statues or other objects imbued with some sort of *mana* or power) might also have contained a life-force and even intention, and thus entered into relationship with the living.

For Malinowski, with his extended fieldwork in the Trobriand Archipelago in Melanesia during the First World War, human psychology was key to understanding religion. The influence here was Sigmund Freud and psychoanalysis rather than the evolutionism of Darwin and Spencer, but the idea of a psychic unity of humanity remained. Malinowski (1922, 1948) reasoned that the psychological need to control an unpredictable physical and social environment gives rise to religious ideas. Religion complements technology by helping people cope with the stresses and uncertainties of everyday life. Malinowski noted, for instance, that whereas the Trobriand Islanders have extensive magical rituals for open-sea fishing, which is full of uncertainty and danger, there are no rituals for the much more reliable and secure lagoon fishing (1948: 14). While paying tribute to Sir James Frazer's *Golden Bough* and to the work of Tylor, Malinowski contended that it was not animism based on an intellectual mistake that was the earliest form of religion. He suggested that we should look instead to belief in a supernatural, impersonal force or *mana*, a dominant notion in Oceania, as the essence of both magic and religion (1948: 3). In African ethnography, notions of witchcraft and sorcery, also based on the idea of psychic and supernatural forces, plays an analogous if not identical role.

For Malinowski, supernatural beings are real for those who believe in them, but purely psychological, and because people are much the same everywhere, the same type of mistakes recur:

> But man in general, and primitive man in particular, has a tendency to imagine the outer world in his own image. And since animals, plants, and objects move, act, behave, help man or hinder him, they must also be endowed with souls or spirits. Thus animism, the philosophy and the religion of primitive man, has been built up from observations and by inferences, mistaken but comprehensible in a crude and untutored mind. (Malinowski 1948: 2)

A more recent proponent of Malinowski's view is Stewart Guthrie, who in his book *Faces in the Clouds* (1995), formulated what he termed the 'hyperactive' or 'hypersensitive agency detection hypothesis'. Guthrie, like Malinowski, argues that we have an innate tendency to see patterns in random formations, such as clouds. We anthropomorphise the world as this comes with an evolutionary advantage. It is better to play it safe and act as if gods exist than to assume that they do not (and Guthrie assumes the latter).

A key proponent of sociological theories of religion, as opposed to Tylor's evolutionary intellectualist theories and the more psychologically based explanations of Malinowski and Guthrie, is Émile Durkheim (1858–1917). Durkheim (1912) saw religion as a social mechanism aimed at maintaining group cohesion. The earliest forms of religion, according to Durkheim, were totemic. Social groups identified with non-human forms, which helped them to envisage themselves as discrete groups in relation to other distinct social groups. Durkheim defined religion not in Tylor's terms of relations with spiritual beings, but as 'a unified system of beliefs and practices relative to sacred things' (1995: 44). This is philosophically quite a different proposition. Durkheim was rejecting the idea that we can know the transcendent thing in itself (God), following the Kantian idea that what we know are representations of the world or *representations collectives*. Durkheim thought that human beings divide the world into the realm of the sacred, comprising sacred objects, sacred beliefs and practices, and a moral community or church, existing in opposition to profane or everyday life. When people come together to perform religious rituals or other collective acts, they are infused with a 'collective effervescence' or unifying force that gives them the impression that they are in contact with something greater than themselves (Durkheim 1995).[3] The idea that religion is socially but not ontologically real, as Durkheim thought, further reinforced an already normative idea within the anthropology of religion.

A particularly British form of social explanation of religion combining the functionalism of Durkheim and structural functionalism of A. R. Radcliffe-Brown (1952) dominated UK universities in the latter half of the twentieth century. Ioan Lewis, for example, wrote some influential texts on religious cults in East Africa (1986, 1989), arguing that if religious practices exist and persist, it is because they serve a social function. In Somalia, for instance, a male-dominated, Puritanical culture, Lewis looked at the female Zar possession cult. It is not that Zar spirits really exist or possess women, Lewis argued, but that as part of a cultic group, disadvantaged women could gain mutual support. Zar spirits speaking through a possessed woman could demand gifts from the woman's husband, providing a legitimate way of redressing an economic and socio-political gender imbalance (1981: 64-71).

The unity of anthropology that Malinowski called for is seldom achieved in one individual, school, or idea, with a movement between the social emphasis on the collective and a psychological emphasis on the individual. Influenced by the structural linguistics of Noam Chomsky's theory of an innate grammar, Claude Lévi-Strauss (1908-2009) argued that biological imperatives give rise to social as well as physical and linguistic forms. Lévi-Strauss argued that humans have a tendency to see the world as a set of binary oppositions—male/female, sacred/profane, pure/polluted, earth/sky, raw/cooked, gods/devils, and so on. He believed that we continually recreate versions of this dyadic universe in our belief systems and social structures because we are hard-wired to do so (Lévi-Strauss 1963, 1970–82). With his interest in myth and history, particularly in the Americas, Lévi-Strauss combined the historical and cultural interests of Franz Boas (1858–1942) with the linguistic insights of Noam Chomsky and Ferdinand de Saussure. Lévi-Strauss was a universalist, interested in features common to humanity rather than cultural differences. He admitted to being more of a theorist with interests in psychology and philosophy, rather than a field-worker collecting ethnographic facts, except insofar as these facts served to 'crack a code' that reveals the logic underlying particular social forms. Also influenced by the eighteenth century French Romanticism of Jean-Jacques Rousseau, Lévi-Strauss believed that modern Western culture had lost its mythical roots, a theme taken up by Mary Douglas (1966, 1973) in her emphasis on the importance of ritual and religious traditions. While giving equal value to developed and small-scale cultures, Lévi-Strauss did not romanticise or essentialise the latter. Cultures are not better or worse *per se*, but each one uses the tools they have to form their ideas and practices, many of which, like gender, are universal (Hufford 1995). In belief systems, as in other cultural practices, we continually recreate versions of a dyadic universe because that is what we are programmed to do. Lévi-Strauss's structuralism did not preclude the notion that religious belief can also have an external source, as Mary Douglas, a life-long Roman Catholic Christian who absorbed both Durkheimian sociology and French structuralism, demonstrated, but it certainly did not necessitate it.

As insightful, brilliant, and influential as many of these explanations of religion and society may be, they generally share the assumption that we live in a material world that can be understood and explained without recourse to metaphysical explanations. Even those who practice some form of religion, if they have grown up or been educated in the Western world, have been influenced by post-Enlightenment positivism. One expression of this is a form of naturalism that assumes a materialist view of nature, including human creations, in which every natural event is the product of other natural events. According to this view of the world, there is no divine cause, no soul, and no prospect of conscious survival beyond death. Religious experience is something that requires an explanation—it needs to be explained away. The question is not so much 'what is happening here' as 'how can we account for the fact that supposedly rational beings persist in believing unbelievable things' (Bowie 2014). What has the power to unsettle these assumptions are the kinds of relatively common experience I described at the beginning of this chapter. A materialist paradigm survives in academia, despite numerous experiences that contradict it, due at least in part to a degree of self-censorship regarding paranormal experiences that do not fit the dominant model.

Philosopher, theologian, and Jesuit priest Bernard Lonergan (1992) developed what he termed the 'generalized empirical method' (GEM) in which he distinguished three acts of cognition: experience, understanding and judgment. It is significant that Lonergan starts with experience, rather than reflection or observation. Cognition starts with a direct experience of being in the world and it is in seeking to understand and then come to a judgment on the nature of that experience that we can move to decision and then action. Experience, whether one's own or that of others, is key to the study of religion, whatever the culture or century in which we live. The sense of contact with a deceased loved one, for example, is universal. The methodological question if we wish to study religion or human beings is what we do about this fact. Anthropologist of religion Edith Turner urges her students to treat all experiences, religious or otherwise, as ethnographic data and to avoid the self-censoring or bracketing of personal experiences that Western culture teaches us to regard as too intimate, embarrassing, or fantastical to share with others.[4] When people have what might be termed religious or paranormal experiences, they can keep quiet, ignore them, or choose to deny them. They can also seek to understand and evaluate them and to adjust or change their beliefs and actions as a consequence. One result of the hegemonic positivism of the West is that people who have had a near-death experience frequently keep quiet about it, even if it has been personally transformative. It is not only academics who self-censor. As researchers have noted, those who have travelled outside their bodies and visited other realms of consciousness tend only to speak about it to a very select group of people whom they trust, fearing ridicule or their sanity (van Lommel 2010: 45-77). Many therefore assume that their experience is unique, not realizing that it is part of the common human heritage.[5]

An Alternative Experiential Lineage

There is an alternative anthropological tradition to the one I have described above, which could be termed the 'experiential lineage'. What these scholars have in common is a *direct personal experience* of what may be called the 'paranormal', 'numinous', 'transpersonal', or 'mystical'. They have reflected on their experience and taken the step of incorporating the insights afforded into their academic explanations of religion. A key figure in this lineage is Andrew Lang (1844–1912), a Scottish classicist, literary scholar, and folklorist who came under the influence of Tylor in Oxford. Although originally a supporter of Tylor's evolutionary theories of religion, Lang's personal experiences led him to doubt that religious faith arose from the misattribution of dreams of the dead being mistaken evidence of soul survival. Neither did he regard belief in an animating force in nature and the existence of unseen forces as evidently mistaken.

In 1869 while walking down Oriel Lane in Oxford, Lang saw a professor who at that moment was some distance away, dead or dying (Stocking 1996: 56). He subsequently saw other 'wraiths' and seems to have been a lucid dreamer, or may have had out-of-body experiences. Lang was a founding member in 1882 of the Society for Psychical Research, a body of some of the most eminent scientists and scholars of the day. He became President of the Society during the last year of his life in 1911, but from 1890 onwards was prepared to describe his own psychic experiences in print. In *Cock Lane and Common Sense* (1894), Lang directly challenged Tylor's view of animism and his notion of survivals. Lang's experience of the Victorian séance room convinced him that at least some of the paranormal phenomena he witnessed were genuine. If this were the case, stories of ghosts and paranormal phenomena in Western societies were not primitive survivals from an earlier savage past, but part of the universal human condition, whatever their origin. Contemporary anthropological theory argued for a progression from belief in spirits and ghosts, through polytheism to monotheism. Lang challenged this view, pointing out that on the one hand, many so-called primitive societies had concepts of a Supreme Being, maker, or judge, and on the other, so-called civilized societies retained a belief in spirits. This suggested, as Lucien Lévy-Bruhl also concluded in his later *Notebooks* in the 1930s (1975), that there are not two different ways of thinking—one primitive and mystical and one rational and civilized—represented by different stages and types of society. There are different ways of interpreting what are in fact real and universal experiences that occur in all societies at all stages of development.

Lang went on to develop his ideas further in what was probably his finest work in this field, *The Making of Religion* (1898), in which he set out to explore the nature of phenomena such as visions and hallucinations. Lang also further dismantled Tylor's theory that high gods and 'relatively Supreme Beings' were derived from a belief in ghosts. In examining the nature of psychic phenomena cross-culturally, Lang drew on recent developments in psychology from writers such as Pierre Janet, Jean-Martin Charcot and William James, as well as from the growing body of data provided by the Society for Psychical Research. Lang made the very reasonable point that extrapolating backward from extant 'primitive' societies to some ancient ancestor is highly tendentious and claimed that we cannot assume that our forebears throughout evolutionary history had the same physiological and psychological makeup as contemporary humans. If, however, abilities such as clairvoyance and telepathy still exist in modern societies, as they appear to do, it is highly likely that they would have given their possessors in earlier times an evolutionary advantage and would therefore have been positively selected.

Unlike Tylor, Lang posed the crucial ontological question: are any of the accounts of ghosts, spirits, and other supernormal phenomena actually true? Rather than a single evolutionary line from primitive to modern forms of religion and ultimately to scientific rationalism, Lang identified two separate strands of religion that coexist in human history. One strand is that of ghosts and ghost-gods, which deals with questions of power and every-day existence. Based on actual experiences of the dead and forms of extra-sensory perception, this strand of religion developed notions such as propitiation and sacrifice, which often became attached to ideas of a Supreme Being as well. Like all experience, it was open to elaboration and could be subverted and exploited for personal gain. Notions of witchcraft in Africa and of *mana* in Oceania would fit well with Lang's 'ghost stream', as they concern psychic powers and ancestors. The second stream, although not necessarily later in time, relates to notions of a Supreme Being. It is more philosophical and focuses on the eternal, moral, and creative elements of religion (Lang 1898: 274; see Stocking 1996: 59). Lang reasoned that because it is hard to imagine a completely non-material being, representations of God are often anthropomorphic and tribal, and in practice these two streams are often interconnected. But Lang did not really deal with the extensive euhemeristic religions of China, in which ancestors become gods as a result of extensive worship and invocation (see Graham 2014; Jordan 1972),[6] which provide a slightly different model or way of connecting these two religious streams or tendencies.

Although Lang's theories of religion seemed to fit the emerging ethnographic data from around the world, including that from Western societies, better than the ideas of Tylor or his other earlier interlocutor, Max Müller (1823–1900), Lang sank into relative obscurity as the twentieth century progressed. Suspicion of Spiritualism and psychic research within academia no doubt played a large part in the decline in his academic visibility (see Moreman 2013), but as a founding father of experiential anthropology, Lang holds a key position and certainly deserves greater attention.

Lang was not the first scholar to write about his own psychic experiences. The ideas, writings, and psychic experiences of the Swedish mystic and scientist Emanuel Swedenborg (1688–1772) prefigured much of what was to come. In *The Economy of the Animal Kingdom* (1740–1741), for instance, Swedenborg developed the idea of the fourfold psyche. The highest faculty was the *anima* or soul proper, the source of truth, law, science, and beauty. The *anima* enters the level below it—the intellect—in the form of light. Below the intellect is the emotional level and finally the physical or material level (Lachman 2012).[7] Swedenborg wrote extensively of his experiences as a psychic and mystic, sometimes in terms that sound very reminiscent of the American psychologist and philosopher James (1842–1910). James founded the first laboratory for experimental psychology at Harvard University in 1872, and is best known for his works on psychology (1890) and his great comparative study of religion, *The Varieties of Religious Experience* (1902). In a paper written in 1910, 'A Suggestion about Mysticism', James also described some of his own experiences of an expanded or mystical consciousness. He likened it to suddenly and spontaneously enlarging one's field of vision. On three occasions he had experiences of perception rather than cognition that took place when he was awake and engaged in other activities, which felt extremely 'real'. The fourth occurrence was in 1906 and involved a series of dreams that occurred over two nights. The dreams seemed to leak into each other in a way that was deeply unsettling to James. In his own words:

> The distressing confusion of mind in this experience was the exact opposite of mystical illumination, and equally unmystical was the definiteness of what was perceived. But the exaltation of the sense of relation was mystical (the perplexity all revolved about the fact that the three dreams *both did and did not belong in the most intimate way together*); and the sense that *reality was being uncovered* was mystical in the highest degree. To this day I feel that those extra dreams were dreamed in reality, but when, and where, and by whom, I cannot guess. (James 1910: 91)

As a practising psychologist, James was sensitized by these personal experiences to the absolute sense of reality that can accompany such phenomena, and he was at least open to the idea that they could have some veridical elements, rather than being merely delusional or pathological in origin.

James had long shared Lang's interest in psychical research. In 1885 his mother-in-law and sister-in-law introduced him to a medium called Leonora Piper from Boston, who had impressed them with the accuracy of some of the information she conveyed from deceased relatives of the sitters. James had more than a dozen sittings with Mrs Piper. Although he was initially sceptical, James was given so much evidential information by Mrs Piper, which could not have been gained through research, that he became convinced the medium had genuine supernatural powers (Tymn 2013). James referred to Mrs Piper as his 'white crow'. Although professionally he preserved a questioning attitude as to the source of information she produced, James was also clear that it pointed to a phenomenon outside the realm of orthodox science.

For James, religious experience was a natural rather than supernatural part of human life. His cross-cultural researches convinced him that there were similar experiences and human responses to them everywhere, despite many differing cultural interpretations. James coined the term 'common-core hypothesis' to explain this observation, putting him in the company of those who believed in an underlying psychic unity and universality within human nature. In this he was in tune with influential German Lutheran philosopher, theologian, and scholar of comparative religion, Rudolf Otto (1869–1937). In *Das Heilige*, first published in 1917 and translated as *The Idea of the Holy* in 1923, Otto described what he believed to be a universal human experience of 'the numinous'. The German *heiligkeit* can be translated as both 'holy' and 'sacred', and for Otto the idea of the numinous was the ineffable core of religion that cannot be translated into anything else. It is the impression of being in contact with something greater than oneself, giving rise to feelings of awe (which can be fearful as well as joyful). Otto coined the Latin term *mysterium tremendum* to express the sense of something wholly other that can overwhelm us with its power, energy and vitality. He sometimes attached the term *fascinans* to the *mysterium tremendum*, indicating that the numinous could be attractive and fascinate us, despite the sense of fear or terror it can invoke. Otto combined the conviction that sensibility to the numinous is universal, although more highly developed in some individuals than others, with the notion of historical evolution. Humanity, he believed, moved from worship of 'daemons' to 'gods' and finally the one God. Although Otto held that Lutheranism had lost some of the sense of wonder and mystery found in other expressions of religion, he nevertheless saw Christianity or monotheism as the purest and highest form of worship.

More recently, David Hufford, an American folklorist and Emeritus Professor of Medical Humanities at Pennsylvania State University, has explored the experiential basis for supernatural beliefs. His work started with his doctoral studies of sleep paralysis and the cultural traditions of the 'Old Hag' in Newfoundland, Canada, but expanded into a much wider general theory of religion (Hufford 1982, 2013, 2015). Hufford's interest in this universal and terrifying phenomenon started with his own experience of sleep paralysis as a teenager. While at the time he thought that his experience was probably unique, he has subsequently researched very similar tales from around the world, both contemporary and historical. Traditions of supernatural assault are given various explanations, from Early Modern versions of the *incubus* and Newfoundland 'Old Hag', to some characteristics of the South African (Xhosa) *tokoloshe* (akin to the European 'brownie') or Inuit *augumangia*. The English term 'nightmare' is itself derived from an Early English term *mare* for a malevolent spirit. Hufford found that whereas cultural elaborations and explanations for the phenomenon of sleep paralysis vary across cultures, the characteristic features of the experience and its rates of occurrence appear to be stable. The frequency is surprisingly high within the general population with as many as 15 percent of those surveyed claiming to have had one or more recognizable 'attacks' (1982: 245). While not claiming a supernatural origin for this universal and terrifying experience of helplessness in the face of attack by an evil entity, Hufford concluded that, 'The contents of this experience cannot be satisfactorily explained on the basis of current knowledge' (Hufford 1982: 246). Sleep paralysis can be seen as one of a number of cross-cultural or 'cultural core' experiences, which 'do not appear to be transmitted by culture itself, arising instead as a spontaneous and primary human experience...at odds with many conventional attempts to account for paranormal phenomena in materially reductive terms' (2015: 290).

Hufford (1982: 14-15) coined the terms 'cultural source hypothesis', 'experiential source hypothesis', and 'experiential source theory' (1995: 28) to account for such phenomena, speculating that the visions and entities encountered during episodes of sleep paralysis play a part in the development of religion and of human religiosity. In this, Hufford is very close to James' 'common-core hypothesis'. It is not necessary to understand the precise origin of universal experiential phenomena in order to see them as giving rise to many of our religious and supernatural beliefs.

A key figure in the experiential lineage is Edith Turner, who with her husband, Scottish anthropologist Victor Turner, spent many years examining ritual and notions of 'communitas', 'liminality', structure, and anti-structure in both Western and non-Western societies. These features of religiosity also appear to be universal and common to human experience everywhere. In 1985 following Victor Turner's death, Edith Turner returned to the Ndembu in Zambia, Central Africa, the site of much of their earlier fieldwork. During a healing ceremony known as *Ihamba*, Turner took part in the ritual as a healer rather than an observer, as on previous occasions (1992). At the climax of the ceremony, much to her surprise, Turner saw a 'gray blob' leave the sick woman for whom the ceremony was being performed, which was 'captured' in a prepared container by the healer leading the ritual. Although a practising Roman Catholic at this point in her life, Turner realised that she had not really taken seriously the possibility that spirits exist, other than symbolically or metaphorically (Turner 2005).

This personal experience was a turning point, almost a conversion, and shaped the direction of Turner's subsequent teaching, writing, and research. In a short paper entitled 'The Reality of Spirits: A Tabooed or Permitted Field of Study' (1993), for instance, Turner challenges the self-censorship within academia when it comes to admitting and analysing experiences that might be considered paranormal, or that lend ontological veracity to the *emic* or insider accounts of informants. In a more recent discussion of the transformative effects of fieldwork, Turner urges ethnographers to attend to their own experiences so as not to reduce 'the phenomena of spirits or other extraordinary beings to something more abstract and distant in meaning' (2010: 224). She raises the possibility that spirits are not only ontologically real for those we study, but possibly for the anthropologist as well. Volumes such as *Extraordinary Anthropology: Transformations in the Field*, edited by Jean-Guy Goulet and Bruce Granville Miller (2006), which is dedicated to Victor and Edith Turner, or *The Social Life of Spirits*, edited by Ruy Blanes and Diana Espirito Santo (2014), owe much to Edith Turner's encouragement to anthropologists to take their own field experiences seriously and to use them as ethnographic data. If we can do this honestly, she believes, we are also more likely to be open to the apparently extraordinary experiences of our informants. This was certainly the case for Paul Stoller (1987), whose apprenticeship to a Songhay magician-healer in Niger, West Africa, laid him open to the jealous and malicious attacks of sorcerers (including an incidence of sleep paralysis). Stoller eventually left Niger fearing for his health, if not his life, as a result of witchcraft activity. Unlike the preeminent Oxford anthropologist, Edward Evan Evans-Pritchard (1902–1973), who 'saw' witchcraft in the form a light travelling to the hut of a man who subsequently died while living with the Azande in Central Africa (1976), Stoller did not try to rationalise or explain away his experience. As with Turner, he allowed it to inform his view of the world and to shape his subsequent work.

It is not necessary to be a psychic virtuoso in order to develop this sensitivity to the experiences of others. Tanya Luhrmann spent several years studying American evangelical Christians, seeking to understand the way they talk to God and how they try to discern the voice of God talking back (2012). Luhrmann did not adopt the worldview of her informants and does not describe herself as a Christian. Like Evans-Pritchard, who found that following the Zande practice of consulting oracles in one's daily life was as good a way as any to make choices (1976), Luhrmann discovered that paying attention to her inner world in the way that her informants did led her to have similar experiences. One reason for this, she observes, is that religion is as much a skill as a belief, a *knowing how*, in philosopher Gilbert Ryle's words (1949), as a *knowing that*. 'It's a different way of thinking about God than the science-religion wars suggest', observes Luhrmann, 'and possibly less divisive' (2015: 71). A similar mimetic quality is illustrated in Mittermaier's study of Sufi dreams (2015: 129), which point to 'an evocative logic in which examples do not merely represent; they also do things'. Religion is also a form of practice, despite the Western tendency to privilege doctrines and belief.

Luhrmann's approach to the ontology of supernatural or non-human entities is similar to that of French anthropologist Jeanne Favret-Saada (1980, 1989), who studied witchcraft beliefs and practices in Normandy, Northern France. She was very concerned with the linguistic as well as the non-verbal ritual and psychological reality of witches and found herself 'caught' in this world as a subject as well as an observer. While treating the ontology of witches as part of a therapeutic and unconscious 'opacity' of the self to itself, Favret-Saada rejected the tendency to deny epistemological status to the ethnographer's personal experiences in the field. For Favret-Saada, participation is key to a real understanding of Normandy witchcraft. Her long involvement with witches and dewitchers allowed Favret-Saada to understand the impact of witchcraft on the lives of her informants as she shared many of their experiences. An observant anthropologist might focus on the drama of ritual, whereas a participant sees the rituals within a much broader context and time-frame, becoming aware of the life and death struggles of those trapped within the discourse of witchcraft struggles, which go far beyond the confines of the séance room (Luhrmann 2015: 106-07). Favret-Saada and Luhrmann remain open to the realities of their informants as a result of a prolonged and full participation in their lives. They do not necessarily adopt the worldview of those they study but retain an openness to experience that is allowed to inform their analysis.

The standard anthropological methodological bracketing of religion and paranormal experiences is often challenged by the seriousness with which researchers tackle the subject. An example of this approach is the work of Nils Bubandt (2009), who treats spirits, embodied in and speaking through spirit mediums, as important informants in the political life of the inhabitants of the Indonesian island of North Maluku. For the local people, spirits are certainly real, influential, and respected entities, and as such Bubandt feels that he cannot dismiss their testimony and treats them as 'methodologically real'. There have been several other recent attempts to expand the range of informants to include non-human or immaterial beings. The 'perspectivism' of Amerindian cosmologies, proposed by Eduardo Viveiros de Castro (1998), invites us to consider the ways in which humans, animals, and spirits view themselves and one another. De Castro's work illustrates a culturally embedded attempt to incorporate 'other-than-human-persons' into the anthropological narrative. Sociologist Charles Emmons (2014) goes even further than this. As a practising medium himself, Emmons is willing to admit that in some cases there is ontological as well as methodological reality to the existence of spirits and that ESP phenomena can be evidential (verifiable). While there is weighty evidence from parapsychology that spirits may be ontologically real (see for instance, Kelly et al. 2010), it is still not often said in print by scholars of religion or within the social sciences.

This self-censorship may be changing slowly, as the so-called 'ontological turn' (anthropology of ontology' in anthropology and cognate disciplines) signals a renewed interest in a post-phenomenological approach to religion. This is due in part to advances in neuroscience and an appreciation of the complexity of the interaction between our biology, culture, and experience—including our experience of transpersonal or trans-human entities. Michael Winkelman is one scholar who tries to combine a cognitive and biological understanding of religion with openness to the possibility of transcendence, arguing that 'the notion that spirits reflect the structures of brain and mind is not to dismiss their ultimate ontological reality' (2004: 91).[8] He is aware of the observer effect as well as of the ways in which our imagination can create the grounds for 'real' events. The desire to divide experience into categories of true or false, real or delusional/imagined is too simplistic. It fails to reflect what we know about a post-Newtonian physics, the messages coming from cognitive neurosciences, or to account for the ways in which we actually experience the world. Speaking about the need for active participation rather than just observation of the objects of study, Winkelman states:

> This engagement with the possibilities provided by the 'other' may be an essential aspect of engaging with these experiences of alternate realities. The mental framework provided by belief and expectation is not merely some self-delusional abandonment of an appropriately empirical or skeptical attitude, but rather a preparation of the mental fields that can enable the manifestation of certain phenomena—much as a magnetic field produced by a magnet provides the organizing framework for the spatial distribution of the affected metal filings. (Winkelman 2012: 200)

Winkelman points to a new methodological approach to the study of religion, treading a fine line between the reflective analytical detachment appropriate for an academic study, and the incorporation of first-hand experience into the data set, whether this is the experience of the ethnographer or scholar, or the experiences of those he or she studies.

An Inclusive Methodology: Cognitive, Empathetic Engagement

Building on much that has gone before in the alternative 'experiential' lineage outlined above, I use the term 'cognitive, empathetic engagement' to describe a methodology for studying religion that attempts to do justice to lived experience, description, and analysis. It is particularly suited to the ethnographic study of supernatural, anomalous, or paranormal phenomena. These are key factors in religion, but are also the most likely to be dismissed, bracketed out, ignored altogether, or explained away. As I have indicated, there are grounds for thinking that these direct encounters with non-ordinary reality (which is in fact quite ordinary for many people) give rise to elements that become formalised in religious doctrines, beliefs and practices. They may remain as suppressed or counter-cultural elements within formal religious traditions, ever suspicious of features not easily controlled. They may merge with or be seen as a shadow side of 'genuine' mystical experience (Mayer and Gründer 2011; Hanegraaff 2012). What out-of-body and near-death experiences, sleep paralysis, encounters with the dead, lucid dreams that appear particularly salient, spontaneous past-life memories, shamanistic and mediumistic practises all share is their universality. This list is not intended to be exhaustive. Whatever culture we look at, past or present, and however such events are interpreted, their occurrence and characteristic features appear relatively stable (Greyson 1983, 1998, Shushan 2011). This strongly suggests that whatever their origin, these key and recurrent phenomena are not the result purely, if at all, of cultural diffusion or transmission (Shushan 2009, 2013). The same can be said of ESP phenomena (clairvoyance, telepathy, psychokinesis) and gifts such as spiritual healing. One could see them as arising from a common, human neurobiological and environmental heritage, or one can regard neurobiology and environment as elements that shape but do not in themselves give rise to these experiences. Whatever the balance between these perspectives, the fact remains that there are some strongly evidential characteristics of paranormal experience that cannot be explained without recourse to theories of the survival of consciousness. They can even lend credence to notions of non-physical beings or other forms of intelligence. Paranormal phenomena are not (necessarily) at odds with a quantum view of the universe, but remain as yet little understood. The mechanisms that enable an object (*apport*) to appear in a séance room, for instance, are not explicable from within our current state of scientific knowledge (Krippner and Friedman 2010).

I have set out the methodology of *cognitive, empathetic engagement* elsewhere (Bowie 2013), thus I will here only give some pointers to what is involved. If we start with *cognition*, I refer to an attitude of openness, not rushing to explanation or prematurely looking for closure. The philosopher Paul Ricoeur (1971) talks about the 'logic of uncertainty and qualitative probability'. Even if definitive answers are not possible, one can weigh evidence and remain open to different possibilities for as long as possible. The ethnographer can engage in a dialogue with the people he or she studies, including texts as well as individuals or communities, and both accept and question his or her own perspective and the perspectives of others. A good starting point is the understanding that all perspectives are limited by their specific positionality. At the same time, it is not necessary to remain apart or at a distance from the subject or object of study. The self and other can be placed in a single ontological, hermeneutical framework. This leads to the element of *empathy* that can arise when the ethnographer tries to see world as others see it. Anthropologist Johannes Fabian (1983) has written at length about the necessity for what he calls 'co-evalness'. By this he means that the ethnographer should not place him- or herself outside the frame, gazing in at those being studied. Data is gathered by people living in the same timeframe as one another, geographically located, engaging in dialogue, and responding to one another. There is no perspective from which the ethnographer can be located as an objective observer, and no objective reality outside our shared existence. Empathy is not the same as liking, but an attempt to accept and understand others. *Engagement* implies that participation does not contaminate knowledge. It exposes the limitations of verbal knowledge and lends itself to bodily engagement with the field that, as Judith Okely (2012: 107) has observed, 'is invariably implicit in participant observation'. The body, and any form of participative engagement, is not straightforward or unproblematic. We are socialised to experience our bodies in particular ways and have to learn and unlearn the limitations of this socialisation in our encounters with others.

Cognitive, empathetic engagement is a method and not a belief system. It is a way of gathering data. Data needs to be interpreted, and whenever possible, interpretation and analysis should be a collective endeavour. There may not be a definitive answer to a research question or investigation, but we may find increasing depth and certainty as the quality and quantity of evidence mounts. We need to be ready to change our working theories as new data emerges and not to be too quick to define the limits of what's possible. It is counterproductive to approach others with the view that they are self-evidently mistaken or fraudulent (a common problem in the study of mediumship), an attitude that is hard to justify scientifically or ethically. We should allow for personal transformation or at least the possibility of it (Young and Goulet 1994).

This approach to religious experience has moved a long way from the Victorian project of cataloguing and correlating an evolutionary religious history. We are no longer looking for 'survivals', those stubborn primitive elements of religion that nevertheless persist in our increasingly rational, material, post-Enlightenment world. It is not so far, however, from the work of pioneering Victorian scholars who were interested in personal experience and the comparative study of religion. An encounter with paranormal reality, whether first-hand or via an unusual receptivity to the experience of others, has opened up the uncomfortable issue of ontology in religion. Writers such as Lang, James, and latterly Edith Turner help to give credence to a study of religion that places experience and interpretation of experience at the heart of the academic enterprise.

Short Biographical Note

Fiona Bowie is Senior Visiting Research Fellow in the Department of Theology and Religious Studies at King's College London. She is an anthropologist of religion with a particular interest in the ethnographic study of the afterlife. She has worked at the Universities of Wales and Bristol in the UK, Linköping in Sweden, and the University of Virginia in the USA.

Notes

1.   The experience of being outside the body and the development of techniques to facilitate this state of consciousness appear to be ancient, relatively common, and probably universal. There are organisations and publications devoted to teaching out-of-body travel and to describing the adventures and insights that can be gained. See, for instance, the work of The Monroe Institute (Monroe 1971; Moen 1997), the International Academy of Consciousness (Vieira 2007; Gustus 2011), as well as Ziewe (2008) and Crookall (1960).

2.   Mediumistically reported accounts from those who have had a sudden or violent death often state that their consciousness left their bodies prior to impact. See, for instance, Galen Stoller's account of his 'fatal' accident (2011: 25).

3.   Edith Turner's recent work, *Communitas* (2012), builds not only on Victor Turner's earlier work on *communitas* (1991), but also develops this notion of Durkheim's, with the important difference that Turner re-enchants the concept, opening it up to a dialogue with external forces or realities. Like Durkheim, Turner deals with contemporary Western as well as small-scale societies, and finds within the undoubted individualism of the West the same longing and possibilities of connection found in many non-Western contexts.

4.   Personal communication. In her 90s, Edith Turner continues to teach at the University of Virginia and to inspire new generations of students to enlarge their understanding of what it means to be human.

5.   There are many excellent works dealing with near death experiences and out of body experiences and their universal characteristics. For summaries of some of this research, see, for example, Fenwick and Fenwick (1995); Shushan (2009); van Lommmel (2010); Carter (2010); Kelly et al. (2010).

6.   Fabian Graham (2014: 341) raises the 'exciting ontological supposition' that in Chinese folk Taoism, 'a spiritual energy can be created through the accumulation of direct spiritual energy (*ling*), manifested through worship and offerings under circumstances where there was no original living or inanimate nature spirit'. In his ethnography of folk religion in a Taiwanese village, David Jordan (1972) illustrates the rather different configurations present in Chinese folk religions, in which there seems to be a greater fluidity between the categories of ancestor, ghost, deity, and Supreme Being than found in other parts of the world.

7.   The fourfold division of the psyche is echoed in much Western esotericism, including Theosophical teachings, with its causal or spiritual body, the mental or intellectual, astral or emotional, and finally the etheric/physical body, all interpenetrating one another (Besant 1939).

8.   See Winkelman's chapter in this book, pp. 33-51.

Chapter 2

Ethnological and Neurophenomenological Approaches to Religious Experiences

Michael Winkelman

Spiritual experiences are often individual and private affairs, perhaps even unique to the person. Such strictly personal experiences would seem to be beyond the purview of scientific inquiry. Religious experiences often reflect the expectations of their respective traditions, and as such, have been seen as requiring no explanations beyond those expectations. Yet both individual spiritual experiences and those induced in the context of established traditions reflect similarities across time and cultures that reject the notion of these being merely idiosyncrasies of personal or institutional biases.

The evidence that spiritual and religious experiences are transcultural is illustrated by reports exhibiting similarities across people, cultures, and time. These uniformities are manifested in the concept of shamanic soul flight found in cultures around the world, in the similarity in possession experiences from many times and places, and in the concepts of a perennial philosophy and psychology underlying transcultural similarities exhibited in mystical experiences. These similarities across cultures in many forms of spiritual and religious experience suggest they are transcendental *noumena* that reflect features intrinsic to human nature. The similarities in the phenomenal forms of many of spiritual experiences attest to an underlying biological nature rather than something strictly individual.

Such claims clearly fly in the face of a longstanding division between science and religion, one in which it has been all too often conventionally accepted that religious experiences have no basis beyond the personal beliefs and faith of the person so fortunate (or afflicted) to have had such an experience. In contrast to this belief is a mounting of body of evidence that points to very different conclusions. These forms of evidence include cross-cultural distribution of phenomenologically similar shamanic, possession, and mystical experiences that have been attested to in comparative religion, transpersonal psychology, and transpersonal anthropology.

These similarities across time and place beg for explanations in reference to human biology. For several decades, increasingly sophisticated biological approaches to altered states of consciousness (ASC) have begun to offer answers to these intriguing anomalies that challenge simplistic dismissals of the reality of such experiences. Instead, we have now entered into an era in which the similar phenomenological patterns of spiritual experiences found cross-culturally are being addressed in terms of neurophenomenological perspectives. These neurophenomenological approaches provide a biological framework for explaining the phenomenal nature of these experiences, their similarities across culture, and the origins of the forms of the experiences themselves by attributing their features to functions of biological processes (Laughlin et al. 1992).

This chapter places religious experiences within an empirical framework through several approaches. The first is through cross-cultural research, specifically ethnological or holocultural research that establishes cross-cultural similarities in religious experiences. These cross-cultural patterns illustrate that these experiences are not merely individual and idiosyncratic, but rather transcend individual factors, personal as well as cultural. Cross-cultural research also serves to establish social predictors of different forms of religious experiences: for instance, the predominance of possession experiences in more complex societies, specifically those with political integration beyond the level of the local community (Winkelman 1992). These kinds of relations help to explain the variable distribution of specific forms of religious experiences in terms of social influences on individual psychology: for instance, those in which the social oppression, violence, and nutritional distress that afflict women contribute to dissociative experiences that play a role in their possession experiences (see also Bourguignon 1973).

A second approach to establishing the empirical nature of religious experiences is neurophenomenological in the sense of a direct, homologous relationship between the nature of a spiritual experience and the specific functioning of the brain system (see, e.g., Laughlin et al. 1992; Winkelman 2010; d'Aquili 1982: 361-83; d'Aquili and Newberg 1993: 177-200, 1999). These relationships illustrate empirically or theoretically that the phenomenology of a spiritual experience is a direct reflection of brain functioning. These relationships of experience and brain functioning are exemplified in the occurrence of epileptic-type seizures in association with possession experiences, during which the involuntary nature of the seizures is reflected in the sense that something external to the person's free will controls (possesses) the person.

A Cross-cultural Study of Religious Experiences:
Alterations of Consciousness

The nature of religious experiences was addressed in a cross-cultural study (Winkelman 1992; Winkelman and White 1987). This formal cross-cultural study was based in a stratified 45-society subsample of the Standard Cross-cultural Sample (Murdock and White 1969: 329-69). The study focused on magico-religious practitioners as documented in the ethnographic literature of pre-modern societies. This paper focuses on the aspects of the data that covered religious experiences, conceptualised in terms of the altered states of consciousness involved in the professional experiences of 59 magico-religious practitioners. These practitioners were perceived by their societies as engaging in personal experiences of the spirit world. Consequently, the data reveal religious as opposed to spiritual experiences assessing the institutionalised practices of the society, rather than the spontaneous, secular experiences of individuals.

The variables used for analyses were based on ethnographic descriptions of magico-religious activities and subjected to preliminary analyses (Winkelman 1986: 174-203, 1990: 308-52). The findings discussed here involved those variables assessing professional religious experiences, including the techniques used to induce these experience, the observable behavioral and cognitive conditions of the practitioners during these experiences, and the descriptive labels attributed to the experiences.

Cross-cultural, Social and Universal Aspects of Spiritual Experiences
The data from this study were subjected to formal analyses to infer universals and to determine cross-cultural patterns and social predictors of religious experiences that were routinely induced in the practices of magico-religious practitioners (Winkelman 1992). All societies in this sample had institutionalised practices for inducing religious experiences through ritual technologies recognised for their ability to produce alterations in consciousness. Features found universally include the use of percussion and music, singing, or chanting to produce these experiences. This notion of a spiritual relationship induced through institutional (religious) practices in repeatable ways contrasts strongly with contemporary notions of religious experiences as spontaneous and involuntary.

Types of Religious Experiences
Religious experiences exhibit cross-cultural patterns in recurrent relationships among their features revealed by entailment analysis that determines which variables co-occur, thereby having implicative relationships (e.g., if A is present, then B is present). These analyses revealed three major forms of religious experiences:

1. *Soul Flight.* The association of conditions of both dancing and periods of unconscious interpreted as a soul flight, corresponding to classic features of shamanic practice;
2. *Meditative Experiences.* The association of sleep deprivation, austerities, fasting, and social isolation constitute the well-recognised practices associated with meditative traditions; and
3. *Possession.* The association of amnesia and convulsions with experiences interpreted as possession, where an external spirits dominates the person; these occur with a spontaneous onset of possession outside of the ritual context which are then subject to ritual control and development, corresponding to classic notions of mediumship. (Winkelman 1986, 1992)

These three types of alterations of consciousness found in association with magico-religious practices worldwide—soul flight, meditative experiences, and possession—constitute transcendental forms of religious experience. These are examined here in terms of their biological and social aspects to help explain their phenomenological features and their differential cross-cultural distribution: shamanic soul flight was the typical spiritual experience of the magico-religious practitioners of hunter-gatherer societies worldwide; the possession and meditative experiences typify the religious professionals of complex societies.

Possession as a Socially Induced Religious Experience

Possession experiences are recognised for their strikingly similar phenomenological profiles across time and cultures, suggesting a physiological basis for possession experiences. These experiences produce dramatic changes in people's behaviors, voices, expressions, movements, and appearances, with the presentation of an entirely different personality than that which is normal for the person. Possession behaviors have been examined in terms of hysteria, dissociation, and other mental illnesses because of associated symptoms of uncontrollable motor activity, tremors and convulsions, glazed eyes, amnesia, anxiety and panic attacks, and episodes of unconsciousness.

Erika Bourguignon (1968, 1976a, 1976b) pioneered anthropological and cross-cultural investigations of possession. She defined possession trances as involving 'alterations or discontinuity in consciousness, awareness or personality or other aspects of psychological functioning' attributed to a belief that a 'person is changed in some way through the presence in or on him of a spirit entity or power, other than his own personality, soul [or] self' (Bourguignon 1976a: 8). Bourguignon also has provided a stronger characterisation of possession as cases 'in which the altered state is

explained as due to a takeover (possession) of the body by a spirit entity'
(Bourguignon and Evascu 1977: 198).

Possession ASC and Societal Complexity

Societal factors responsible for the incidence of possession experiences
were first established by cross-cultural analyses reporting the association of possession with social stratification, jurisdictional hierarchy, and
agriculture (Bourguignon and Evascu 1977). These findings were confirmed by my replication, which further identified political integration as
the only variable that independently explained significant variance in
the societal incidence of possession (Winkelman 1992). The societal incidence of possession manifested by culturally recognised religious practitioners is associated with specific psychophysiological, psychological,
and social conditions (Winkelman 1986, 1992). There are also individual-
level relationships of possession in magico-religious practitioners with
the presence of psychophysiological symptoms associated with pathological conditions, such as amnesia, tremors, seizures, and convulsions and
agitated, uncontrolled behavior. The presence of these conditions also
accounts for substantial variance in the societal incidence of possession
experiences, indicating that there are biological contributions to the individual and societal incidence of possession experiences.

I simultaneously assessed the predictive power of both biological conditions (temporal-lobe symptoms) and social conditions (political integration) and reported findings that show both variables have independently
significant predictions of possession experiences, but that the physiological measure (temporal-lobe discharge) predicted more variance than did
political integration (Winkelman 1992). This suggests that psychophysiological factors are central to the production of possession experiences, but
that these also reflect individual conditions produced by social circumstances. Societal practices can produce epilepsy, dissociation and temporal lobe conditions. Possession experiences predominate among abused
women of the lower classes whose deprived conditions cause physiological conditions that produce the resultant experiences (Winkelman 1992).

The predominance of possession cults and experiences occurs where
women lack adequate nutrition, have dietary deficiencies that produce
abnormalities in the central nervous system, and suffer from metabolic
imbalances such as hypocalcemia and hypoglycemia that cause emotional
disturbances, tremors, and seizures (Bourguignon 1973). Thus, social conditions creating dietary deficiencies appear responsible for triggering
physiological conditions that predispose individuals to seizures and the
interpretations of their conditions as possession.

These relationships of spiritual experiences, religious practices and
social conditions reveal a specific dynamic of the neurophenomenology

of religious experiences. When people experience oppressive social conditions that cause physiological conditions predisposing them to dissociation, they and their societies are disposed to accept interpretations of possession. In this sense we can attribute the form of the spiritual experience, as well as its contributing factors during induction, to socially induced, individual psychophysiological conditions.

Psychophysiological Perspectives on Possession

The presence of amnesia is a controversial and significant feature of religious experiences, especially possession. My cross-cultural research found a strong association of possession and amnesia, while amnesia is absent among shamans experiencing soul flight (1992). This reflects a distinctive physiological profile associated with possession episodes that are generally first manifested spontaneously and outside the ritual context, during which the person is beset by tremors, convulsions, seizures, and uncontrolled compulsive motor behavior, as well as amnesia. There is a temporal-lobe personality syndrome, also referred to as an interictal personality, that has symptomology similar to that of epilepsy with features of increased emotionality and philosophical and religious preoccupations (Schachter 2006). A second physiological mechanism of possession is reflected in a similar psychiatric diagnosis of multiple personality disorder (dissociative identity disorder).

The interictal personality syndrome underlies an association of pathological symptoms with divine experiences because the temporal lobe syndrome is found in association with mystical and religious experiences among normal populations. There are a number of parallels of possession experiences with the dissociative identity disorder, which like possession, manifests a separate personality dissociated from the ego and with mutual amnesia between different personalities. Goodman (1988) suggested that the behavioral similarities of possession with these disorders is a reflection of a common underlying capacity for dissociation.

The association of these physiological features and religious experiences suggests that these predispositions were selected for in human evolution. The functional aspects of dissociation reveal the nature of possession as a human adaptation. Dissociation is an evolved mechanism that provides a means for escape from extreme emotional stress in one's interpersonal relations. Rebecca Seligman and Laurence Kirmayer (2008) note that stressful parental relationships can disrupt the integration of consciousness, resulting in the formation of a separate dissociated identity. Dissociation involves a separate stream of consciousness that results from selective suppression of memories. This adaptive reaction enables a person to continue to function in relation to parents, while dissociating from the stress experienced in relationship to them. This dissociation produces an emotional distancing that inhibits the normal flight-or-fight response, enabling the child to remain and seek adaptive solutions in the relationship. Such dissociative detachment of the psychological self from the social self is facilitated by the personalities of possession spirits that mediate an identification with the idealised social norms they represent.

The predominance of women experiencing possession worldwide is a reflection of a socio-psycho-dynamic response of dissociation produced by abuse and conditions of powerlessness (Bourguignon 1976a, 1976b; Winkelman 2010). Possession experiences are a culturally acceptable avenue for expressing unconscious or repressed desires. The alternative selves manifested through possession allow for sublimated self-expression, with the powerful spirits that are manifested providing tools for influencing others, particularly their husbands, by using the spirits to convey what are the women's own wishes.

Possession in Neurophenomenological Perspective

Possession experiences result from a variety of predisposing biological factors derived from marginalisation and how it affects wellbeing in ways that cause dissociation and facilitate alterations of consciousness (Bourguignon 1976a; Lewis 1971; Winkelman 2010). The association of possession with a psychiatric profile and distinctive physiological conditions (an epilepsy-like temporal lobe syndrome) appears to be the consequence of political and social processes responsible for prompting the possession conditions. The symptoms of central nervous system dysfunction, such as seizures and amnesia, can result from trauma and nutritional deficiencies, disease, injuries from physical abuse, psychological distress, marginalisation, and oppression that produce dissociation and other predisposing and precipitating features that contribute to temporal lobe and epileptic syndromes. The phenomenology of possession, manifested by being controlled by another personality, is a direct reflection of the activation of biological mechanisms that affect consciousness outside the control of the person. This may also explain the association with amnesia as a symptom of a biologically based disorder (but see Buhrman 1997).

Shamanic Soul Flight and the Archetypal Structures of Consciousness

Shamans' alterations of consciousness take a variety of forms, with soul flight, soul journey, or magical flight considered a central and defining feature. Eliade (1964) characterised typical shamanic ecstasy as an experience in which the person's soul was believed to depart from the body, traveling to the heavens or underworld. Other forms of the shaman's religious experience may involve a vision quest, during which a neophyte seeks a direct encounter with the spiritual powers, especially animals; a death and rebirth experience, during which the initiate experiences being killed and dismembered by animals and later reconstructed with new powers; or a transformation into an animal, during which the shaman loses sense of his/her own body and surroundings and instead experiences the world as an animal.

Individuals from virtually all societies have reported the experience of a separation of the personal consciousness and identity from the body and its entry into another world—a central feature of the shamanic soul flight. In shamanism, these experiences are thought to involve some personal aspect of the person, identified as his/her soul or personal spirit that departs from the body and travels to spirit worlds. A significant feature of the soul journey is the persistence of the practitioner's personal consciousness while appearing unconscious to observers, but nonetheless actively engaging in an experiential realm with memory of experiences shared upon return to ordinary consciousness.

Soul Flight as an Archetypal Structure: A Neuroepistemological Perspective

Central phenomenological features of the shaman's soul flight have substantial parallels with phenomena studied in modern psychology, such as out-of-body experience (OBE) and anomalous body experiences, as well as medically studied near-death experiences (see, e.g., Lopez et al. 2008; Metzinger 2009; Greyson 2000). A main feature of these varied OBEs is one's personal subjectivity and sense of self experienced in a location distinctly different from the physical body. In OBEs there is a separation of the self, body, and visual perspectives, with the visual field often of a nonordinary reality that takes precedence over the somatic field.

Thomas Metzinger (2005, 2009) shows that in these OBEs and similar body-self dissociation experiences we see a separation of the underlying architecture of the human self and consciousness, which is distorted by a dissembling of the normal unity of the elements of self experience, in which one's self and body are experienced as being in the same place as one's visual perspective. This visual experience can be understood as an early form of symbolism—a presentational symbolism (Hunt 1995a) in which one experiences a separation of various components that underlie the functional and phenomenological properties of the proto-concept of mind.

OBEs can be studied in people who can induce them voluntarily, as well as through inducing them with electrical brain stimulation and with false visual feedback that provides erroneous information regarding tactile stimulation and positions of the body. The neural correlates of these experiences implicate interference in the temporo-parietal junction, resulting in a failure of integration of body-related information involving a functional disconnection of the motor, somatic, and balance areas of the brain from the frontal cortex processing areas. This interference in the normal body information integration can produce a variety of anomalous body experiences involving the disintegration of the normal body and self model (Lopez et al. 2008). Such biological interference is a contributing destabilising factor that disables normal self functions and permits the cultural programming and intentions of the shaman to guide the internal visual experiential encounter with the supernatural. The visual experiences of the self and strange environments that occur during the OBE are a result of the disengagement of the mechanisms managing the visual field and body proprioception. This separation of aspects of the person's self and body allows for the illusion of movement through a pseudo-body experienced as a spiritual body.

Shamanic practices apparently induce such experiences through repetitive drumming and dancing that interferes with the normal integration of the various senses (vestibular, proprioceptive, visual and tactile) through effects of habituation (a failure to respond to stimuli caused by overstimulation). The over-stimulation of the temporo-parietal junction may also result from the extensive physical activities of the shaman involving extreme exertion in dancing to the point of collapse. Because medical literature indicates that similar to OBEs, near-death experiences can occur as a result of physical trauma, drug overdoses, or even extreme fright, a variety of shamanic ritual activities may contribute to this experience of separation of the self and perception from the body.

Soul Flight as Presentational Symbolism: A Visual Epistemology

OBEs exhibit features of complex synesthesia integrating perceptual modalities (Hunt 1995a). This capacity reflects the visionary aspects central to shamans' religious experiences that are manifested in an internal flow of images. These visual experiences reflect one of the most fundamental functions of the human brain, an ancient mode of imaginal consciousness (Baars 1997). Such experiences result from the match of sensory input with a mental image, also manifested in memories, dreams, and other internal visual experiences. This visual cognition, primarily based in imagery from a reactivation of past sensorimotor experiences (Newton 1996), constitutes what Harry Hunt (1995a, b, c) proposed is a fundamental modality of symbolic cognition: presentational symbolism.

Presentational symbolism has a central role in shamanic and mystical visionary experiences, in dreams, in near-death experiences, and in other 'hallucinatory' experiences that occur as a consequence of illness, trauma, and drugs. Presentational symbolism reflects a natural symbolic system manifesting the structures of abstract intelligence in the imagistic mode. It emerges spontaneously out of the unconscious in the arts, dream imagery, and religious visions. These visionary experiences are a natural symbolism of the brain expressed as a consequence of a disinhibition of the regulation of the visual cortex, resulting in hyperactivity of the visual region experienced as visual panoramas full of meaning.

Shamans' practices are intrinsically linked to dreams by their overnight nature. Shamans explicitly sought to integrate dream processes within their rituals in order to integrate the potentials of dreaming. The functional basis for this shamanic use of dreams is revealed in the evolutionary and functional roles of dreams and the nature of dream cognition (Winkelman 2010). The nonverbal body-based aspects of dreaming reveal their connection with a pre-egoic and pre-linguistic level of symbolisation, with the dream content representing complex manifestations of presentational symbolism that play a key role in memory formation and integration, as well as exploration of alternative scenarios and problem solving.

Shamanic visionary experiences engage forms of knowing made available by the alterations of consciousness, constituting a special epistemological approach (Krippner 2000; Rock and Krippner 2011). Shamanic experiences engage processes of deciphering images to infer meaning relevant to diagnosis, cure, planning, and many other informational needs (see also Winkelman and Peek 2004). The contributions of shamanic ritual to human cognitive evolution involved abilities to make symbolic interpretations of images, using this information for adaptations involving the prediction of future conditions and responding to those challenges.

In shamanic experiences, the alterations of consciousness have central roles in engaging analogical modeling processes through use of image-schemas that provide foundational meanings embodied in archetypal forms. These potentials are accessed through shamanic visions, in which the visual symbols experienced were based on information processes of our ancient reptilian and paleomammalian brains (Winkelman 2010). These pre-language processes of knowing accessed through shamanic alterations of consciousness enable the integration of normally unconscious information into the symbolic processes mediated by the frontal brain.

Such forms of knowledge provide biological explanations of many features of the shamanic experiences. These include the visual nature of the experiences and their association with animalistic forms of consciousness and self experiences. The separation of self, perspective, and body experienced in soul journey and other anomalous self-body experiences reveal the fundamental archetypal and functional structures of consciousness and provide mechanisms for the spiritual experience of self dissociated from body as manifested in soul flight.

Neurotransmitters and Shamanic Neuropsychology

I have proposed that shamanic rituals and practices have direct effects on the major neurotransmitter systems, which are reflected in the experiences (Winkelman 2016, 2013). Behaviorally induced as well as drug-induced technologies produce alterations of consciousness through effects on the serotonergic, dopaminergic, and endocannabinoid neurotransmitter systems.

Shamanic ritual practices enhance dopamine through general effects on the autonomic nervous system produced by dancing and drumming, as well as a variety of other aspects of ritual such as exhaustion, temperature extremes, and night-time activities. Fred Previc (2009) proposed that the effects of dopamine account for a variety of features of shamanic practices and that diverse mechanisms that alter consciousness involve a disinhibition of dopaminergic extrapersonal brain systems in the ventral cortex and the limbic areas. The parasympathetic action of dopamine produces the physical collapse experienced that precipitates shamanic soul flight. The neurochemical dynamics of the shamanic visionary experiences likely reflect dopamine transmission, which is implicated in visionary experiences such as hallucinations and dreams.

These higher-order sensory processing activities and cross-modal sensory experiences, typified in the shamanic soul flight, are mediated through dopamine association areas. Extensive activation of dopamine produces a dominance of extrapersonal cognition such as context-independent cognition that processes information about distant objects and events. Enhanced dopamine stimulates extrapersonal cognition, augmenting intelligence, achievement orientation, and confidence, as well as underlying the typical charisma of shamans by provoking intensely aggressive drives, creative genius, a sense of invincibleness, delusions of grandeur, and magical ideation regarding the ability to control others and future events (Previc 2009).

Mystical Experiences as a Perennial Psychology and Neuroepistemology

There are several typical forms of mystical experiences manifesting similar phenomenological patterns across time and cultures. These various types of mystical experiences represent *noumena*—transcendental realities existing apart from the particular tradition's conceptualisations of them. The transcendental status of these experiences are exemplified in the use of broad labels such as introvertive versus extrovertive mysticism and similar descriptive terms to represent them—concepts such as bliss, void, and oneness.

The commonalities found cross-culturally in meditative practices and traditions include similarities in their views of processes of the mind and specific stages of development of consciousness. The cross-cultural distribution of these experiences attest to their innate basis in qualities intrinsic to human nature, rather than merely some arbitrary cultural construction. These commonalties have been discussed as a perennial psychology and a perennial philosophy involving cross-cultural or universal beliefs about human consciousness (Smith 1975, 2000; Schoun 1977; Wilber 1977, 1980). The perennial principles reflect neurognostic structures and reveal neuroepistemological foundations of mystical experiences and knowledge (Winkelman 1997, 2000, 2010; d'Aquili 1982; d'Aquili and Newberg 1993, 1999).

Neurognostic features are reflected in similar features of the stages of consciousness recognised across meditative traditions. Ken Wilber (1977, 1980, 1986), who based his model on the Vedic perspectives, postulates a universal hierarchy of transpersonal development that extends Piaget's four initial stages of cognitive development (sensorimotor, preoperational, concrete operational, and formal operational thought) into a series of transpersonal development stages that he labeled vision logic, psychic, subtle, causal, and ultimate or absolute levels of consciousness. These developments are based on changes in the forms of self that mediate experience.

A similar model of the development of consciousness based on the Maharishi Mahesh Yogi's Vedic psychology specifies advanced states of consciousness they call transcendental, cosmic, glorified cosmic, and unity consciousness (Alexander, Davies et al. 1990; Alexander, Robinson et al. 1994). C. Alexander, J. Davies et al. characterise mystical modes of knowing as providing more invariant knowledge of reality by an increasing differentiation and hierarchical integration of cognitive structures. A new self mode allows liberation of consciousness from the habitual symbolic representations of language, permitting the integration of the affective functions with intellectual operations.

I have proposed that these mystical experiences and the perennial psychology represent developmental stages involving distinctive epistemic processes (Winkelman 1993, 2010). Epistemology is a necessary and fundamental perspective for understanding differences among forms of consciousness, exemplified in Jean Piaget's (1971) genetic epistemology. Piaget proposed that we understand the development of consciousness in terms of the epistemic structures and concepts that the person employs to understand experiences. Knowledge and experience are mediated by epistemic structures—assumptions about the nature of the knower's capacities and what can be known. This process constrains knowledge because epistemic structures assimilate experiences to their own forms and principles.

Meditative practices change self-awareness and results in the suspension of automatised epistemic structures used for organisation of experience and consciousness. Engagement and disengagement of basic neural systems and psychological processes can explain major aspects of the phenomenology of mystical experiences. The levels or stages proposed for mystical development are analysed here in terms of epistemic structures and basic brain functions, proposing neuroepistemological relationships for various stages or states of meditative consciousness in terms of differential activation of various functional systems of the brain.

Neurophenomenological Views of Mystical Experiences

Neurophenomenological bases for the phenomenal content of mystical experiences are exemplified in research on various physiological parameters associated with meditative practices. Features of meditative traditions such as control of attentional, perceptual, emotional and conceptual processes are reflected in their control of associated physiological responses (see Taylor et al. 1997). The physiological parameters of meditators' brains coincide with their phenomenological descriptions of the experiences, which is to say that their conditions of greater attention, focus, and coordination reflect similar effects on brain waves that exhibit greater coherence, synchronisation, and power.

Meditation and Brain Synchronisation

Meditation results in decreases to alpha and theta ranges in brain wave frequency, manifested in increased alpha and theta amplitude and regularity in the frontal and central brain regions (Winkelman 2010: ch. 4). These typical changes in brain waves involve an increase in alpha waves, followed with a decrease in their frequency to theta rhythms. These changes in overall theta activation reflected proficiency in meditation practice. The alpha enhancement of meditators involves permanent alpha slowing and increased theta activity and power. This increase in theta power is reflected in frontal lobe activity and enhanced mindfulness, internalised attention and mindfulness (Takahashi et al. 2005). Meditation-induced alpha and theta EEG waves are also the modulators of the hypersynchronous high-frequency gamma waves (35-44 cps) associated with binding of signals and activities from diverse areas of the brain. Alpha EEG of meditation reflects the brain's processes of information transfer and integration that underlie high-level cognitive processes.

The increased interhemispheric synchronisation and greater coherence across cortical areas during meditation reflect what the mystical traditions consider to be the effects of meditation. Increased theta activity substantiates attentional development, reflecting the role of sustained low amplitude theta in sustained attention. Enhanced interhemispheric synchronisation reflects activation of attentional processes of the lower brain structures and the lower brain discharges that synchronise different cortical areas. These are neurophenomenological correspondences, or concordance between physiological conditions and phenomenological experiences (Winkelman 2011).

Attention and Awareness

Commonalities across meditative traditions include enhanced control of attentional processes, and the resultant changes in the operation of perceptual processes produce variations that underlie mystical development. Meditation enhances pre-attentive processes, a result of the retraining of attention that increases awareness and the ability to concentrate and focus attention for extended periods of time (see, e.g., Taylor et al. 1997). This increase in awareness and attention results in a disinhibition of the personally and culturally programmed structures of perceptual and cognitive categorisation.

The concentrative techniques of controlling attention to constrict the perceptual field leads to recognition of the constructed nature of perception and an awareness that the objects of perception are derived from the mental models employed to interpret them. This deconstruction of perception also permits central features of mystical experiences: the perception of universals of the human mind. This insight into the nature of mental operations enables an internal locus of control and awareness of the habitual perceptual and cognitive processes, resulting in a reduction of unconscious projective and associative processes.

Epistemic Processes and Mystical Consciousness

The control of attention can lead to suspension of basic epistemic processes. For instance, Walter Odajnyk (1993) noted the ability of meditative practices to inhibit operation of basic psychological functions such as sensations, intuitions, feeling and thinking. As a consequence of the deautomatisation of the habitually employed constructs underlying these processes, one develops an ability to observe these constructs and then abandon them. Enhanced attention increases awareness of unconscious mental processes and of the more basic nonverbal, imagistic and somatic processes. Recognition of perceptual and cognitive programs results in reevaluations of one's personal identity and changes in cognitive processes that can lead to development of further levels of consciousness. For example, increased awareness leads to another cross-cultural feature of meditative states: the notion that our sense of self is false, that who we think of as our personal identity is mistaken.

The suspension of epistemic processes leads to several of the basic principles of mystical consciousness:

1. Awareness of the constructed nature of perception leads to the ability to suspend the habitual personal and cultural programming embodied in the routine processing performed in the structures of attention and perception, permitting the development of awareness of the inherent neurognostic structures;
2. Realisation of the false nature of one's sense of self and ecstatic emotional experiences resulting from suspension of the participating self as the point of reference, and the emergence of identification with the 'observing self' and its liberation from attachments; and
3. Suspension of conceptual thought and language descriptions, leading to transverbal and transconceptual apperceptions that result from suspension of both learned concepts and innate neurognostic structures, and leading to experiences such as void and awareness without content (contentless awareness).

Subtle Consciousness

Subtle consciousness involves developments that depend on the changes in perceptions regarding the self produced by separation of the participating self and the observing self. As a consequence of unlearning of habituated conditioning of thought, increased self-awareness results and leads to a re-evaluation of self. This re-evaluation results in a deconstruction of the sense of self and abandonment of false beliefs derived from a mindless, automatic and unconscious information processing. Discarding habitual identification with thought and behavior permits awareness that the permanent and continuous sense of self is an arbitrary construction and only one of many possible selves.

Richard Castillo (1991) characterised this meditative development in Hindu yogis as involving the creation of co-conscious selves that produces a divided consciousness. In addition to our ordinary personal self, called *jiva*, which participates directly in the world, there is also an uninvolved observing self, called the 'true self', 'witness', or *atman*. The participating self that engages with the world is experienced as the mind: one's personal thoughts, emotions, and sensations of the body and memories. The *atman* develops an observing consciousness by being an uninvolved witness of reactions of the personal and physical selves. I. K. Taimni (1968) discussed this witness as seer, *purusha*: the essence of the subjective the power of consciousness to function through the vehicles of the mind.

The control of attention achieved in meditation—focus to the point at which only the experience of attention exists—permits the separation of these two streams of awareness. This dynamic enables a permanent meditational attention in addition to the habitual focus on everyday activities.

Meditators experience both aspects of consciousness simultaneously through the separation of the observing self from the participating self, resulting in a sense of liberation. This liberation is the consequence of the observing self, which only witnesses events rather than engaging or participating in them, and consequently is freed from the suffering that comes from identifications made by the personal self.

Cosmic Consciousness

Alexander et al.'s (1990, 1994) assessment of the Vedic cosmic consciousness, described as involving rapture, bliss, love, and compassion, is attributed to a unification of self and the world, but is an unbounded or nonattached self that does not identify with thought. Vedic psychology attributes a central role to feelings in interconnecting levels of the mind, particularly 'the interface between mind and senses and between the intellect and ego' (Alexander, Davies et al. 1990: 304). Hunt (1995a, 1995b) characterised mystical experiences as involving an affective development that integrates underlying valuation, feelings, and personal experiences of others.

Piaget's recognition that affective development lags behind intellectual development because it lacks a fixed point of accommodation is addressed in transpersonal development through accommodation provided by the affective perspectives derived from the observing self. This self underlies the permanent sense of presence, openness, and compassion and provides the basis for formal affective operations (Hunt 1995b). The roles of feelings in early development and emotional attachments are suspended in meditative development, permitting joy and bliss independent of surrounding circumstances and the operation of their intuitive modalities that are holistic and more rapid. Freedom from pain and suffering results as a consequence of the ability to suspend emotional attachments.

Eugene d'Aquili provides neuroepistemological perspectives on the extreme positive affect associated with meditative states by linking these experiences of positive affect to differential patterns of stimulation and disruption of right-hemisphere and limbic processes (d'Aquili 1982; d'Aquili and Newberg 1999). Stimulation of the peripheral parasympathetic system produces a profound quiescence, with ecstatic and blissful feelings emerging from the reverberation of circuitry connecting the posterior superior parietal lobe with the prefrontal cortex, a stimulation of both divisions of the autonomic nervous system (ANS) resulting in saturation and habituation. The role of the limbic brain apparently first involves specific activations to produce the ecstatic rapturous emotional states and then subsequently the suspension of these limbic processes, producing equanimity and nonattachment.

Causal Consciousness

Wilber (1980) attributes to causal consciousness the experiential features described as the unmanifest realm or void, a form of consciousness that is without objects in awareness. This widely recognised form of contemplative consciousness, often referred to as Void, is a state achieved by completely controlling awareness and cutting it off from the outer world. With this experience, all forms of awareness are radically transcended, so that nothing arises in consciousness. This void consciousness is generally considered to be beyond description and concepts—a perception of reality without personal, cultural, or linguistic conceptualisation that is free of conditioning and all conceptual distinctions. This transcendence of ordinary perceptions of separate self and isolated objects is produced by suspension of the imposition of concepts on the undifferentiated reality, in essence reflecting the abandonment of all learned processes for processing perceptions.

Odajnyk (1993: 66-67) proposed that meditation eliminates the reductive and selective operations of the brain to a point that the nervous system and sensory apparatus cease operations. The role of selective segregation or deafferentation of input from brain systems in producing mystical experience is proposed by Eugene d'Aquili and Andrew Newberg's (1993) examination of what they call Absolute Unitary Being: an awareness that is unlimited by senses of self, time, or the environment and is accompanied by emotions of bliss. D'Aquili suggested that the neurophysiological mechanisms underlying the experience of absolute unity are a result of activity of the parietal lobe of the non-dominant hemisphere (1982: 375). D'Aquili and Newberg (1993) proposed that these experiences are produced by interference with the brain's processing loops, the normal functions of tertiary association areas that analyse and integrate information, particularly somaesthetic (body), visual, and auditory information. D'Aquili and Newberg (1993) further proposed that deafferentation, involving a functional blocking of input into a structure that is caused by inhibitory fibers, accounts for specific features of mystical experiences. A consequence of deafferentation of a neurological structure, such as pre-frontal cortex inhibition of input from language-processing areas, can impede formation of words and concepts, resulting in the ineffable aspects of mystical experiences.

Conclusions: Religious Experiences as Intrinsic Forms of Knowing

The dominant view of religious experiences has been that they reflect the person's religious traditions and cultural beliefs and expectations that determine the phenomenological content of the experiences. It is true that cultural and religious traditions shape the experiences and their reports. However, as Robert Forman (1998), Frithjof Schoun (1975), Wilber (1980), and others have shown, there are cross-cultural similarities found in the spiritual experiences of advanced devotees from many different theological traditions. These cross-cultural and universal features of mystical experiences cannot be explained simply as a result of cultural influences. Such findings falsify the traditional constructivist hypotheses and support instead a neurophenomenological view of mystical experiences as a biologically structured experiences.

While the neuroepistemological approaches are biased towards biological explanations, they also recognise the role of cultural learning in the formation of the structures and functions of the brain during development (Laughlin et al. 1990). In essence, cultural structures (i.e., language) are embodied in biology during neural development. But the universality of certain features such as the classic mystical and shamanic experiences reflect the predominant if not exclusive role of biology in the phenomenology and structure of the experiences. Culture nonetheless plays a role in facilitating access (or blocking) these experiences through cultural ideologies and practices, which contribute to the interpretation and utilisation of these experiences.

This constructionist view of experiences as being the result of the cultural and personal features is, however, proposed by meditative traditions for characterising ordinary consciousness as a construction produced by the mental models that provide the basis for interpretation of experiences. Meditative experiences reveal the constructed nature of ordinary perception and lead to a deconstruction of these habitual processes and permit the emergence of neurognostic structures. Mystical experiences relieve repression of these early systems of knowing, which are reintegrated in mystical developments. Meditative practices involve suspension of the processes of habituated attention, emotional detachment, self-concepts, and formal conceptual structures that are assumed as epistemic structures in the development of the stages of cognitive development proposed by Piaget (1971). The initial meditative development involves the suspension of the ethnocentric cultural assumptions embodied in realisations of cultural relativism. Next, at the subtle levels, there is the suspension of habituated perceptual habits. At the cosmic level there is the suspension of emotional attachment and self-identity, followed at the causal level by the total suspension of conceptual structures.

While the idea of unmediated experiences and experiences without content ('contentless experience') that are free of any personal or cultural programming flies in the face of most contemporary psychological and anthropological theories, these kinds of perceptions are central claims of many mystical traditions. The ability to link such experiences to the suspension of certain neurological processes is what enables a neurological account of mystical experiences. This perspective allows an understanding of the nature of mystical experiences in terms of a suspension of mundane conceptual structures, enabling an experience without normal conceptualisation that embodies the essence of the unspeakable sacred.

Short Biographical Note

Michael Winkelman was an Associate Professor (now retired) at the School of Human Evolution and Social Change at Arizona State University, former President of the Anthropology of Consciousness section of the American Anthropological Association, and founding President of its Anthropology of Religion Section. His research focusses on cross-cultural and interdisciplinary research on shamanism and alterations of consciousness.

Section Two:
Methodological Challenges for the Study of Religious Experience

Chapter 3

Fieldwork and Embodied Knowledge: Researching the Experiences of Spirit Mediums in the Brazilian Vale do Amanhecer

Emily Pierini

The apprenticeship of a medium or a shaman involves, along with the acquisition of knowledge and techniques taught by instructors, teachers, or spirit guides, the development of the capacity of becoming a mediator of knowledge of the spiritual worlds. The body is at the core of this mediation and, therefore, of the process of learning and knowledge production. Studies on shamanism, spirit mediumship, and possession are certainly fertile ground for the scholarly interest in the body, emotions, and the self. Since the emergence of the paradigm of embodiment (Csordas 1990), particularly in the field of anthropology, a progressive shift of focus has taken place towards the sensorial ground of experience and the role of the body in producing cultural meanings. Proceeding along these lines, my research among mediums in the Brazilian Spiritualist Christian Order Vale do Amanhecer (Valley of the Dawn)[1] addresses the cognitive, sensory, and emotional processes involved in mediumistic development, and how these inform the notions of the self. After introducing the mediumistic practice of the Vale, I will discuss the debates regarding the categorization of these phenomena, progressively shedding light upon the centrality of the body and the self in mediumistic experience. Subsequently, I will reflect upon the bodily dimension of the ethnographic encounter, questioning the assumption of 'going native' and the notion of 'belief', exploring the potential of focussing upon bodily experience. This focus allows us to avoid reproducing those dichotomic categorizations and pathologising reductions which characterised earlier approaches to mediumship and possession.

Encountering Spirits: From Categories towards a Multidimensional Phenomenon

The Vale do Amanhecer (Valley of the Dawn) was founded in 1959 by Neiva Chaves Zelaya (1925–1985), known in Brazil as the clairvoyant Tia Neiva

(Aunt Neiva). While working as a truck driver in the construction of the federal Capital Brasília, Brazil, Tia Neiva began to manifest spontaneously mediumistic phenomena with a revelatory character through which she established the sacred spaces, ritualistic practice, and foundations of the Doctrine of the Amanhecer. Since its foundation, the Order has opened more than six hundred temples throughout North and South America, Europe, and Japan. The main temple, which is located near Brasília, has grown from a small farm into a town of almost 10,000 inhabitants. Open daily with a great variety of healing rituals, the temple is now considered a place of 'spiritual first aid', rather than a place for worship, where mediums rapidly pass from one ritual to another in order to assist patients and spirits in need of spiritual assistance.

Mediumship is understood in the Vale as a universal feature of human beings, the practice of which is culturally shaped according to the purposes of different religions. The process of mediumistic development is a complex path through which a medium learns how to control his or her own mediumship and to use it for the healing of others. The spiritual treatment of patients is offered free of cost and is referred to as 'disobsessive' healing, which involves the release of causal spiritual agents understood as affecting (obsessing) the patient. For the purpose of disobsessive healing, two complementary types of mediumship are developed in the Vale: those of the medium *apará* and of the medium *doutrinador*, who always work in pairs in healing rituals. The *apará* embodies spirits through a semiconscious trance described as being similar to dream sleep. These may be spirit guides bringing guidance, protection, and healing from the higher spirit worlds, such as: *pretos velhos* (spirits of old African slaves), *caboclos* (spirits of Amerindians), *médicos de cura* (spirits of doctors), *ciganos* (gypsies), and *orixás* (known in the Afro-Brazilian context). Or, they may be suffering spirits who remain trapped between the planes after death and may affect human beings. The *doutrinador* in a conscious trance does not embody spirits, but rather directs the rituals and indoctrinates the suffering spirits embodied by the *apará*, helping them to move further in the spirit world.

In different cultures, spiritual beings are variably represented as enunciators of knowledge about the afterlife, as guides bringing healing and assisting the living with their lives on earth, or as attendants accompanying the specialists of the sacred through the spirit worlds. Some spirits are otherwise understood as opposing forces or pathogenic agents that need to be exorcised or removed from a particular person or place. Whether welcomed or not, these spiritual agents are understood as being able to communicate through, to be embodied by, or to influence human beings to differing extents. I refer to mediumistic practices by addressing the many ways and techniques through which this type of communication, embodiment, or influence may happen in different cultures in more or less controlled ways, assuming local features and conceptualizations. For many people in a great variety of societies around the world, including the Western ones, these phenomena are part of an everyday life in which the boundaries between the world of the living and of the dead, spirits, or deities are conceived as permeable.

According to a major cross-cultural survey conducted by Erika Bourguignon drawing on George Murdock's *Ethnographic Atlas* and using a sample of 488 societies around the world, 90 percent of these groups had socially structured forms of altered states of consciousness (ASC) usually within religious contexts, 74 percent of which attributed ASC to spirit possession (Bourguignon 1967, 1979). The way the interaction between human and spiritual beings has been interpreted has produced different sets of categories determined by variables such as control, ASC, and desirability of the phenomenon.

The control variable has been widely used in the definition of different typologies of spirit possession. For example, a classical categorisation was proposed by Raymond Firth in his study of the Tikopia of Melanesia. By focussing on the control aspect, he distinguished between three different phenomena: spirit possession, when the spirit is controlling the person's actions provoking abnormal behaviour; spirit mediumship, which is the use of abnormal behaviour to communicate with the spirit world; and shamanism, when the person is controlling the spirit (1967: 296).

Ioan M. Lewis (1971) provided a wide-ranging comparative investigation on mystical experiences involving shamanism and spirit possession in different religions. He drew a distinction between *unsolicited* possession, which is involuntary and uncontrolled, and *solicited* possession, which conversely is voluntary and controlled. These types of spirit possession may also be approached as two consequential phases. The primary phase is understood in many contexts as being a sort of mystical call from spirits involuntarily manifesting in the person, and in some cases it may be accompanied by illness, thus requiring therapeutic action. The secondary phase may be linked to a further stage in which the individual gradually learns how to control the spirit's behaviour for purposes of communication or for healing spirits afflicting others (Lewis 1971: 55).

Bourguignon (1967) focussed on the presence or absence of trance behaviour, distinguishing between possession *trance*, which implies an ASC with the loss of conscious awareness and a spirit taking over the person's body producing observable changes, and *possession*, which is characterised by the absence of ASC but with a spirit producing changes in the person's behaviour or health. The kind of social response to a behaviour attributed to a supernatural being would then determine a further distinction in *positive* possession—that which is socially valued—or *negative* possession—that which is socially abhorred, because it is often considered to be pathological and linked to a dissociative identity disorder (DID).

Although still widely used in the literature on possession, this distinction focussing on trance has been considered problematic. Michael Lambek (1981), for instance, argues that trance is merely one aspect of spirit possession. He provides the example of meditation to illustrate how trance and ASC do not always involve spirit possession. Dismissing the pathological aspect used by Bourguignon in her definition of possession, Lambek, in his study of possession in Mayotte society (Comore Islands), describes 'manifest possession' as the moment in which the relationship between humans and spiritual beings becomes manifest in rituals of spirit possession, that is, when the deity manifests itself actively possessing the host's body. This moment is generally characterised by an ASC. In contrast, 'latent possession' refers to the everyday life of the possessed during which the deity does not manifest actively (Lambek 1981). Most studies on mediumship and possession, particularly the psycho-physiological ones, are focussed primarily on manifest possession as the tangible indicator of the relationship with the spirits. However, spirit possession is not confined to the 'extraordinary' and dramatic manifestation of spirits in rituals; it is rather embedded in the experience of 'ordinary', everyday lives of the subjects (Boddy 1988).

Furthermore, the relationship with gods and spirits is complex and changeable according to the life circumstances of the individuals. The desirability or legitimacy of these phenomena determine the classification proposed by Peter Claus in his study on the Siri and Mayndala cults in southern India (1979). He described spirit mediumship as the 'legitimate, expected possession of a specialist by a spirit or a deity, usually for the purpose of soliciting aid...for human problems', and spirit possession as the 'unexpected, unwanted intrusion of the supernatural into the lives of humans [which] generally creates disturbance and is regarded negatively with concern and apprehension' (Claus 1979: 29).

The exploration of the underling cognitive structures that may account for the cross-cultural recurrence of concepts of possession is currently a major concern of cognitive anthropologists addressing these phenomena. Emma Cohen has proposed two types of possession:

> *Pathogenic* possession concepts result from the operation of cognitive tools that deal with the representation of contamination (both positive and negative); the presence of the spirit entity is typically (but not always) manifested in the form of illness. *Executive* possession concepts mobilise cognitive tools that deal with the world of intentional agents; the spirit entity is typically represented as taking over the host's executive control, or replacing the host's 'mind' (or intentional agency), thus assuming control of bodily behaviours. (Cohen 2008: 103)

According to Cohen (2008), in pathogenic possession the spirit is perceived as a contaminating substance, and beliefs about contamination are universal and accompanied by conceptions of purification. Thus, she recognises that executive possession may be a prescribed treatment for pathogenic possession, a consideration that is in line with the above-mentioned consequential phases described by Lewis (1971) and later by Bourguignon (1979). Cohen (2008) makes a further distinction within executive-possession concepts. Exploring spirit possession in the Afro-Brazilian cult Tambor de Mina in Belém, Brazil, she distinguishes between the modes of *displacement*, in which the spirit's agency replaces the person's agency and takes control of the body (and the medium's identity is perceived as sleeping or journeying out of the body), and *fusion*, in which the agencies of the medium and the spirit are merged in the person's body and the two entities form another being (Cohen 2007, 2008). In both cases, the medium is in a state of unconsciousness. Cohen's approach, however, raised criticism regarding the disentanglement of conceptual categories from the embodied and perceptual dimension, as if possession beliefs are the product of the acquisition of concepts by disembodied minds. Whilst Cohen claims a context-sensitive analysis, it has been argued that she does not adequately address how the process through which concepts are transmitted may vary contextually and how social, cultural, and religious interactions produce changes in the conceptualisations of possession (Espirito Santo et al. 2010).

Researching in a cult house of the same Afro-Brazilian religion in northern Brazil where Cohen conducted her fieldwork, Daniel Halperin (1995) explored mediums' discourses concerning memory and states of consciousness in spirit possession. He examined the emic conceptions of conscious and unconscious possession. He noted that in Afro-Brazilian religions' discourses, unconscious possession is related to the perception of authenticity of the deity's manifestation in the medium's body, and it is expected to be accompanied by the medium's amnesia, that is, retaining no memory of what happened during the deity's manifestation. Incomplete possession is often associated with fake, simulated possession. However, Halperin provided some ethnographic examples of conscious possession. Interestingly, some mediums reported that in certain cases they were not completely unconscious, but only 'radiated' by the spirit during rituals; thus, they were aware of what was happening around them while in trance. That is to say, they described their experiences of incomplete possession as a radiation of the spirit, which leaves an intuition in the medium's mind about what to say and what to do. These experiences, which do not meet the common expectations of total unconsciousness, might lead mediums to doubt the authenticity of their possession, but seldom would they publicly admit it. Some mediums, however, suggest that conscious mediumship may be conceived as a more developed form of mediumship, because it would not allow spirits to dominate and control the medium's body. Halperin attributed the transformation in the conceptualisation of possession, and thus the growth of the phenomenon of conscious mediumship, to the influence of the spread of Kardecism in Brazil.[2]

The discourse about mediumship in the Vale do Amanhecer is similar to the understanding of conscious mediumship because through initiatory learning two types of mediumship are developed: the semiconscious one of *apará*, and the conscious one of *doutrinador*. Some mediums I have met in my research lamented the fact that they felt that both journalists and researchers were attributing labels to them that did not reflect their meanings and practices. Their concern involved an issue that several anthropologists have repeatedly warned about: direct translations of a set of categories from one culture into another are often misleading (Evans Pritchard 1976 [1937]; Lienhardt 1961; Goldman 2006; Holbraad 2008, 2009; Bowie 2012). Context-sensitive approaches propose that when applying a native category, the ethnographer should use one that mediates between the two different sets of categories—even though the mediation itself is understood as 'positioned' (Goldman 2006)—or should create new concepts that reflect the native ones (Holbraad 2008, 2009).

The categories of 'possession', 'mediumship', and 'shamanism' appear to be used interchangeably in the anthropological literature about these phenomena in different societies. Different forms of mediumship and possession are described as being accompanied by out-of-body experiences or astral travels, or as mastery of spirits, which are features of the classical categorisations of shamanism. Similarly, shamanic practices are not limited to ecstatic kinds of conceptualisations; they may also include the incorporation of spirits. Through the category of possession, scholars have addressed a variety of practices involving crossing the physical boundaries of the human body, variably featuring channelling, mediumship, shamanism, or astral projection; however, not all practices that involve a direct relation with the spirit world are locally understood as possession. In Brazil, for instance, the category of possession is not commonly used or understood everywhere in the same way, given the widespread nature of Spiritism and the influence of its conceptualisations of human-spirits relations in different religious practices. These ritualised relations are consequently referred to as 'mediumship' (*mediunidade*) or 'mediumistic practices' (*práticas mediúnicas*). When the relation is interpreted negatively, it is referred to as 'obsession' (*obsessão*) by a spirit. Not only Spiritists, but also members of the Vale and leaders of some centres of Umbanda and Candomblé I visited during my research did not use the term 'possession'. Whereas in Europe and North America the word 'mediumhip' is often associated with the practice of communication with the dead, in Brazil mediumship involves a great variety of practices, including spiritual healing. These are practices in which either the self or the body mediate between different material and immaterial dimensions or beings.

What has emerged from this discussion is the difficulty in and the inadequacy of providing an exhaustive conceptual classification, and in systematising these phenomena in one single theoretical framework. Particularly, the current debate highlights the need for moving beyond preconstructed dichotomies, such as: 'Eliade's division between possession and trance, the gender roles within ecstatic practice generally...and the fundamental Western paradigm of mind-body dualism' (Huskinson and Schmidt 2010: 12). The methodology I have outlined is based on an interdisciplinary approach that promotes a dialogue between different perspectives (Huskinson and Schmidt 2010: 12). Furthermore, this debate highlights the extensive character of a phenomenon able to embrace and embody heterogeneous meanings, values, needs, practices, and discourses within the same process. This is a complex phenomenon that is related but not reducible to identity, morality, ethics, social organisation, history, politics, notions of personhood and of the body, conceptualisations of the afterlife, and different modalities of relation to the sacred of each particular society.

Discerning Spiritual from Pathological Experience

The current anthropological discourse rejects the classical hypothesis that related possession, mediumship, and shamanism to the Western categories of 'primitive pathology', which were a legacy of the nineteenth-century evolutionist debates that were perpetuating the dividing lines between 'us' and 'them'. Previous psychophysiological perspectives explained some manifestations of these phenomena in different cultures through the use of Western psychiatric definitions. Primarily, they focused upon trance and ASC and approached spirit possession as pathology. They have, in turn, associated the alterations of behaviour with hypnotic states, hallucination, hysteria, schizophrenia, epilepsy, neurosis, and psychopathology (Oesterreich 1930; Nina Rodrigues 1935; Kroeber 1940; Devereux 1961; Ward 1989).

Some of the earliest works among the pathological explanations were permeated by evolutionist ideas about race. Traugott Oesterreich (1930) considered spirit possession as a form of autosuggestion characteristic of the instability of 'primitive' personality. His theories based on racial psychology have now been dismissed given the speculative assumption of an existing correlation between mental illness and a 'primitive' race. The Brazilian psychiatrist Raimundo Nina Rodrigues, who studied the phenomena of spirit possession in Afro-Brazilian cults 'considered them all the outcome of "hysterical phenomena" allowed by the "extreme neuro-pathic and hysterical" and "profoundly superstitious" personality of the Negro' (in Krippner 2008: 4). Several studies have compared schizophrenic and shamanic behaviours suggesting that they are generated by similar cognitive processes although differently interpreted in both Western and 'primitive' societies (Silverman 1967: 21). Lucy Huskinson and Bettina E. Schmidt considered the 'negative association' related to possession as a legacy of either a colonial perspective or of the early scholarly focus on the aspects of pain and suffering which led to interpretations of possession as 'evil' through a Judeo-Christian perspective (2010: 8). A direct criticism of approaches concerning mental illness was made by Vincent Crapanzano, who argued:

> To emphasize 'pathology', 'mental illness', 'psychosis', and 'neurosis' in case of spirit possession...is to raise essentially misleading, though culturally expectable, responses to an 'uncanny' encounter... Such diagnoses may well blind us to the dynamic of spirit possession. The question that must be asked is this: what, besides a protective shield, do we gain from calling a shaman schizophrenic..., an individual possessed by a spirit a paranoid..., a neurotic..., or an hysteric? (Crapanzano 1977: 13-14)

According to Crapanzano, 'spirit possession provides [the individual] with an idiom for articulating a certain range of experience' (1977: 10), that is, it renders an event meaningful through its construction. Therefore, the spirit idiom should not be reduced to the Western psychological one, because self-articulation is oriented differently within the individual in the Western perspective and outside the individual in societies that use the spirit idiom. Hence, because spirits are located outside the individual in non-Western societies, we should not consider them as if they are merely projections of inner feelings and desires that are not recognised by the individual. Crapanzano ultimately suggested analysing the ways in which the idiom is constructed and used in different societies.

Several cross-cultural studies stressed the absence of mental disorders among initiated shamans or participants of possession cults (Eliade 1964; Lewis 1971). Shamanic states and schizophrenia cannot be considered 'as transcultural versions of the same psychological state' because the former does not meet the criteria for the diagnosis of the latter; thus, the schizophrenic metaphor is untenable (Noll 1983: 447). The shaman voluntarily enters ASC, and his activity is balanced with social activities that require a strong sense of self. The shaman is also able to make a distinction between the two worlds he or she inhabits, a distinction that the schizophrenic cannot make (Noll 1983: 454). Márcio Goldman, who addressed possession in Afro-Brazilian Candomblé, proposed investigating shamanism from the standpoint of notions of personhood, rather than reducing it to 'pathology', such as dissociation of personality, which he noted is a term reliant upon the Western notion of the indivisible self (1985: 30). Rather, pathologies may lead a person to a religion, and 'If we assume that a disease may be lived through as an experience of division of the person, we may understand possession as a technique of its symbolic construction' (Goldman 1985: 50).[3]

Recent developments in psychiatric research advocated the need to discern between spiritual and pathological experiences. Among the causes of these explanatory reductions, J. Hageman et al. identified 'methodological pitfalls' in psychiatry, such as 'assuming that experiences based on superficial similarities are identical' (i.e., mediumship and dissociative identity disorder) and identifying a particular brain region as the cause of spiritual phenomenon merely because it is involved in the experience without considering that bodily experiences may have different etiologies (2010: 87). However, neurological experiments based on EEGs of mediums in Brazil have excluded abnormal electrical activity in the temporal lobes or epileptic disorders (Hageman et al. 2010: 105). Brazilian psychiatrists Alexander Moreira de Almeida and Francisco Lotufo-Neto proposed methodological guidelines specifically for the study of ASC that include avoiding pathologising the unusual; multiplying the concepts of 'pathology' and 'normality'; extending research into non-clinical populations; considering the cultural contexts as well as the cultural meanings of terms; considering the limitations of psychiatric classifications; and wherever possible using phenomenological description (2003: 24). Clinical studies exclude psychopathological perspectives, revealing that people with mystical experiences score higher than control groups on the psychological wellbeing scale (Lu, Lukoff, and Turner 1992; Moreira-Almeida 2009).

Clinical studies particularly demonstrated that mediums had a low prevalence of anxiety, mental disorders, borderline personality symptoms, and use of mental health services, and that they had high socio-educational levels, consistent employment, and good social adjustment (Moreira-Almeida et al. 2007). Clinical studies and ethnographic data therefore stress a distinction between spiritual and psychopathological experiences. This non-pathological character of mediumistic experience becomes clearer through the use of ethnographic methods that examine lived experience and notions of the body and the self. These notions are the product of a specific historical and cultural context and of a particular embodied experience, which in turn inform the interpretation of that experience (Pierini 2016a).

Through an analysis of the learning process that unfolds along different levels of initiation of mediums in the Vale do Amanhecer, namely the mediumistic development, I have argued that the somatosensory experience of these phenomena determines the articulation of a sense of body and self and the notions produced by it (Pierini 2016a). My ethnographic research suggested that the embodied knowledge produced by the process of initiatory learning might have informed the therapeutic process in some particular cases in which mediumistic development was used as a complementary treatment in patients with mental disorders and alcohol and drug addiction. It is noteworthy that only a small number of mediums encountered in my research reported a past history of schizophrenia, anxiety, panic disorders, or alcohol and drug addictions. Most mediums arrived in the Vale as spiritual seekers or simply in search of spiritual assistance for a wide range of emotional, material, or health issues. Being that the assistance is free of charge and exercised according to the principle of charity, participation is quite heterogeneous in terms of social composition of patients and members of the Order (Pierini 2016b). Therefore, the category of developed mediums should not be reduced to a condition of 'controlled pathology' or 'wounded healers'. However, some patients who arrived with symptoms of disorders or addictions were advised by spirit guides to develop their mediumship in the Vale or in other religions. Mediumship is, indeed, understood in the Vale as an energy common to all human bodies, originating in the blood flow. If this energy is produced in excess it accumulates, affecting the medium physically, whilst when this excessive energy is distributed amongst others, it is said to heal. Hence, the practice of mediumship is considered by mediums to be shaped differently according to the aims for which it is used to channel this energy in each religion.

Through mediumistic development in the Vale do Amanhecer one may learn to become aware of one's mediumship, to control it, and to direct the energy in excess for the healing of others. When a patient decides to undertake the development for therapeutic purposes, this practice is understood as complementary to the biomedical therapies of each particular case. The instructors in charge of the special therapeutic cases observed how, in cases of addiction, the chances of relapses were lower when progressing along the development and the initiatory steps. The percentage of relapses drastically fell after the last initiation as a consequence of increased control, awareness, and personal responsibility that the medium seemingly acquires at that stage. Particularly, the experiences reported by mediums suggested that through the process of learning and the acquisition of specific techniques of the body, they developed a transformation in their perception of the body as permeable and of the sense of self as multidimensional and extensible towards their spirit guides. These 'embodied notions' seemed to have triggered a healing process, which was then reinforced by the shift of their social role from patients to mediators of healing.

Embodied Encounters: Educating Perception in the Field

The process of apprenticeship may be understood not only in terms of knowledge transmission, but particularly in terms of production of embodied notions that have a transformative potential for the individual. Specific forms of encounter with spiritual beings through the body are learned in the mediumistic development through a process of 'enskillment' intended, in Tim Ingold's terms, as an education of perception (2000).

In discussing how participants in the Xangô cult in Brazil learn to be possessed by their *orixás*, Arnaud Halloy argues that 'possession is lived through patterns of affects, percepts' shaped by contextual factors (2012: 195). The focus upon bodily experience in the production and transmission of spiritual knowledge is accompanied by a methodological reflection upon the bodily experience of the ethnographer in the field and in the process of production of ethnographic knowledge. This dimension—which has always been a significant part of the experience of field research, although not made explicit in ethnographies—is currently becoming considered as a resource in the approach to practices based upon embodied forms of encounter with the sacred. Hence, within this context, the education of my own perception became relevant for the ethnographic encounter.

In my earlier conversations with a medium in the field, I often noticed that in the middle of the discussion, he would often shut down communication or drastically change a topic, leaving me with a sense of impatience and frustration. However, as a medium, intuition and perception guided him in his every interaction involving topics related to the spiritual. The unfolding of our conversations depended on his *feeling* what issue should be developed or not at that moment. It was only later that I came to understand that energy was always in movement in each conversation, that the topic could change energy as much as energy could change a topic, and that an interruption in conversation could be interpreted as energetically influenced, meaning the topic should not be discussed.

The Brazilian expression *sentir* frequently emerged from mediums' narratives in order to convey their experiences. *Sentir* means both 'sensing' and 'feeling'. Claims for a more sensuous and embodied scholarship are also echoed among scholars. Paul Stoller has noted how 'mind has long been separated from body, sense long severed from sensibility' (1997: xii). Arguing against a 'disembodied observation', he proposed a 'sensuous scholarship in which writers tack between the analytical and the sensible, in which embodied form as well as disembodied logic constitute scholarly argument' (1997: xv). Stoller has fully engaged his body in the field by training as an apprentice sorcerer among the Songhay People of Niger (Stoller and Olkes 1987).

Similarly, Judith Okely pointed out that the 'bodily experience of the fieldworker as a research process and source of knowledge has been under-scrutinized' (2007: 66). She stressed that the anthropologist learns of another culture 'through all the senses' (Okely 2007: 79). *Sentir* moved beyond observing and listening towards a 'participant observation' that included the observation of my own sensations and emotions. Thus, with renewed attention to my bodily feelings in rituals, I gained insight about what mediums claimed to be the difference between the vibrations of the energies channelled by the different spirits they incorporated. In experiencing rituals as a patient, I could feel that my body responded differently to each ritual.

Fieldwork is an interplay between various levels of proximity and distance. The range of positions the ethnographer assumes during fieldwork results in different responses from his or her interlocutors. Furthermore, Renato Rosaldo (1984: 193) has stressed that the individual experience of the ethnographer may inhibit or enable particular kinds of insight. During my fieldwork, I have adopted multiple perspectives by experimenting with different positions. I participated in rituals firstly as patient and, in the last five months of my fieldwork, I followed mediumistic development, gaining another perspective on how knowledge was transmitted and the practice was learned. Particularly, I was able to grasp those 'features of experience', which in Kirsten Hastrup's words, 'have no immediate reflections in language, but which still have to be spoken about in the anthropological discourse' (1990: 52).

Eventually, being reflexive about my experience constituted a common ground for interaction with mediums. Indeed, the kind of information passed on by informants is determined by what they perceive we recipients are able to grasp or understand, and by what they think our ideas are about their practice. Being able to engage our feelings, our senses, and our perceptions in the field and to share and discuss our insights with mediums also provides them with the opportunity to reflect more in depth on their own experiences, producing sophisticated accounts of their practices and the way meaning is attributed to them. I was then able to identify a change in reports from the first part of my fieldwork to the second. My questions became more focussed, and mediums' reports became more layered and coloured with different nuances and details. We entered another level of reflection, attempting to put in words what is not always translatable: embodied knowledge. Indeed, as Okely notes, '[C]raft and bodily knowledge confront misconceptions and limitations of verbal knowledge. It can integrate the two' (Okely 2012: 77).

In addition to the limitations of verbal knowledge in the field, anthropologists have also tackled the limitations of visual modes of knowing. Sarah Pink proposed that 'the notion of ethnography as a participatory practice is framed with ideas of learning as embodied, emplaced, senso-rial and empathetic, rather than occurring simply through a mix of obser-vation and participation' (Pink 2009: 63). She noted how the visual mode of understanding has dominated ethnographic practice and stressed that a 'sensory ethnography', on the other hand, helps understanding 'experi-ence as multi-sensorial and as such neither dominated by nor reducible to a visual mode of understanding' (Pink 2009: 64). In participant observa-tion, vision is the dominant sense. However, it should be stressed that there are fields in which vision is *not* the dominant sense, whereby approaching other people's experiences requires a step further in engaging with other senses in the field. The core of the mediumistic experience of *aparás* hap-pens when their eyes are closed. However, their reports of these experi-ences unfolded through images, sounds, and bodily perceptions. By closing my eyes and experiencing rituals, I allowed myself to explore other ways of knowing through an expansion of perception and increased intuition.

Okely noted that among ethnographers 'the fear of total participation is the fear that observation will cease', however, she stressed that 'there is always the need to take notes... If note taking and the relevant anthro-pological analysis cease, then so does the research' (2012: 78). Additional-ly, I argue that participation can never be complete, and observation does not cease. Indeed, I had to struggle to close my ethnographic eye, as I was engaged in a continuous process of observation and interpretation even when my eyes were closed. On the one hand, this kind of participa-tion has allowed me to consider the role of the researcher's body in the construction of ethnographic knowledge while discussing the emplaced and embodied knowledge (Stoller and Olkes 1987; Desjarlais 1992; Okely 2007; Pink 2009) gained from engaging my own body and senses in the process of learning mediumship. On the other hand, it has led me to ques-tion the assumption of 'going native', as this kind of participation does not imply that the ethnographer accepts beliefs at face value, because not even mediums do so when they approach the practice. It rather implies reflecting critically upon one's bodily experience and the insights gained from it and discussing them with research participants establishing a par-ticular kind of rapport (Favret-Saada 1990; Goldman 2003, 2005), and thus using this reflexivity as a common ground of interaction with research participants. Therefore, considering the embodied knowledge produced in mediumistic practice, the notion of 'belief' needs to be questioned in favour of that of 'experience' (Pierini 2016a). Moreover, the category of 'native' may not be considered as internally homogeneous: because mem-bers of the Vale are participants in a new ritualistic practice with differ-ent socio-cultural backgrounds, not only was my experience informed by my cultural background, but all mediums' experiences are. I had to train my 'somatic modes of attention' (Csordas 1993), as every medium had to. It is widely agreed that even full participation does not allow the ethnographer to reach the full understanding of meanings, practices, and experiences as an insider would. Robert Desjarlais, for instance, when comparing his experiences of trance to those of Nepali healers, noted that his anthropological background determined his interpretation of the experience. Although bodily experience may be similar at the level of the senses, the tension between worldviews and symbolic systems of the participants becomes clear, and he argued that it is precisely within this tension that the anthropological insight emerges (Desjarlais 1992).

In my own experience of learning mediumistic states of consciousness, on certain occasions I felt whilst being in a semi-conscious state during the ritual as though I was placed in a particular seat, and when opening my eyes afterwards, I realized that I was rather placed one row of seats in front or behind where I had imagined. In discussing this sensation with other mediums, they reported similar sensations of displacement during trance states, such as seeing themselves in another seat, or observing the ritual from a side perspective. Indeed, the conscious and semi-conscious modalities of mediumship allow mediums to be aware of different feelings and emotions, such as the multisensory images they experience during their trance states.

These conversations provided us with the opportunity to explore the production of embodied notions in the process of learning. It gradually emerged that these experiences of *partial* displacement appeared to be more recurrent than experiences of astral travel. I emphasise 'partial' because the feeling is described as being on one level somewhere else and on another still present in the body, suggesting a partial presence of proprioceptive sensations. A medium instructor explained to me that according to the Vale's discourse, the spirit of the medium *apará* is projected about one and a half metres out of the body, whilst spirits project their aura within the medium's body leaving the messages and the stimulus for bodily movements in the *apará*'s intuition, according to a conceptualisation of the self as multidimensional. Hence, a notion of the body emerged as a place of shared emotions and sensations.

In a reciprocal movement, bodily experience in rituals informs the notion of the self, providing it with attributes of extendibility and multidimensionality, which in turn inform the conceptualisation of trance. In the Vale do Amanhecer, spiritual knowledge and religious principles are transmitted primarily through practical learning and through the mediums' bodily experiences, rather than through doctrinal teaching. As the instructor explained to me, 'you have to *feel* spiritual knowledge: it is not a study (*estudo*), it is a state (*estado*). Therefore, cosmology and spiritual knowledge become significant for mediums according to the way they are perceived and experienced, by the way they are embodied and act upon mediums producing a transformation in their cognition' (in Pierini 2016a: 307-08).

Extraordinary experiences in the field, such as dreams, seeing spirits manifesting, accounts of reincarnation, and so forth, may or may not change the belief of anthropologists; however, scholars agree upon recognising the value of such experiences for their research and attempting to treat informants' claims seriously (Young and Goulet 1994; Goulet and Granville Miller 2007). Jeanne Favret-Saada (1980, 1990) and Goldman (2003, 2005, 2006), who researched witchcraft in the the *bocage* of Normandy and Candomblé in Brazil respectively, have remarkably shown how their experiences of 'being affected' may not have radically changed their beliefs, but they certainly favoured the establishment of a new form of communication or rapport with the people who were part of their research.

Whilst researching witchcraft, Favret-Saada got involved in 'unbewitching' sessions, which opened up a specific perspective that helped her in highlighting the complexity of the system of witchcraft attacks and unbewitching therapy. She stressed the importance of having access to informal moments and spontaneous discourses, and how her participation allowed her to describe a therapeutic device extending beyond rituals (Favret-Saada 1990: 196). Goldman (2003) described an event from his fieldwork in Brazilian Candomblé when he accompanied a funerary ritual offering performed in the forest. On that occasion he heard the sound of drums playing. Other participants confirmed having heard the same in other rituals, and they associated this event with souls of the dead that play drums as a sign that they have accepted the ritual offering. Goldman stressed that it was not the mystical nor materialistic explanation that were important, but the fact that he had been affected—although in a different way from informants—which allowed a new and 'involuntary form of communication' along with the articulation of new interpretations of different spheres of the life of Candomblecistas (2003: 450). Drawing upon Favret-Saada (1990), Goldman suggested that 'being affected' by what affects the native does not rest upon a complete identification with the native point of view, with emotional or cognitive empathy, nor with 'conversion' or 'substantial transformation'. It is rather a process of 'becoming', which 'is not resemblance, imitation or identification;...it is a movement by which a subject leaves her own condition through a relation of affections that she can establish with another condition' (Goldman 2003: 464).

Some researchers' choices to adopt a participatory methodology involving their bodies in the process of fieldwork or in part of it was accompanied by a critical and reflexive approach to their experiences in the field and especially in the phase of analysis. In these cases, participation, affection, or the bodily involvement in the field produce a particular kind of ethnographic knowledge. Indeed, these embodied encounters engender different levels of understanding that, in the context of these spiritual experiences, may refer to the phenomenology of mediumistic practices, or to different notions of body and personhood, illness and health. The increased attention towards lived and somatosensory experience promoted by the ethnographic method firstly allows moving beyond misleading conceptions, allowing us to discern between spiritual and pathological experiences; secondly, it undermines the notion of *belief* in favour of that of *experience*, which, according to Goldman (2003), allows moving beyond differences in terms of belief, between the categories of the researcher and those people with whom he or she studies. This approach to spirit mediumship and possession ultimately reframes cognition within the bodily dimension of the encounter with the sacred.

Short Biographical Note
Emily Pierini is Honorary Research Fellow at the University of Wales Trinity Saint David, lectures at the American University of Rome; PhD (Bristol) in Social Anthropology with a thesis on the Spiritualist Christian Order Vale do Amanhecer in Brazil; research about spirit mediumship, spiritual healing and mental health, religious experience, religious learning, embodiment, and the self.

Notes
1.   The ethnographic fieldwork upon which this discussion is based was conducted in Brazil in 2004, and between 2009 and 2012 in the main temple of the Vale do Amanhecer in Brasília. It also included fieldwork in temples in North-East and Southern Brazil, Portugal, the UK, and Italy between 2012 and 2016. This research has been funded in different stages by The Spalding Trust, the Read-Tuckwell Scholarship (University of Bristol), and the Royal Anthropological Institute's Sutasoma Award. It also benifited from the institutional support of the Faculdade de Médicina of the Universidade de São Paulo (Medical Anthropolgy).

2.   The European Spiritist doctrine widespread in Brazil since the early twentieth-century is also known as Kardecism, which is named for its founder, Allan Kardec, a pseudonym of the French educator Hippolyte Léon Denizard Rivail, who systematised the Spiritist doctrine in the 1850s. Spiritism grounds its practices in the communication with spirits through mediums.

3.   Translated by the author from Portuguese.

Chapter 4

Cultural-Linguistic Constructivism and the Challenge of Near-Death and Out-of-Body Experiences

Gregory Shushan

Introduction:
Near-Death and Out-of-Body Experiences Across Cultures

In the mid-seventh century BCE, the Chinese provincial ruler Muh of T'sin recovered from an illness and reported that he had undergone an enjoyable journey to the home of the Emperor of Heaven. He was given precognitive information which was later verified after his return to life (de Groot 1892: IV, 113-14). This is the earliest of many such accounts from ancient and medieval China. A single source (*Taiping Kwang chi*) enumerates 127 up to the tenth century CE (de Groot 1892: 123).

Over 700 years later and over 5000 miles distant in Greece, Plutarch recounted the experience of Thespesius of Soli who, in c. 81 CE, apparently died then returned to life three days later. Thespesius claimed that his soul had left his body and traveled to a place where stars radiated light 'on which his soul was smoothly and swiftly gliding in every direction', and he 'could see all around himself as if his soul would have been a single eye' (Plutarch in Platthy 1992: 74). He met spirits of deceased relatives, one of whom took him on a tour of otherworldly places of reward and punishment. Previously wicked, avaricious, and given to 'lewd and illegal acts', Thespesius returned transformed into an honest, devout, faithful man and 'altered the whole course of his life' (Plutarch in Platthy 1992: 74). At least a dozen such narratives survive from Classical antiquity.

Three accounts were related over 500 years later in the *Dialogues* of Pope Gregory I (c. 593/4), each involving out-of-body journeys to other realms, encounters with spiritual beings and with souls of dead individuals known previously on earth, and a return to life characterized by a positive transformation of beliefs or lifestyle (in Gardiner 1989: 47-50).

Over 900 years later and more than 6000 miles away, Spanish missionary and early ethnographer Bernardino de Sahagún (1547–69: IX:3, II:498, 181, n.20) recounted the experience of Quetzalpetlatl, daughter-in-law of the 15th-century Mexica ruler Moquihuix. Quetzalpetlatl reported having died, then being led by a youth to the land of the dead. There she encountered deceased relatives and the deity Tlaloc, who gave her the ability to heal the sick upon her return to earth.

Over 2000 miles across the North American continent and more than a hundred years later, English astronomer and explorer Thomas Hariot (1588: 37-38) related the experience of an Algonquin man he met. The man reported that he died and left his body during his own funeral, seeing his corpse below him. He walked along a path lined with houses and abundant fruit trees, and met his deceased father who sent him back to his body to tell his people about the happiness of the other realm.

Over two-and-a-half centuries later in his journal of 1838–56, George Charter, a missionary working on the Polynesian island of Raiatea, recounted the experience of a woman named Terematai who had lain unconscious for a number of days. When she revived, she described a trip to a heavenly realm where she saw spirits of deceased people she had known in life. She wanted to stay in the other world, 'but God sent me back to exhort my family that they may be saved' (in Gunson 1962: 218). She returned 'in a very happy state of mind and appeared wholly absorbed in spiritual subjects' (in Gunson 1962: 218).

In southern Africa over a hundred years later, the missionary W. C. Willoughby (1928: 99) recounted the experience of a BagammaNgwato boy who died, 'went away', and saw his brother as well as his father and uncle. The latter told him he must return to earth because he should not leave his mother. The boy concluded, 'they sent me back with great peace,' and he revived with 'new life' fully recovered from his illness (Willoughby 1928: 99).

Spanning two-and-a-half millennia and originating in seven different parts of the world with seven very different religious traditions, these are all examples of a phenomenon that would later be termed 'near-death experience' (NDE) by psychologist Raymond Moody in 1975. Prior to that time, the phenomenon was scarcely known in contemporary Western cultures. Since then, however, NDE-type narratives have been identified from Ancient Greece, the Biblical Near East, Medieval through modern Europe, ancient through modern India, China, Japan, pre-Columbian Mesoamerica, modern Mexico, 18th century through modern US, 12th century through modern Tibet, modern Thailand, and the Philippines (Belanti et al. 2008; Shushan 2009), and in 16th-20th century missionary, explorer, and ethnographer accounts of indigenous societies in the Pacific, Asia, the Americas, and Africa (Shushan forthcoming).

Although no two NDEs are exactly alike, and none contain all the defining elements, they are made up of a number typical sub-experiences. These include out-of-body experience (OBE), existence in quasi-physical form, entering darkness, bright light, exceptionally vivid senses, distortions of time, universal understanding, peace and pleasant feelings, joy, a sense of universal unity, being in another realm, encounters with mystical beings and deceased individuals, evaluation of one's earthly life and/or replays of scenes from the past, ESP, having visions of the future or obtaining pre-cognitive information, impressions of having returned 'home', reaching a border or limit, being instructed or choosing to return to the body, and positive transformations of the individual following the return (Greyson 1983; Fox 2002: 100f).

Comparative research establishes that while accounts of NDEs share many common elements worldwide, those elements are embedded in matrices of clearly culture- and individual-specific material. This suggests that NDEs begin as pre- or non-cultural *events*, which cause experiences that are both culturally contextualized *and* cross-culturally thematically stable. Like any experience, NDEs are rooted in the cultural environment of those who have them. They are processed live by an enculturated individual, then recounted in socially, religiously, and linguistically idiosyncratic ways. In other words, *how* the experience is *experienced* varies by individual, resulting in narratives being interpreted and expressed in highly symbolic local modes. It is a symbiotic relationship in which culture-specific beliefs and individual expectations influence universal experiences and vice versa (McClenon 1994; Kellehear 1996; Belanti et. al. 2008; Shushan 2009, forthcoming). Local attitudes towards death and the afterlife affect receptivity to NDE phenomena and determine how the experiences are undergone and subsequently symbolically expressed.

NDEs and OBEs clearly reflect established local beliefs *and also* share apparently universal structural similarities. Cross-cultural differences are attributed to the experiences being mediated, interpreted, and elaborated upon within individual and cultural contexts. Nevertheless, the similarities clearly demonstrate that (1) there are common experience types regularly interpreted in religious terms across cultures; (2) not all such experiences can be attributable entirely to cultural expectation; and (3) such experiences can lead to new beliefs and change preexisting ones. These conclusions are in direct opposition to currently dominant paradigms in the study of religions, which regard religious phenomena of all kinds as purely cultural-linguistic constructs.

Constructivism, Categories, and the Culture of Disbelief

In the academic study of religions, it is widely accepted that any so-called 'religious' experience cannot be independent of its cultural-linguistic context, and indeed that experience *per se* is entirely culturally and/or linguistically constructed. Because languages, cultures, and religions differ, there can be no such thing as an experience type that can by definition be considered 'religious' or 'mystical'. Although such notions lack empirical validation and are thus more accurately seen as philosophical stances, they are nevertheless treated by many scholars as axiomatic (e.g., Proudfoot 1985; Cupitt 1998; Sharf 1998; Bocking 2006). Near-death and out-of-body experiences present serious challenges to these ways of thinking and indeed may be seen as the tools that dismantle the philosophical houses of cards upon which the axioms are built.

First is the idea that we cannot separate a narrative of an experience from the experience itself, and indeed that there is no actual experience underlying a description of it. Robert Sharf (1998: 286) considers it a 'mistake' to treat 'representations' of ostensible experiences 'as if they referred back to something other than themselves', i.e., to the kind of experience which they purport to describe. At the same time, Sharf does not deny subjective experience, nor does he explain how a person can have such an experience but not accurately 'represent' or 'refer' to it in narrative form (1998: 286).

It is obvious that any narrative will not be the same as the actual experience it intends to describe: some individuals will embellish more than others, while descriptions, symbols, similes, and interpretations will vary widely by one's culture, individuality, and preexisting beliefs. This does not, however, indicate that the individual did not have something like the kind of experience he or she describes. This is demonstrated by the existence of specific, identifiable, extraordinary experience types such as NDEs and OBEs. Despite cultural and individual idiosyncrasies, the kinds of narratives described above share many thematic, structural similarities: apparently dying, leaving the body and traveling to another realm, encountering supernatural beings and deceased relatives, being instructed to return, and coming back to life followed by a subsequent spiritual or other positive transformation. Not only do NDEs have cross-culturally stable phenomenologies, *they also share cross-culturally consistent, locally-ascribed interpretations*: that the individual really died, left the body, had a variety of unusual experiences, and returned to body.

Sharf (1998: 280-82) questions whether there is any reason to assume that reports of mystical experiences are 'credible' as 'phenomenological descriptions'. But is there any reason to assume they are not? Categories of specific experience types are constructed through phenomenological observation and comparison. Terms such as 'near-death experience' are possible because similar *types* of narratives of experiences have been identified and generically categorized in consistent ways by numerous and diverse scholars.[1] Certain narratives of experiences that occur in return-from-death contexts contain a particular set of similarities that leads to their identification as NDEs. Phenomenological and contextual similarity across cultures and throughout history is evidence that the narratives share some structural phenomenological credibility, despite cultural and individual difference, showing that there is such a pan-human experience type as the NDE. Conversely, it is difficult to imagine what kind of proof there could ever be that the masses of descriptions of NDEs and OBEs found cross-culturally do not actually refer to any experiences.

These observations apply whether we subscribe to a psychological, neurophysiological, or metaphysical explanation of the nature of the phenomena. All attempts to explain NDEs in materialist terms involve *physical* events, such as REM intrusion, anoxia, hypercarbia, and other epiphenomena of a compromised brain. These events cause experiences with identifiable, predictable, and consistent phenomenologies, enabling critics of the veridicality of NDEs to formulate theories predicated on their universality. NDEs also share a similar phenomenology with the effects of the drug ketamine, according to individuals who have had experiences of both (Jansen 2001). This similarity demonstrates an objective phenomenology of two experience types. To accept one on the grounds that it has medically identifiable origins (ketamine) and not the other on the grounds that some claim it does not (NDE) would be an example either of cognitive dissonance or an anti-scientific privileging of philosophical commitments over evidence. Obviously, the empirical study of NDEs and OBEs would not be possible if there were no such experiences to fit these categories. Research that measures neurological data while NDEs are in progress and pinpoints the timing of their occurrence as well as the ostensible observations during them (Parnia et. al. 2014), experiments in OBE induction (e.g., Blanke et. al. 2003; Metzinger 2005: 76), and survey- and fieldwork-based studies on the relationship between experiences and beliefs (e.g., Shiels 1978; McClenon 1994, 2002; Yao and Badham 2007) all demonstrate that these experiences are temporal, finite, actual *occurrences* (see, e.g., Davis 1989: 19-22) that can be referred to and described like any other.

Critics (e.g., Katz 1978; Proudfoot 1985; Sharf 1998) also object to the notion that our particular terms for experience types may not have counterparts in other languages, which means that the phenomenon we term 'near-death experience' may be unknown in a given society. The lack of a term in a given language for a particular experience type, however, does not indicate that the experience itself is unknown to speakers of that language. Taken to its illogical extreme, this line of thought would imply that speakers of Malayalam or Russian, for example, do not experience having hands on the grounds that they have no separate word for 'hand' (it is considered a part of the 'arm'). Put simply, linguistic differences do not negate the possibility of common human experiences (see, e.g., Forman 1990: 18). Concepts, objects, and experiences are all cross-linguistically expressible, even if translation from one culture/language can never be 100 percent exact. Individuals in contemporary China have extraordinary experiences (including NDEs) phenomenologically consistent with those known elsewhere, and commonly associate them with religious ideas and beliefs (Yao and Badham 2007: 28ff). And although Tibetans consider everything to be part of the natural order and do not have a term for 'supernatural', they nevertheless 'consider certain phenomena as beyond normal consciousness, outside the realm of ordinary experience' (McClenon 1994: 1). The fact that experiences sometimes *are* described and interpreted in similar ways across cultures enabling their categorization suggests that it is more a question of how people culturally and linguistically negotiate these experiences rather than whether or not they actually have them. While NDEs were only formally named in 1975 by Raymond Moody, and OBEs in 1943 by mathematician and physicist George N. M. Tyrrell, we have many accounts prior to those dates of experiences that phenomenologically correspond to those that came to be called 'NDEs' and 'OBEs', and they should thus be properly considered as such. The notion that the existence of terms is somehow equivalent to that to which they refer is unsupportable. In other words, the existence of an experience type is not predicated on the existence of a term for it.

Wayne Proudfoot (1985: xii-xiv, *passim*) argues that seeing religions in terms of religious experience, and indeed the concept of religious experience *per se*, can be traced only as far back as Friedrich Schleiermacher (1799). Thus, Sharf (1998: 271) summarizes, such notions should not be applied earlier because to do so 'anachronistically imposes the recent and ideologically laden notion of "religious experience" on our interpretations of premodern phenomena'. However, NDEs and OBEs are clearly described in pre-Schleiermacher *religious contexts* around the world, confirming that they are neither late nor exclusively Western, and that they are regularly interpreted in religious terms cross-culturally. In addition to the examples cited earlier, many religious texts relating to life after death show an awareness of the concepts of NDEs and OBEs and involve an individual's soul temporarily traveling to afterlife realms. Such texts are often intended to prepare the reader for what to expect after death, and they provide instructions about behaviour types that will ensure a positive fate, indicating that they were believed to be based on first-hand knowledge and actual experiences. This is the case with the continuous strand of otherworld-journey narratives spanning the range of Vedic literature (*Rig Veda* X.135; *Shatapatha Brahmana* XI.6; *Jaiminiya Brahmana* I.42-44; *Katha Upanishad* I-VI) and is overtly the case with the Tibetan *Bardo Thodol*. The 10th century BCE *Atharva Veda* (VIII.1-2, VII.53.3) contains instructional texts for retrieving a soul from the underworld, and OBEs are described in the *Jaiminya Brahmana* (c. 900-700 BCE, I.46) and *Chandogya Upanishad* (VIII.12.1-2). There is an important, perhaps foundational connection between NDEs and Pure Land Buddhism in China and Japan, with many prominent figures in the traditions reporting them (McClenon 1994: 182). Much shamanic poetry and other narratives from ancient China contain descriptions of OBE journeys to other realms.[2] In light of these and many other examples, it is clear that NDEs and OBEs were part of human experience long before they were named by Western researchers and were seen in religious terms long before Schleiermacher.

Ultimately, there is no psychological, neurophysiological, or anthropological evidence to support the notion that experience is dependent upon language. On the contrary, there is evidence that both emotions and cognition (i.e., kinds of experience) can *precede* language (Downey 2010; McClenon 2002: 161). If some experience types can precede language, it is logical to assume that others can as well. Furthermore, it is objectionable to characterize those who claim to have had these kinds of experiences as uncritical products of their belief systems at best (see, e.g., Barnard 1992) or liars at worst. To adopt the stance that 'we are not obliged to accept' their testimonies as 'phenomenological description' (Sharf: 1998: 283; also see Cupitt 1998: 33) creates a culture of disbelief that places critics in an unwarranted superior position to those they study. To question the credibility of representations of religious experience is to question the credibility of the individuals relating them and to effectively stigmatize them. Disregarding emic testimonies and self-understandings of NDEs and OBEs is to privilege specific etic interpretations *de facto* over those of the individuals who provide us with our data in the first place, while also to deflect attention away from the very phenomena we are studying. Likewise, the distinction between experience and narrative is obvious (Rennie 2000: 108), and to anyone who has any kind of experience, having it and relating it are not the same. Implying that certain individuals—by virtue of the fact that they claim to have had an unusual experience—cannot make such distinctions, or are unable to differentiate between experience types, or lack the critical faculties to interpret rationally their experiences, is groundless.

Language and the Mediation of Experiences

Further problems with linguistic constructivism are revealed when we consider that OBEs and NDEs are often characterized as being ineffable by those who have them. Mark Fox (2002: 134-35) raises a highly significant question: if language is the primary factor in the creation of such experiences, why is it that experiencers often do not have the 'language' to describe them? As with mystical experiences described as Pure Consciousness Events, with NDEs there is often a 'disjunction' between the event and the later attempt to describe it, and it is this disjunction that the experiencer refers to as 'ineffable', that is, non-linguistic (Forman

1990: 41). Likewise, according to Larry Short (1995: 665), mystical practices are essentially designed to 'interfere with language use' and 'disassociate sound from meaning, signifier from signified', resulting in a non-linguistic state. This does not necessarily mean that the experience is unmediated—only that the mediator is not language. Language is important for 'our understanding of the non-linguistic experience' (Short 1995: 670), however, and of course in relating the experience. The act of telling or writing about the experience will be reliant upon and limited by 'the conventions of our language' (Short 1995: 668). As Fox (2002: 134-35) concludes, 'Far from being a product of language and/or cultural-linguistic expectation', the core elements of the NDE 'stand prior to and independently of their culturally acquired expectations of what death might be like'.

The inadequacy of language to express OBEs and NDEs suggests that the experience originated prior to the attempt to put it into language, while the existence of cross-cultural similarities indicates that they originate in phenomena that are independent of culture. Diffusion or intertextuality cannot explain the structurally similar narratives describing contextually stable experiences from such different times, places, and cultural-linguistic backgrounds (Shushan 2009: ch. 2).

The idea of a pre-cultural, pre-linguistic origin of NDEs and OBEs is supported by two further considerations. The first is that the experiences often conflict with the expectations and cultural-religious background of experiencers (Fox 2002: 115-16). The second is that they can be spontaneous, with no associated religious practice, no expectation, and indeed often with total ignorance of the phenomenon. An experience cannot conform to expectation if one does not expect it. An early twentieth-century Zuni Native American NDE, for example, included encounters with deceased relatives and bright light—motifs that are inconsistent with Zuni afterlife conceptions (Wade 2003: 94-5). Medieval Chinese, Japanese, and European NDE narratives often conflicted with the theological conventions of their times and places (McClenon 1994: ch. 9), and atheists have NDEs consistent with those of theists. Conversely, certain themes that we might expect to find in the NDEs of individuals of specific religions are rarely reported. For example, salvation, physical resurrection, and reincarnation do not commonly feature in NDE reports at all, whether from Buddhists, Christians, Hindus, Jews, or Muslims. Significantly, while NDErs report a number of sub-experiences from a recognized repertoire, variability between accounts is often attributable to identifiable, specific cultural and individual factors[3] (Shushan 2009: 39-50). This means that NDEs can conflict with the expectations even of those *with* prior knowledge of the phenomenon, who may wonder, for example, why they did not go through a tunnel or have a life review.

This is not to suggest that language and culture play no role in mediating NDEs and OBEs. Narratives of experiences are obviously culturally-embedded artefacts. However, accepting that experience is culturally *mediated* is not the same as accepting that it is entirely culturally *fabricated*. Mediation is often seen as being at odds with true mystical experiences and thus enlisted as proof that they cannot occur, as if the only type of experience that could be accepted as mystical must be a pure-consciousness event wholly transcending culture and individual. Short, however, argues that mediation actually *enables* experience, and is a central component to the process of understanding it. Indeed, as ontologically human beings, 'We come with given physical, perceptual, and neurological equipment', as well as common experiences of 'time, space, and causality'—essentially pre-linguistic mediators that filter all experience (Short 1995: 661-64). This indicates a degree of commonality of all human perception, and thus of the ways in which we experience.

The possibility of NDEs and OBEs having pre-cultural origins is not predicated on their being wholly unmediated. Rather, it is more productive to see such experiences as having interconnected universal, individual, and cultural layers: a universal 'event' is experienced by, filtered through, and processed live by a biological, enculturated individual, who subsequently attempts to make sense of it according to his/her socio-cultural-religious situation, or indeed by innovating away from it (King 1988). As universally human beings we have universal experience types, and as enculturated human beings we process and express those experiences according to our specific cultural-linguistic modes. As a self-conscious, analytical species, we have the ability to discern one experience from another, to generalize about them in order to construct categories of experience types, and to analyze, interpret, and describe them in culturally and individually diverse ways.

Accepting that there are cultural and individual idiosyncrasies in NDEs and OBEs indicates neither that they are solely products of cultural-linguistic construction, nor that truly unmediated experience is impossible. Fox (2002: 125-26) emphasizes that mystical experiences are typically described as 'a state which bypasses normal modes of sense and apprehension'. Exceptional experiences such as leaving the body and encountering spirits of dead relatives are commonly regarded by those who have them as occurring beyond the physical senses, therefore not subject to physical laws, and thus beyond our ability to understand through our usual constraining modes of materialist analysis and interpretation. In other words, while direct, unmediated experience is not *normally* possible, it is at least philosophically conceivable that in certain exceptional states it is. While we cannot assume that these experiences are identical for everyone, this does not mean they are incomparably different or that certain elements of the experience *may* have been truly unmediated (Evans 1988: 54-55).

Although claims of the total narrative construction of experience and of the impossibility of unmediated experience are without empirical validation,[4] they are nevertheless widely accepted in the study of religions. Without empirical underpinnings, however, such claims should more correctly be regarded as philosophical speculation rather than as scientific fact. Indeed, there seems to be no rational justification for giving default ontological primacy to language/culture over experience.

NDEs, OBEs, and the Experiential Source Hypothesis

If there were no such things as universal experience types that people cross-culturally widely consider to be religious, it would be pointless to look for some kind of religious experience that might help us account for the origins of religious beliefs. Brian Bocking (2006), for example, believes that Sharf's cultural-linguistic constructivist 'argument is, or should be, unsettling for anyone who naively thinks that religious beliefs are grounded in religious experiences'.

Among the range of experiences humans have are ones that *within their cultural contexts* are commonly considered religious, mystical, or otherwise extraordinary, and inexplicable without reference to a supernatural, metaphysical, or otherwise non-quotidian cause or agency. Cross-culturally, indeed perhaps universally,[5] NDEs and OBEs are considered exceptional within the contexts in which they occur, and they are given special, often elevated status. There is clearly a difference between the quotidian sensations of one's awareness being in the body and interacting with other tangible human beings, and non-quotidian sensations of one's awareness being out of the body and interacting with spiritual beings. Regardless of whether or not these things veridically occur, people around the world have been reporting them throughout recorded history and regarding them as being in a separate category to everyday occurrences. This pattern of consistent ascription is an important indicator of the cross-cultural stability of such experiences.

There are certain types of human experience that are obviously most relevant to certain types of beliefs, and as such they are logical candidates to help us explain the origins of those beliefs. There is, in fact, direct evidence in the form of historical, ethnographic, and contemporary personal testimony that people around the world regularly base beliefs concerning an afterlife and mind-body dualism upon NDEs and OBEs. Such cases validate what David Hufford (1982) termed 'the experiential source hypothesis', that is, that extraordinary experiences often lead to new religious, spiritual, or supernatural beliefs. Hultkrantz (1957: 235-37) presented a great deal of evidence to support his conclusions that Native American afterlife beliefs were widely based on NDEs. When asked about such beliefs, informants from various tribes related ostensibly factual NDEs, both to give a phenomenological description of dying and the afterlife, and to lend their beliefs experiential authority. In the late 19th century, Ghost Dance revitalization movements originated with the NDE of Paiute shaman Wovoka (Mooney 1896: 701-02, 926-27), and the Indian Shaker Church was founded by John Slocum following instructions given to him during an NDE (Ruby and Brown 1996: 7-9, 752). Recent ethnohistorical research has unearthed over twenty 16th-early 20th century Native American claims that local afterlife beliefs were grounded directly in NDE phenomena (together with roughly 40 additional NDE accounts), as well as examples from the Pacific and Africa prior to conversion to non-indigenous religions (Shushan forthcoming). This substantiates ethnologist and psychologist Holger Kalweit's (1984: 70) generalization that individuals across cultures claim that they gained their knowledge of the afterlife 'from the experiences of those who have returned [i.e., NDErs] and from shamans'.

Staunch materialists and atheists have also had their convictions challenged by their NDEs and OBEs. Such cases are effectively microcosms of Hufford's 'experiential source hypothesis'. While publicly admitting only that his experience had 'slightly weakened' his conviction that death is the end of consciousness, shortly after his fairly typical NDE, philosopher A. J. Ayer told his doctor, 'I saw a Divine Being. I'm afraid I'm going to have to revise all my various books and opinions' (Foges 2010). Before his own experience, mathematical physicist and psychologist John Wren-Lewis (n.d.) regarded mysticism as a form of neurosis. Not only did his NDE run contrary to his expectations, it also resulted directly in new spiritual beliefs, namely 'that proponents of the so-called Perennial Philosophy are correct in identifying a common "deep structure" of experience underlying the widely different cultural expressions of mystics in all traditions' (Wren-Lewis n.d.).

As a single, discrete experience (as opposed to the composite NDE), OBEs are perhaps even more problematic for cultural-linguistic constructivism. Whatever its cultural-linguistic context, OBE is by definition always and unambiguously considered a dualistic state in which consciousness is separated from the body. While Sharf (1998: 277) may be correct that Western perceptions and assumptions about religious experience lie in Descartes' 'notion of mind as an "immaterial substance"', what is being described in all OBE reports is a *kind* of mind-body dualism. Phenomenologically speaking, it is irrelevant whether OBE is understood in philosophically Cartesian, Upanishadic, or Salteaux terms. Cultural models of mind-body dualism need not be identical in order to be grounded in the same experience type.

Explicit descriptions of OBEs are found in Eastern and Western narratives throughout history (as cited above), and mind-body dualism, often exemplified by descriptions of OBEs, is a common element of nearly every branch of Egyptian, Ancient Near Eastern, Zoroastrian, Græco-Roman, Jewish, Christian, Muslim, Buddhist, and numerous other theologies.[6] Dean Shiels (1978: 699) found that of the 67 small-scale societies he reviewed, 95 percent believed in OBEs, and that they were consistently described in remarkably similar ways. He concludes that the most likely explanation for this wide cross-cultural occurrence of OBE belief was that it 'results from a common experience of this happening' (Shiels 1978: 699). Sociologist James McClenon's fieldwork (1994, 2002: 106-31) provides a mass of cross-cultural evidence that demonstrates that NDEs and OBEs often lead directly to beliefs in an afterlife and in mind-body dualism.

From a neuroscientific perspective, Thomas Metzinger (2005: 57) also theorizes that dualistic beliefs cross-culturally originate in OBEs, which 'can be undergone by every human being and seem to possess a culturally invariant cluster of functional and phenomenal core properties.' OBEs 'almost inevitably lead the experiencing subject to conclude that conscious experience can, as a matter of fact, take place independently of the brain and the body' (Metzinger 2005: 57). Metzinger (2005: 78 n.8) cites other studies that support his hypothesis, including one (Osis 1979) in which 73 percent of survey respondents claimed that their beliefs had changed as a result of their OBEs, and another (Gabbard and Twemlow 1984) in which 66 percent claimed that their OBEs caused them to adopt a belief in life after death. Metzinger concludes:

> Although many OBE reports are certainly colored by the interpretational schemes ordered by the metaphysical ideologies available to experiencing subjects in their time and culture, the experiences as such must be taken seriously. Although their conceptual and ontological interpretations are often seriously misguided, the truthfulness of centuries of reports about ecstatic states, soul-travel and second bodies as such can hardly be doubted. (Metzinger 2005: 78 n.8)

NDEs and OBEs have been largely ignored by most cultural-linguistic constructivist critics of religious experience.[7] One exception is Carol Zaleski (1987: 190), whose work is marked by logical inconsistencies that appear to result from adherence to a preconceived constructivist interpretation, even when it conflicts with her own data. For example, she carefully draws parallels between modern and Medieval NDE narratives, but because similarities are problematic for her conclusion that the NDE is wholly imaginative, they are left unexplained in order to focus on the differences. Zaleski (1987: 127) further argues that imposing Western descriptive terms such as 'being of light'[8] upon NDEs cross-culturally denies the testimonies of experiencers who describe a radiant Jesus or Buddha specifically. However, Zaleski herself denies insider testimony comprehensively and deliberately by concluding that NDEs are imaginary. She also sidesteps the fact that NDErs describe these entities in phenomenologically similar ways (radiating light), regardless of cultural ascription.

In his discussion of Wren-Lewis' NDE, Bocking (2006) writes that the author differentiates the experience he had from an NDE because it 'had none of the classic NDE features of tunnel, light etc.' and because 'it stayed with him permanently'. However, while Wren-Lewis (n.d.) was indeed puzzled by elements that he believed were inconsistent with so-called classic NDEs, he himself referred to his experience as an NDE. Furthermore, his description actually does feature some typical elements of NDEs,[9] including the fact that 'it stayed with him permanently': NDEs commonly remain vivid long after the experience and have lasting positive aftereffects, such as loss of a fear of death and increased spiritual orientation (Noyes et. al. 2009)—both of which Wren-Lewis described. Other common NDE elements found in Wren-Lewis' narrative include time slowing down, indescribable bliss and joy, universal understanding and feelings of unity, returning to a home or origin state of being, ineffability, being 'pure consciousness' beyond space and time, and dramatic impressions of light and darkness, an 'almost palpable blackness that was yet somehow radiant'. While NDEs are not central to Bocking's (2006) arguments,[10] he nevertheless employs a biased straw-man methodology by selecting an isolated example of an NDE allegedly inconsistent with other NDEs in order to imply that consistencies do not exist in general, while (similar to Zaleski) also ignoring consistencies actually found within that example. Wren-Lewis' change of beliefs concerning mysticism as a direct result of his NDE is ignored, even though it challenges Bocking's assertion that beliefs cannot be grounded in experiences.

NDEs and OBEs are specific, stable pan-human experience types, and their basic consistent interpretations cross-culturally have been attested, helping to explain certain structurally common themes found in religious beliefs in diverse societies around the world. The generalizations being made here about NDEs and OBEs are contextually relevant to the cultures that produce the narratives of the experiences: they are seen locally as being related to consciousness leaving the body and/or surviving physical death. To be clear, the experiential source hypothesis does not in itself attempt to define the ontological status of the experience and can be used to support both theological and reductionist interpretations (as seen in the quote from Metzinger above). We can accept narratives of experiences as phenomenological descriptions of experiences without necessarily accepting experiencers' interpretations. Whatever their ultimate nature, individuals have experiences that *seem* like they leave the body and travel to another realm, and such experiences can alter their pre-existing beliefs. We do not necessarily need to believe that the person genuinely did leave the body in order to respect and take seriously his or her narrative.

Conclusions

For a variety of reasons, NDEs and OBEs present major challenges to the types of criticisms discussed above:

(1) A great deal of empirical and social scientific research on these phenomena has been undertaken, and they are widely accepted as pan-human experiences by researchers from the most reductionist to the most theological of orientations. Narratives of NDEs and OBEs are found throughout history and in all parts of the world. Their occurrence is not in general dispute, only their origins and meanings. This demonstrates that they are phenomenologically classifiable and distinguishable as a particular type of experience.

(2) NDEs typically occur under similar, generally physical circumstances: an individual is close to death, apparently dies, subsequently revives, and reports having undergone unusual experiences. A particular originating event (being near death) is thus a common catalyst for generating the structural effects of the NDE. This means they have an objectively, cross-culturally stable originary context and indicates a pre-cultural origin.

(3) The fundamental interpretation of NDEs appears to be universal—not only in general religious, mystical, or otherwise supernatural terms, but specifically in the belief that *this is what happens when we die.*

If there is no common experience underpinning narratives of religious experiences, cross-culturally consistent narratives of these specific extraordinary experience types should not exist, and certainly should not have the same apparently universally ascribed basic meanings. These considerations not only help reveal how cultural-linguistic constructivist perspectives rely on a number of mutually-reliant unproven axioms, but also demonstrate that these axioms do not stand up to scrutiny: (1) experience cannot precede language/culture, (2) narratives of experience do not refer to actual experiences, (3) religious experience is meaningless as a cross-cultural category, and (4) religious beliefs cannot be grounded in religious experiences (Shushan 2014).

NDEs and OBEs also reveal some broader theoretical and methodological problems with cultural-linguistic constructivist assumptions about religious experience. As seen above in relation to Schleiermacher, the study of religious experience is often critiqued through a lens of postcolonialist discourse. However, cultural-linguistic constructivist perspectives can also be seen as a legacy of Western cultural-imperialist domination and indeed may themselves derive from colonialist thinking. For example, certain Christian missionaries refused to accept indigenous claims that local afterlife beliefs stemmed directly from personal NDEs. Chrétien Le Clercq (1691: 207) wrote that Mi'kmaq Native American statements to this effect resulted from 'error and imposture', and Jean de Brébeuf (1636: 141) was 'astounded' that anyone could believe the narratives he heard from the Wyandot. In his exploration of the historiography of the psychopathologization of spiritual experiences, Hufford (2005: 21-25) pointed to 'Enlightenment skeptics such as David Hume who saw supernatural belief as inherently not rational'. Protestant and Calvinist theologies after the Middle Ages encouraged negative views of spiritual experiences, which were downplayed in favour of 'non-cognitive,' non-rational faith. The contemporary cultural-linguistic constructivist critiques may thus have roots in Catholic missionary ethnocentric justifications of colonialism, Humean skepticism, and Protestant/Calvinist theologies in (a) their culture of disbelief and mistrust of experiencer testimony and negatively evaluative assertions about narratives of experience; (b) their portrayal of the 'other' as untrustworthy, non-rational, and ignorant (inventing narratives of experience, being unable to understand or distinguish between experience types, and being uncritical products of belief systems); and (c) their privileging of their own preconceived philosophical paradigms (i.e., beliefs) over evidence.

Finally, a nearly exclusive focus on cross-cultural difference has become *de rigueur* in the study of religions, largely through politically motivated attempts to discount observations of similarity made by comparativist scholars of universalist orientations (Shushan 2013). The cross-cultural occurrence of NDEs and OBEs and their widespread interpretation in religious terms show that comparison and focus on similarity are valid and potentially fruitful avenues of research. They also bring to light an essential conflict in contemporary assumptions about religion and religious experience: the widely held perspective that religious *beliefs* are wholly culturally situated and cross-culturally meaningless conflicts with claims of the total cultural-linguistic construction of religious *experience*. Thus, if afterlife beliefs cannot be objectively and meaningfully similar across cultures, how can *dissimilar* beliefs result in cross-culturally *similar* NDEs? If one were to claim that there are no cross-cultural similarities of either NDEs or afterlife beliefs, the mass of evidence to the contrary would need to be proven false. Because these experiences and their relationships to beliefs imply that there *is* a type of human experience that is regularly interpreted in religious terms cross-culturally, similarities cannot be dismissed as conceptually unintelligible Western scholarly subjectivities. Contrary to decades of theoretical claims to the contrary, it seems we may have categories of phenomena that can logically and generically be called 'religious' after all (notwithstanding debates concerning the meaning and usefulness of the term 'religion'). This provides validation for the study of 'religion' as a category distinct from other aspects of human culture. The acknowledgement of cross-cultural similarities in these experiences and beliefs also calls into question the value of emphasizing difference to the exclusion or denial of even basic similarity in postcolonialist discourse, for such a focus can be divisive and potentially foster ethnocentrism.

Rather than being comprehensive explanations in and of themselves, language and culture are more productively seen as contributing factors in the formation, processing, and expression of experiences. To recognize and engage intellectually with the cross-cultural occurrence of NDEs and OBEs is little different from doing so with any other type of human experience. Grief at the loss of loved ones, for example, is universal although culturally expressed (Stroebe and Stroebe 1987: 53-54). The fact that people commonly ascribe to certain experiences religious, spiritual, or otherwise supernatural meanings does not make them beyond our ability to research or show that they are meaningless as pan-human categories. Both cross-culturally stable, structural features and culturally idiosyncratic features (i.e., similarities and differences) between experience narratives require explanation (Shushan 2013). The most likely way of achieving a more thorough understanding of NDE and OBE phenomena is through an acknowledgement of common non-cultural factors (i.e., universal human experience types) together with local cultural, linguistic, and environmental factors (Shushan 2009). Likewise, acknowledging the existence and significance of extraordinary experiences will help us achieve a more thorough understanding of the formation of religious beliefs across cultures.

Acknowledgements

Many thanks to the Perrott-Warrick Fund for a generous grant that has enabled the wider research project in which the present article is situated (Shushan forthcoming), and to the Ian Ramsey Centre for Science and Religion, University of Oxford, for hosting the project. Thanks to Gavin Flood, Peggy Morgan, James McClenon, David Hufford, Giovanni Casadio, Hrvoje Cargonja, Wendy Dossett, Mark Fox, Maya Warrier, Richard Moore, David Rousseau, Jeffrey Kripal, Viktoria Kovalevskaya, and anonymous reviewers for sharing their work, thought-provoking discussions, suggestions, and/or encouragement.

Short Biographical Note
Gregory Shushan is an Honorary Research Fellow at University of Wales Trinity Saint David, previously Research Fellow at the Ian Ramsey Centre

for Science and Religion, University of Oxford (supported by a grant from the Perrott-Warrick Fund, Trinity College, Cambridge), and at the Centro Incontri Umani (The Cross Cultural Centre) at Ascona, Switzerland.

Notes

1.   As of April 2016, a Google Scholar search for articles and books concerning NDEs yielded 15,200 results and 8,550 for those concerning OBEs. On ScienceDirect.com, the figures are 651 (NDE) and 687 (OBE). On PubMed (limited to medical literature) there are 133 and 71 results, respectively.

2.   See, for example, 'Ai shi ming', 'Yuan You', 'Zhao hun' in *Chu ci*, 4th-2nd centuries BCE; *Li ji* I.II.1.32, II.I.I.20, 5th century BCE; and throughout the *Zuangzhi*, c. 319 BCE. See also Shushan 2009 (Ch. 6 for India, Ch. 7 for China, 168) for numerous further examples with summaries, references, and fuller discussions.

3.   And perhaps to the duration of the experience—see Stevenson and Greyson (1996: 203-04).

4.   For 'illustrative and dramatic purposes' Proudfoot (1993: 793) employed Schachter and Singer (1962), a study that has been highly criticized and effectively refuted by further research over a half century (Barnard 1992: 234-35; McClenon 2002: 161-63). While Proudfoot (1993: 793) later clarified that his argument is not dependent upon that article's conclusions, we are still left with a lack of empirical evidence to support his claims.

5.   I know of no narrative from any time or place in which an NDE is casually accepted or seen to be an everyday occurrence.

6.   See, for example, Pilch 2011; Metzinger 2005; Badham 1997; Couliano 1991; Zaleski 1987; Bremmer 1983.

7.   Sharf (1998: 284f) raises NDEs, but only to criticise inconsistencies in Zaleski (1987).

8.   In an attempt at neutrality, NDE researchers use the term 'being of light' for what NDErs may identify as a *particular* radiant entity (the Buddha, Jesus, etc.).

9.   David Rousseau (pers. comm.) has calculated that it rates a 9 out of 32 points on the Greyson scale, and 7 is enough to qualify as an NDE.

10.   He uses Wren-Lewis' example to illustrate his points about distinctions between mystical experience and mystical teaching.

Chapter 5

Provincializing Religious Experience: Methodological Challenges to the Study of Religious Experiences in Brazil

Bettina E. Schmidt

The label 'religious experience' refers to a range of practices that is difficult to study. Anthropologists studying spirit possession and similar phenomena that come under this label have discussed the study of experiences 'behind the veil' of non-ordinary reality since decades (e.g., Harner 1982). However, as Bonnie Glass-Coffin (2013) explains in a recent article, anthropologists still have problems with the study of non-ordinary experiences. She argues that cultural relativism, at the core of anthropology, allows us to step aside from the core question of transpersonal. She even criticises the tendency of anthropologists to contextualise local accounts of non-ordinary reality because it would only serve 'domesticating and dismissing them, colonializing knowledge even as they claim to honour the truth of the Other' (Glass-Coffin 2013: 117).

Her critique is also at the heart of my article though I take a different approach. I argue in favour of local accounts that we should embrace in the same way that we accept academic interpretations of what we observe in the field. I focus here on spirit possession as one specific type of religious experience and include ethnographic information from my recent research in Brazil. I begin with an excerpt from an interview that was taken on the eve of the final part of an initiation ritual for a Candomblé community. Candomblé is an Afro-Brazilian religion that is centred on the worship of African deities called *orixás*. My interviewee describes in the following how difficult his path towards an acceptance of the *orixás* was and also how the experience enriches his life.

> When I turned eighteen, I talked to my mom and told her that from that moment I wanted no part in that religion [his family belongs to Jehovah's Witness]. They were very sad, but it was a decision I had to make for myself... And I stopped attending any kind of religion. But about two years later I felt the need to seek spiritual guidance but did not know how. A friend who knows Pai Z. [a priest of the Candomblé community]

said 'Why do you not ask the shells [i.e., a form of oracle reading]? It can help you. You are passing through a very difficult phase of your life, and I think it might do you good.' I said 'Oh no, I do not believe in those things. I learned that these things were wrong. I want to learn, not to play.' But one day I decided that I would do it, I would ask the shells, and was surprised when he [the priest] told me what the shells told him about me, about my private life, my past, how I was raised, and other things that only I know, no one else knew. And it really confused me when he told me that I had to do spiritual work... But I was like, 'I do not do it... I do not know if I do it...' But in that week, while I was at my house, *Egum* took me [this is a common way to describe an initial possession]. I was at home, normal, lying in my bed, and suddenly I felt as if something jumped on top of me and started to shake me. I got stiff, fell to the ground, I opened my bedroom door and when my friend who lived in the same house saw me, I was all red-purple, choked... Since then, since that time, twenty years ago, I never let go of Candomblé.

He continued his narrative by explaining how spirit possession has enhanced his life, despite his initial reservations:

It was love at first sight, you know, it made me complete. And I had serious problems with possession, because I did not believe in it. I thought it was all a lie, did not think anything would happen. Because I did not feel anything at ceremonies, I thought it was a thing of the imagination. Until it happened to me the first time... It totally changed my life. But I believe now that my first spiritual manifestation, my first trance happened when I was seven years old. But I had no idea then what I know today—Candomblé gave me the insight to see. I was seven years old when I lost consciousness, and my parents thought I had a seizure but in fact it happened only once in my life, when I was seven years. And I did tests, CT scans, electro, a lot of tests and they never found anything... I believe that it was the first manifestation of the *orixá* when I was seven years old and without the knowledge of my family—without anyone knowing, not even myself, because no one knew, my family did not practice it... And the feeling I had when I fainted was the same feeling when I started, the loss of consciousness, the same feeling...

It is a complete world within Candomblé; to me it is very important. It changed my character, my personality, my social life, my patience, understanding of what is religion, understanding the limits of other people. I do not want to prove to people that my religion is better than others. I think you show that you have a good character through actions, and behind this is the religious principle, in a certain way.

The fact is, you help us preparing clothes and when you see the *orixá* out, fully dressed, you will say 'Wow,...the *orixá* is happy, dancing, people feel pretty'. I mean, look at all this, I think it's a form of a God who manifests, I think it is a message from the *orixá*. Just imagine a religion in which God, the gods come dancing with you and manifest in you, it is unique, it is very unique. (Excerpt from an interview with M. on 23 April 2010)

M. demonstrates the struggle to understand what happens but also the joy the experience can provoke. The question of what to do with these narratives, however, remains crucial because of the complex context of Brazil and the danger of using these narratives only as illustrations. In the first part of the article I outline these two problems and offer a solution by introducing a new way to provincialise experience. The second part explains in detail what I mean by 'provincialising experience' and why it helps to understand religious experience as a deictic concept.

The Methodological Problem with Personal Narratives of Religious Experience

Personal accounts help us contextualise the religious experience. The Jungian psychotherapist José Jorge de Morais Zacharias, whom I interviewed about his involvement in Afro-Brazilian religions, explained, 'If a person experiences something unusual and is not given an explanation [by his/her surroundings], it will cause anxiety and disorder, even mental instability. It is only when a culturally embedded explanation is delivered that the experience becomes meaningful and structured' (interview with Zacharias in São Paulo on 15 April 2010). The narratives provide therefore an important framework that helps us understand the experience.

However, there are several different explanations in Brazil within one culture, every one of them representing a specific ontological framework. In Umbanda, one of the widespread Afro-Brazilian religions, there is a fine line between an experience involving *orixás* and an experience involving spirits that have derived from specific *orixás*, while in Candomblé the ontological understanding of the *orixás* prevents bodily incorporation. Candomblé priests speak instead about a merger of the divine and the human. This understanding is very different from Spiritism because Spiritists refer to their practice as a means of communication between two worlds and point towards the importance of the message instead of the experience. On the opposite side of the spectrum are Brazilian Pentecostals who regard the *orixás* as demons causing despair and suffering. For them the only solution is to exorcise the spirits and *orixás*. However, although the explanation and interpretation are very different from Umbanda, the bodily experience shows fundamental similarities (see Schmidt 2016). These ontological differences increase the importance of differentiating the contextual frame and allowing polyphonic views instead of one monolithic context.

The second problem is more widespread. Anthropologists tend to tell stories usually from the field. As I just did above, anthropologists like to include accounts from participant observation and interviews as supporting evidence for the case we want to make. It is seductive to illustrate our publications with photos taken during rituals and with excerpts from interviews or our field diary. The problem is to go one step further. Instead of using them only as illustrations I want to make the case that we need to include information from interviews in the analysis. To be honest, this problem has also affected my own approach to religious experience. While I have studied traditions with mediumistic elements since the 1990s, I have avoided looking 'behind the veil', or, as I wrote in my PhD thesis (Schmidt 1995), I have tried to step through the looking glass. I felt enchanted by the drumming, the movements, and the colours but kept my distance because I could not accept the presence of the spirits and deities. Despite my obvious fascination with possession rituals in Vodou and other religions, I focused my research on identity, ethnicity, migration, gender, and other issues when studying Puerto Rican Spiritism and Afro-Caribbean religions. And I only included observations from rituals and excerpts from interviews as background for the traditions. In my work on the Caribbean diaspora in New York (Schmidt 2008), I even made the French school of *ethnoscénologie* my main empirical approach. It allowed me to include various forms of data such as descriptions of public performances (e.g., carnival parade, theatre productions, jazz sessions in a pub, dance and music workshops) as part of the public sphere of Caribbean religions into my interpretation.

However, when I decided to go to Brazil to investigate the understanding of spirit possession, it was time to change my approach. Instead of referring to my observations, I had to find a way to include the emic understanding into the analysis. While I still do not share the beliefs in spirits and deities, the Brazilian environment made me realise that this was *my* problem, not that of the participants of these rituals. Brazilians in all sections of the society have a very open-minded attitude towards so-called paranormal phenomena. The only difference is how the non-ordinary reality is experienced and interpreted. The openness towards these experiences includes therefore a relatively widespread tolerance towards varieties of forms of understanding. A presence can be even experienced in a similar bodily manner but interpreted as empowering or suffering. The academic understanding is therefore just another way to interpret the experience, although most scholars have the disadvantage of not experiencing the reality themselves.

I do not want to disqualify here the academic understanding—quite the opposite. Anthropology is in its heart a secular discipline. I am not arguing in favour of Rudolf Otto's approach, which would lead only to the well-known pitfall of a non-critical, biased 'religious by sympathy' understanding. The academic frame is not only necessary to remain in the scholarly field; it also widens our understanding. It is, however, important not to limit the scholarly field to the debate in the West. Brazilian scholars have much to offer to the understanding of mediumistic experiences and must be included in the analysis. My research in Brazil included therefore ethnographic research among participants of possession rituals as well as research in libraries and discussions with scholars and participants. Hence, I attended as many rituals as possible in various traditions. I interviewed devotees of these traditions and collected their personal narratives about the experience. Whenever possible I discussed my observations with Brazilian anthropologists and other colleagues. In addition, I studied Brazilian academic interpretations of these rituals and discussed them with my interviewees, some of whom were scholars or students studying for a degree. They, too, were keen in gaining a wider understanding of what they experienced. In my interviews I noticed an impressive awareness of academic publications, from well-known scholars such as Jung, whose archetype concept seems widely accepted, to more specialised scholars such as Ruth Landes, whose book *City of Women* (1947) represents one of the earlier anthropological studies on gender and Candomblé. Interviewees referred sometimes explicitly to her work or others in order to challenge academics whom they criticized as being biased towards a limited Western understanding. By referring to their own experiences, they offered an alternative reading that challenges the academic view.

I argue therefore that the personal narratives are more than just illustrations. They allow us a view behind the veil and enable us to gain a fuller view of spirit possession with its polyphonic interpretations. To use the narratives only as illustrations of academic interpretations disqualifies the emic understanding as secondary to the academic debate. As Ann Taves already noted in her study of Anglo-American Protestants (1999), the academic boundary between experiencing religion and explaining experience, between scholars and participants, is blurred and obscures reality. The same is the case in Brazil where there is no boundary between these groups. Not only Kardecists, who are, according to the Brazilian census, the group with the highest rate of people with higher education, but also people involved in Candomblé and other Afro-Brazilian traditions are educated people who read and comment on any publication about their practice. It is therefore 'antithetical' (Taves 1999: 6) to insist on a dualistic view that divides experiencing religion and explaining experiences. Taves promotes a threefold typology and includes a third position, 'the mediating tradition' (1999: 348). Taves refers here to the work of William James and writes that mediators 'believed that the way in which they accessed religion was scientific rather than simply a matter of faith and that the character of their methods legitimated the religious reality of that which they discovered as a result of their method' (1999: 349). While her language indicates her distance in accepting these views, she urges us nonetheless to follow James's interest in the interplay between theories of religion and living religion. She writes that although theories are 'the farthest removed and the most fragmented', they inform the 'making and unmaking of experience at the level of narrative in varied and complicated ways' (Taves 1999: 361).

While I agree with her critique of the dualistic view that separates experiences and scholars, her threefold typology does not solve the dilemma that is at the core of the research into non-ordinary experiences. Despite promoting a third way, she remains reluctant to accept the mediators' way of understanding reality.

Provincialising the Experience

In this article I present an alternative approach that addresses both problems outlined above. With reference to Michael Lambek's article on provincialising God, I argue for an understanding of religious experience as *deictic* term, hence provincialising the experience by embracing locally specific features. This approach allows us to disregard contradictory explanations (e.g., whether the experience is empowering or requires exorcism to stop suffering) and also the complex but dualistic interplay between scholars and experiencers. It enables me to speak about spirit possession by presenting the interpretations of the experiencers, although I am not one of them. In the end, it allows us to maintain anthropology as a secular discipline and have a glimpse 'behind the veil' nonetheless. As Lambek argues, we have to overcome the binary logic of either/or that influences the Western way of thinking. Rather, we should embrace the possibility of both/and which allows more than one answer, more than one truth, as the following quote shows:

> We cannot subscribe exclusively to European meta-narratives or analytic stances they presuppose or generate, but we cannot do without them either. What I want to provincialize is not all aspects of the Abrahamic religious traditions but rather their dedication precisely not to such a pluralistic logic of both/and but rather to a binary logic of either/or. Indeed, it is this binary logic of mutual exclusion that also poses the alternative of secularism: either belief in, and invocation of, religion—or not. In a cultural universe characterized by both/and, scepticism and rationalism are simply part of a larger repertoires of attitudes and positions, invoked according to shifting practical considerations, rather than a matter for strict adjudication. (Lambek 2008: 123)

Lambek rejects here the Western idea of religion, which is centred on the Abrahamic tradition that 'belief in God requires rejecting alternatives', but he also disagrees with secularism because 'the secular is by definition a perspective that imagines it can look at religion from the outside' (2008: 124-25). Both positions seem fundamental faulty because they privilege one stance over others: either the religious or the external. Rejecting the binary thinking of either/or in favour of both/and gives us therefore a crucial methodological advantage. As Steven Sutcliffe and Ingvild Gilhus outline in the introduction of their book on New Age spirituality, 'Religion does not exist in a pure form in cultural processes'; the separation between religion and secular is artificial and unstable (2013: 12). My own research also shows that 'The empirical data about religion are impure and reactive and potentially mix with everything else' (Sutcliffe and Gilhus 2013: 12). Rejecting the traditional understanding of religion in opposition to secular allows us therefore to embrace all kinds of activities, whether they are located in a designated religious sector of society or not. It leads us also towards a polyphonic reading of any form of religious experience.

Religious Experience as a Deictic Term

'Deixis' is a linguistic term that describes the problem that the meaning of certain words depends on a given context. A typical example of deictic terms are the words 'here' or 'now', because the determination of their referents depends on the context in that sentence or situation. Lambek highlights the significance of 'deixis' for anthropology by referring to Edward Evan Evans-Pritchard's work, in particular his book *The Nuer* (1940) but also his book on Azande witchcraft. Evans-Pritchard is well-known for his contribution to the anthropology of religion. In his book *The Nuer* he points eloquently to the significance of cultural translation, the core of anthropology. But Lambek criticises Evans-Pritchard for overlooking the depth of the problem concerning cultural sensitivity. In support of his critique, Lambek points towards Evan-Pritchard's translation of the Nuer word *kwoth* with God. Alhough Evans-Pritchard acknowledges in his book that the Nuer language is highly deictic, he fails to see that the meaning of *kwoth* depends on the situation. Lambek argues that *kwoth* is also a deictic form of speech. Because of this mistake, Evans-Pritchard consequently also misinterprets the question of whether the Nuer religion can be regarded as monotheistic or polytheistic. For Lambek, the solution is to describe *kwoth* as deictic deity. Only then we can avoid further misinterpretation. Lambek argues that the misreading of deictic terms has led to the transformation of these terms from context-dependent concepts into stable, objectified referents. The outcome is that religious practices have been misinterpreted, not only in the context of African religions. He insists that 'a deictic world is one that is open and inclusive, characterized by a both/and rather than an either/or logic', and continues that 'attention to deixis implies putting practice ahead of belief' (Lambek 2008: 137). The result is the acceptance of locally specific features—what Lambek labels 'provincialization of God' (2008: 120).

Lambek's anthropological reflection on God provides me with an analytical frame for understanding religious experience and in particular, spirit possession. The understanding of spirit possession as a deictic form of speech highlights that the meaning of spirit possession depends always on the situation, not only on the cultural and historical context of the situation but also on the community, on the gender of the experiencer, and more—hence on the ethnographic moment of the specific experience. We need to provincialise the experience itself. As Paul Johnson (2011) has already outlined in detail, theories of spirit possession must remain superficial and limited as they originate against the background of the Western idea of religion. The only way to move forward with an understanding of spirit possession is to embrace locally specific features of the experience. As I demonstrate elsewhere in detail (see, e.g., Schmidt 2016) the Brazilian Spiritist idea of mediumship will always remain different from the Candomblé idea of merging the realm of the *orixás* with the human realm in the moment of possession trance, or the Umbanda idea of incorporation will always differ from the Pentecostal idea of demonic possession and divine experience with the Holy Ghost. The differences between these ideas do not make one of them less valuable than the other, nor are they incoherent; rather, every one of these ideas makes an equal contribution to a wide range of positions. I even argue that the sometimes opposing readings can further our understanding of the experience because they show us the danger of generalisation.

The use of ethnographic present tense in anthropological publications supports—perhaps subconsciously—the idea that the culture described in such a way remains unchanged. Subsequently, spirit possession is regarded as unchanged since the time of Landes (1908–1991). Landes was an American anthropologist in the tradition of Franz Boas and Ruth Benedict, her PhD supervisor. Landes was in Brazil between 1938 and 1939 and investigated spirit possession in collaboration with several Brazilian scholars, especially Edison Carneiro, Bahian Candomblé, mainly with regard to gender roles. The outcome of her research is the much acclaimed book *City of Women* (1947), in which she presents Candomblé as a religion centred on women and homosexual men. Her book had a vast impact on Afro-Brazilian studies, mainly but not only among US anthropologists. Her findings confirmed a general impression that ascribed spirit possession, as Mary Keller wrote, 'to women, the poor, and the religious other (the "primitive", the "tribal", the third-world woman, the black, the immigrant)' (Keller 2002: 4). However, as research in the last decades have shown, possession rituals are not always limited to the powerless, and even when the two coincide, they are not always causally linked (Cohen 2007: 93). As I have argued elsewhere (Schmidt 2016), Brazilian society changed dramatically during the twentieth century. These changes influenced the meaning of the experience for people involved and the discourse about it. Nowhere is the impact more visible than when discussing the social dimension—gender as well as race. Hence, by comparing studies from the first part of the twentieth century with my own research, we can see the impact of the social changes on the gender distribution and even on the growing racial diversification of the membership. While some scholars disregard Landes's interpretation, I argue that we have to look at it as context-dependent—in this case, dependent on a different historical and social context. And the changes have an impact on the experience itself. Spirit possession today varies therefore from spirit possession in the 1930s, despite a relatively identical belief concept.

Today we see in Brazil the presence of a highly sophisticated debate among practitioners about their experiences. The growing social diversification of the communities supports an impressive intellectualization of the membership. Numerous practitioners pursue further training (e.g., in the *Faculdade de Teologia Umbandista* in São Paulo) and even higher-education degrees at universities. Consequently, we can find an impressive number of publications, conference papers, and lectures by members of the priesthood and other devotees that exceeds those in any other country. The application of the Jungian archetypes to the *orixás* is also firmly established. And recently the attention shifts to debates about empowerment, embodiment, and cognition. Provincialising the experience on a conceptual level allows the co-existence of these and more discourses as equally relevant contributions to the debate. Ioan M. Lewis is wary of this development and warns that when following 'the current fashions of anthropological theory...the voices of those we seek to report are in danger of being silenced as we pursue our own ethnocentric preoccupations' (2003: xii). He overlooks here that also the experiencers follow trends.

Spirit Possession as Practice

The argument to treat spirit possession and other types of religious experience as deictic terms has another advantage because it shifts the attention from belief to practice. The outcome is the acknowledgement of the specific Brazilian situation in which it does not matter whether someone self-identifies as agnostic, Christian, or atheist. It only matters what people *do*; their *practice* is important. Perhaps this is why the current rise of secularism in Brazil has had little impact on the continuity of possession rituals. Although spirit possession is located in the Western framework in the religious sector of society, this is not always the case in Brazil, where it is widely linked to secular healing and well-being (see also Greenfield 2008). The focus on practice also helps to avoid the conceptual trap of explaining religious experience as 'unreal' or 'irrational'. Spirit possession has suffered throughout the decades under the Western focus on rationality, as Paul Johnson writes:

> Discourses and legal actions naming and constraining 'spirit possession' over the past four centuries helped to create the dual notions of the rational individual and the civil subject of modern states. The silhouette of the propertied citizen and free individual took form between the idea of the automaton—a machine-body without will—and the threat of the primitive or animal, bodies overwhelmed by instincts and passions (or the two merged, as in Descartes' 'nature's automata', animals-*as*-machines (2003: 24, 29, 66). The balance between the lack of will and its unchecked excess has been considered through the prism of the dangers of spirits in relation to persons and objects at least since the mid-seventeenth century. (Johnson 2011: 396)

My aim is not to find an explanation for what happens during spirit possession. In line with Johnson I disagree with the dichotomy of the Western rational civil religion on one side and the irrational other on the other side. If we put aside any notion of a 'correct belief' or a 'correct scientific explanation', questions about whether one believes in the spirits, or in the *orixás*, or in science become irrelevant. Spirit possession relates to the relationship between human and non-human beings and not whether the spirits, the *orixás*, or God exist. The corporeal experience during possession is a key aspect of how to maintain this relationship, while the interpretation of it depends on the situation. Hence, spirit possession as a deictic term enables an ambivalent, sometimes even contradictory usage, without an essentialist meaning.

I explain what I mean by referring again to personal narratives. I focus here on the concept of consciousness and agency and the controversy around the term 'semi-consciousness'. From a scientific level, semi-consciousness does not exist. One is either aware of one's surroundings or not, hence, either conscious or unconscious (Klass 2003: 79-80). From the emic perspective, however, the debate about consciousness and semi-consciousness offers an insight into what happens during the experience. I begin with an excerpt from an interview with a medium who declares to be unconscious:

> In my first contact with Dr Marsec I was 18 years old. My mother had a seizure and she was bedridden. I woke up very early to go to work and when I said goodbye to her at five in the morning she could not move in her bed; she only moaned in pain. I told her 'Mom, I'll say a prayer because I need to go to work. I'll say a prayer for you to calm down, and I'm going to work.' When I started praying, I lost awareness of what was going on, and the Doctor came for the first time. When I came to, my mother was sitting up in bed and had nothing, no pain. She told me what happened and I was very scared because someone had entered my body, took over and

did this to me. I was angry, happy to see her well, but very upset because
this was not right.

Then with time, I understand that it was not someone coming into my
body, but it is a psychic power that is now almost instinct... I gradually
understood that my psychic power was not the same as with most other
mediums, who are conscious or semi-conscious. In the beginning everything was very difficult, because sometimes when I returned I was off balance. Sometimes I had the impression that I was missing my legs and I
would fall. Not today, today I think that training and extensive work with
these brothers has given me a physical strength and knowledge... But I
always need someone to hold me. (Interview with a Spiritist on 17 April
2010)

This medium describes here her first experience with a spirit and her
progress in handling this 'collaboration'. The woman is the co-founder of
a small Spiritist centre that specialises in various types of healing. While
the other mediums working in the centre remain aware of what is going
on, she is an exception, not only in her centre but among other Spiritists as well. Spiritists insist that mediums are always responsible for what
happens during trances. While an untrained medium might not be able
to control the spirits, to work as a medium is allowed only after intensive
training and with approval of the spirits.

Despite the differences between Spiritism and Afro-Brazilian religions,
a common feature of most narratives is the inability to control one's own
body, despite being aware of what is going on. This following excerpt is
from an interview with a medium in an Afro-Brazilian centre:

I do not remember anything about the first time except that the sensation
was a strong heat, the sensation of heat and sleep at the same time. I felt a
huge weight in my back and neck, and I began to feel my heart. The heart
accelerated! And it was the sensation of two hearts beating inside me.
There was a kind of force in my throat, a very strong energy in the throat,
and I felt like it was about to speak. But in that moment, at the first time,
I was very afraid, because when it began to happen, I had doubts about
whether it would be good or bad. I tried to stop it and I was left with the
sensation that it would begin the communication in a trance. (Interview
with a medium on 21 May 2010 in São Paulo)

The interviewee was quite unique, as he grew up within a Catholic family
but became reborn into a Protestant Evangelical church where he experienced at various times the Holy Spirit. One day, however, he became possessed by a very different kind of divine entity, the so-called *encantados* of
the Afro-Brazilian tradition Tambor de Mina. For a while he was not sure
which path to follow and attended church as well as ceremonies in Tambor
de Mina. When I met him, he attended regular ceremonies at home as well
as in a small community in São Paulo, although not as a main member of
the community. In my interview I repeatedly came back to the differences

between his experiences, but he avoided my probing questions. As I could observe later when we attended together a ceremony during which he suddenly became possessed, he did not remember anything afterwards. Even his body could not remember that he had eaten dinner during the possession, and he immediately asked for food when he recovered from the possession.

Other interviewees made precise distinctions between the experiences with different entities, and in particular between spirits and *orixás*. The following is an excerpt from an interview with an Umbanda priest:

> I feel differences between the spirits in Umbanda. When I incorporate some spirits, I do not feel anything. And I have other spirits that make me feel ecstatic, even though I did not enter them. The feeling is different from my normal waking state. But when I incorporate an *orixá*, I usually I have no control of my movements. In most deities, in the Yoruba tradition, I have no control of my movements. Often when I am conscious, I want to stop, but I cannot...
>
> Sometimes I feel as if my arms fall asleep, or my legs, and sometimes I even feel as if I'm having a heart attack. With each *orixá* I have a different feeling. Sometimes it begins with dancing, quite violent, but I'm still conscious. Nevertheless, I can control myself, or stop dancing, and I intend to stop dancing and stand, but when I least expect it, I lose control again. In my first session, I wanted to stop dancing... But I could not stop and began dancing with the other leg. (Interview with an Umbanda priest on 14 April 2010 in São Paulo)

This priest describes what people mean by 'semi-conscious': to be aware of what is going on but not in control. However, the degree of awareness varies and depends often on the level of initiation and experience. Steven Engler writes that Umbanda mediums enter 'an unconscious trance state and are more likely to require subsidiary rituals to free them from the spirit that has possessed them' (2009: 486). However, an Umbanda priestess differentiates between three types of trance, depending on whether a medium is unconscious, conscious, or semi-conscious. She said:

> In Umbanda we believe all mediums are semi-conscious because we know what is happening, we just cannot control the body. We speak in a different voice and say things that we had not thought of before. New things come to mind, with a different body language and movement. Sometimes we see people who are ill or are old doing things that people would not do naturally. (Interview in São Paulo on 22 March 2010)

That lack of control does not excuse every action was a common feature in my interviews with priests and priestesses. They insisted that mediums have certain responsibilities for the situation because properly trained mediums can initiate, allow, or prevent the incorporation. The priestess quoted above explained that while mediums previously were unaware of what happened during trance, over time it came to be seen as problematic when a medium was unconscious, because it exempted this person from any liability. She even said that being unconscious would prevent a medium from enriching her or his own life as the medium would be unaware of the messages from the spirits. According to her, Umbanda mediums are now usually semi-conscious.

The position towards agency is even regarded as the dividing line between traditions or between houses. One priest positioned his own tradition of Candomblé in contrast to Umbanda by arguing that only spirits in Umbanda take complete control of the human bodies. Consequently, he and other Candomblé priests use the term 'spirit possession' only when speaking about Umbanda but not when they address their own tradition. In Candomblé the experience is described more as 'divine transformation'. A human being is transformed into a new being who embraces the divine, the *orixás*. The key here is that the *orixás* are regarded as too powerful for human beings to incorporate. They are perceived as forces of nature. And because it is impossible for a human being to become a thunderstorm or a flash of lightening, it is also impossible to become possessed by one.

The Candomblé concept has inspired the Brazilian anthropologist Márcio Goldman to develop an elaborate explanation for what happens during the encounter between humans and *orixás*. He argues that being possessed in Candomblé means that a person has become an 'almost' divine entity (Goldman 2007: 114). The world of the gods and the humans converse; human and *orixá* almost overlap and create two new agencies together: a person and an individual *orixá*. Goldman argues that a person 'is presumed to be multiple and layered, composed of agencies of natural and immaterial elements', including a main *orixá* and a number of secondary *orixás*, ancestral spirits, and a soul (2007: 111). Prior to the initiation that firmly links *orixás* and human, a human being is incomplete. Only the initiation finishes the creation process and transforms an unfinished, undifferentiated human being into a structured person (Goldman 2007: 112). For Goldman this explanation is the reason why each possession is different. Each initiation ritual creates one specific being within the human; possessed agency and possessing agency become inseparably merged and create a unique entity. The question about agency and responsibility become invalid as the initiated person includes elements of the *orixás*.

Conclusion

These excerpts recount private recollections of the possession experience. Despite the focus on agency and consciousness, they highlight well the diversity of the interpretations. While these excerpts represent only some of the common Brazilian traditions (Spiritism, Umbanda, and

Candomblé), they point towards some common features, such as lack of control, loss of memory, and an awareness of an extraordinary presence in their body. The commonality is therefore the reference to something extraordinary, outside oneself, and often outside the human body.

This awareness challenges the dualistic understanding of body-mind in the Western discourse. I argue that we need to embrace physical, cognitive, and cultural elements if we want to understand any form of religious experience. Whether it is called cultural biology (Greenfield) or bioculture (Armin Geertz), the important point is not to limit our view to one aspect alone (mind or body) but to look at all elements. And this includes the corporeal feature, because experiences such as spirit possession cannot be understood without taking the body into account. The body, however, is not only the brain or blood components but the *whole* body and, to use Marcel Mauss' terminology, its bodily techniques, such as dancing and speaking. Roberto Motta defines Candomblé and other Afro-Brazilian traditions consequently as 'religion of the body and the image' and writes that these religions 'encourage the display of the body with all its drives and tendencies' (2005: 301, 299).

Both dance and speech are common means of communication between human beings and supernatural entities, the spirits and *orixás*, but they are performed in distinct ways depending on the tradition, the community, the situation (time and place) and function. It is impossible to extract the essence of spirit possession. We need rather to embrace its many local features.

'Body trance', to use Motta's term, is vital for the relationship between humans and non-humans. Mark Münzel compares the dance during trance with the performance of a dressage horse guided by the rider through elegant and difficult figures (1997: 153); without the rider the horse would not accomplish its complex task as well and vice versa, without the horse the rider could not carry on. We cannot see, touch, or communicate with the 'rider' (the spirit or *orixá*) without the 'horse' (the medium). We are even unable to confirm its existence with scientific measures, although subjectively we can feel and observe the impact. But the main point here is to highlight the importance of the local features of the experience. The embodiment demonstrates the interrelation—and interdependence—of body and mind, which must be regarded as a unity within a polyphonic context.

Short Biographical Note

Bettina E. Schmidt is a cultural anthropologist, professor of study of religions at the University of Wales Trinity Saint David and Director of the Alister Hardy Religious Experience Research Centre in Lampeter, research on religion and identity in Latin America, the Caribbean and its diaspora.

Section Three:
Theological and Philosophical Approaches to the Study of Religious Experience

Chapter 6

Immediate Revelation or the Basest Idolatry?
Theology and Religious Experience

Robert Pope

The French novelist Alexandre Dumas, author of *The Three Musketeers* and *The Count of Monte Cristo*, among other works, is credited with coining the aphorism 'all generalisations are dangerous, even this one' (in Swatridge 2014: 153).[1] Despite his warning, I am going to begin by offering a dangerous generalization: on the whole, theologians tend to be ambivalent about 'religious experience'. As one theologian has expressed it: 'One needs to be very careful in speaking of religious experience. It is notoriously difficult to construct a meaningful theology on the basis of it' (Jones 1999: 21).

Of course, much depends on how 'theology' and, perhaps more significantly 'religious experience', are defined. In this chapter, I will begin with a brief examination of what scholarship, particularly in the twentieth century, has identified as constituting 'religious experience', and then I will discuss theological approaches, which first, consider 'experience' to be fundamental and second, consider the claims of 'experience' to border on the idolatrous. In conclusion, I will tentatively suggest that, while there might well be a disparity between what commentators mean by 'religious experience' and the experiences with which the Christian tradition is replete, it remains possible to see that 'experience' plays a part in theological construction.

Defining Terms

Religious Experience

Recognizing both that 'there is no simple thing that can be bottled and neatly labelled a "religious experience"' (Cole 2005: 6), and that the singular term 'religious experience' might well be too narrow to cover all the phenomena attributed by those who experience them to 'religion',[2] there are, nevertheless, various possible definitions of the term 'religious experience'. For example, Ninian Smart suggested that 'a religious experience involves some kind of "perception" of the invisible world, or involves a perception that some visible person or thing is a manifestation of the invisible world' (1969: 28), while F. W. Dillistone asserted that religious experiences consist of 'a state of mind or feeling induced by something beyond ordinary explanation' (1983: 205). One further definition will suffice. Reaching his conclusions from a study of descriptions, which the authors acknowledged to comprise religious experience, Alister Hardy goes slightly further than either Smart or Dillistone in suggesting that religious experiences consist of 'a deep awareness of a benevolent, non-physical power which appears to be partly or wholly beyond, and far greater than, the individual self' (1979: 1). All three definitions raise questions for theological reflection.

The primary problem is that Smart, Dillistone, and Hardy all take the idea of 'religion' beyond the realm of the 'religions'. While those who have the kind of experiences they describe might belong to a specific religious tradition, or might be led, subsequent to their experience, to involve themselves in a particular religious organization, adherence to a religious tradition is not deemed essential. In other words, a distinct religious interpretation, couched in doctrinal terms, is not the crucial factor in defining religious experience. While the existence of the 'invisible world', 'something beyond ordinary explanation' or 'a benevolent, non-physical power' is *axiomatic*, it is clearly not important to identify any of these with Yahweh, the God and Father of the Lord Jesus Christ, Allah, or any other deity, even if those explaining their experiences might employ such language. In this way, the *religions* become possible expositions of *religion*, the former being logically and culturally defensible human constructs concerned with teaching, worship, ritual, doctrine, and so forth, but the latter being what corresponds to the highest, or possibly basic, realities of the universe and is known only through experience. Even when it is admitted, as by William James, that 'religion' is not a common 'essence' but 'many characters' (1923: 26), it remains the case that 'religion' is the shorthand reference to the experience of the multifarious elements of that which constitutes ultimate reality. It might be possible to convey something of this reality through doctrinal statements, but it is *knowable* fundamentally through experience.

As a result, commentators such as David Hay have argued for the priority of experience, partly because emphasizing doctrine in a milieu in which the religious dimension to life cannot be presupposed contributes to the continuing decline of institutional religion. Nevertheless, Hay's argument is predicated on the belief 'that these [religious] experiences are part of being human, have always been there, and indeed are a major root, or *the* major root of religion' (1990: 61-62). His insistence on the priority of religious experience is thus in turn based on the axiom that religious experience is fundamental in human experience, and doctrine is consequently relegated to a secondary position as a historically and culturally dependent exposition of 'religion'. As with other scholars, Hay's axiom is based on a reasonable and logical account of how religious systems emerge, on a sense that what is real and true must be universal, and on the conviction that when the real and true are experienced, they are mediated by historically and culturally generated forms that give rise to different and possibly conflicting religious claims. It is, of course, impossible to demonstrate beyond all conceivable doubt that the axiom is misplaced. It is nonetheless necessary to acknowledge that it is possible to begin with a different axiom based on a similarly reasonable and logical argument, which places doctrine and religious experience in quite a different relationship, as will be seen below.

Definitions such as those of Smart, Dillistone, and Hardy and arguments such as that of Hay endorse the view that a 'subjective turn' has occurred since the Enlightenment and is to some extent associated with the work of thinkers such as René Descartes, Friedrich Schleiermacher, Immanuel Kant, and Søren Kierkegaard. Although the detail of their systems varies significantly, in their thought, the self—the experiencing, thinking, feeling, rational subject—rather than any external referent, such as 'God' or the scriptures, becomes the primary source for understanding reality. It might appear simplistic or obvious to say so, but it is important to acknowledge that 'religious experience' has come largely to be understood as first and foremost the 'state of mind or feeling' experienced by the subject, which might well be 'induced by something beyond ordinary experience' whose significance is largely rooted in the 'state of mind or feeling', thereby induced in the individual who records having the experience. Religious experience, then, is focused squarely on the one who experiences it, her or his attempt to understand and articulate it, and the effect that the experience and its interpretation might subsequently have on the experiencing subject. This can be observed in descriptions of religious experience. Take, for example, the following (admittedly curtailed) descriptions, self-identified as religious experiences,[3] which can be found in the collection of the Alister Hardy Religious Experience Research Centre:

> I heard nothing, yet it was as if I were surrounded by a golden light and as if I only had to reach out my hand to touch God himself who was surrounding me with his compassion. (Rankin 2008: 116)

> I have a growing sense of reality, and personal identity, which comes from being united to something more powerful than myself, something that is helping me to be what I want to be. (Rankin 2008: 134)

On first view, both examples appear to include what could be termed an external referent. In the first example, there is a 'golden light' as well as a reference to God, who is felt to be surrounding the person with compassion. In the second example, the language is perhaps less personal and less traditionally religious: the external referent is 'something more powerful' than the self, and the result of the experience is one of personal transformation or fulfilment. Smart's 'invisible world', Dillistone's inducement of a state of mind by something 'beyond the self', and Hardy's 'benevolent, non-physical power' are clearly represented in both examples. What is clearest, however, is that both examples contain an attempt by the experiencing subject to find a language considered adequate to express the ineffable. The experience itself is believed to constitute an immediate sense of the transcendent, but the attempt to describe the experience must draw on paradigms of thought, which might have developed as a result of sensory perception, as a result of pre-existing categories in the human mind, as a result of nurture into prevailing intellectual (or religious) systems, or as any combination of all three factors (and possibly others). However formulated, it is clear that the attempt to articulate a religious experience is inevitably dependent on some form of epistemological paradigm. As a result, it might seem appropriate to some to name what they experience 'God', while to others it is more accurate to consider 'something more powerful than myself'. It is likely that these are in some ways analogous descriptions, but they cannot be considered synonymous because both potentially hold a host of other meanings that might—or might not—be assumed. What is unclear from the description alone is whether or not this paradigm is *forced* upon the experience[4] or is in itself *prompted* by the experience, which is *sui generis*, as Rudolf Otto argued (see, e.g., Otto 1950: 7, 44, 120, etc.). Nevertheless, both examples revolve around the belief, prompted or confirmed by the experience, that there exists something greater than the physical realties we observe and encounter, which is not beyond immediate perception but is at best hidden and at worst absent from our everyday lives—something that Christian theologians would also wish to affirm, as will be seen below. More significantly, however, both descriptions also revolve around the *ego* of the person who experiences such phenomena, and it is the effect on individuals of their perceived experiences that comes to the fore: in the first description, the person feels surrounded by God's compassion; in the second, the individual is firmly set on a path to personal fulfilment.

Thus the term 'religious experience' has come to represent something extraordinary that occurs in an individual's life, which is explained by appealing to a sense of immediate contact with the divine, the ineffable, the real, or God. It provides an authoritative moment through which individuals who have such experiences are enabled to reach conclusions about themselves, life, the universe, and everything, even if those conclusions are expressed in religio-cultural terms belonging to predominant paradigms existing within each person's particular context. The possibility exists for these conclusions to be negative, but on the whole, religious experiences tend overwhelmingly to lead people to a positive account of themselves and the world in which they live.[5] What, then, of theology?

Theology

Theology is usually associated with a specific religious tradition, which most prevalently in western contexts is Christianity. In technical terms, theology is a *second order discipline* because it is always predicated on certain axioms or preconceptions that have priority. Theology seeks to explore, to understand, and to construct its claims on the basis of those axioms and, depending on the theologian's standpoint, it uses particular tools, such as the Bible, the Christian tradition, other fields of intellectual enquiry, critical reasoning, and so forth in order to fulfil its task. Theology, then, struggles with religious experience in part because it concerns the 'religions' (or one of them), while 'religious experience' appears to go beyond the specificity of the 'religions' and makes axiomatic a sense of 'religion', which does not constitute the theologian's usual field of interest, apart from the initial experiences that are fundamental to the religious tradition itself. Theologically speaking, Jesus might well have had an experience of what has been described here as 'religion', but the claims of the apostles are based on the perception that they had experienced something through the presence of Jesus. In this way the theological tradition has been constructed not specifically on the religious experiences of its major figures or on those of the mass of its adherents, but on Jesus, who he was, what happened to him, and what Christians believe he accomplished. At least on the surface, theology is not the introspective exploration of the human condition, but the attempt to understand what it means to have been subject to God's address in the history of a particular nation (Israel) and the life, teaching, death, and resurrection of a particular person (Jesus). Gareth Jones, for example, argues that theology is the attempt to understand the fundamental Christian confession that 'God is present in this world, as was revealed in Jesus Christ' (1999: 11).

If God is present in the world, then all experiences have the potential to convey something about what it is to be subject to God's address, as Gareth Jones acknowledges (1999: 55), and the work of Friedrich Schleiermacher (1768–1834) to some degree accomplishes this by basing theological claims on religious experience. Influenced by the Pietist (specifically Moravian) movement, as well as Romanticism, Schleiermacher recognized that the affections, including emotion, experience, and 'feeling' were fundamental to both human being and to religion itself. Thus 'true religion is the sense and the taste for the infinite' (Schleiermacher 1994: 39). Creeds, texts, rituals, and other aspects of religious systems are outward and secondary matters that attempt to give expression to the core experience of the divine. This experience is *sui generis*, because it is inaccessible to philosophical enquiry and because it is separate from matters of morality. It has its own integrity and appeals to 'the aesthetic and affective character of the religious life' (Proudfoot 1985: 2). It therefore retains significance and relevance to religion's 'cultured despisers' because it is not the *core* of religion that they truly despise but its secondary, *outward* aspects. Thus Schleiermacher calls on them to 'turn from everything usually reckoned religion, and fix your regard on the inward emotions and dispositions (1994: 18).

Schleiermacher's work was pioneering for a number of reasons. First, it could be said that he was the first to consider 'religion as such' or 'religion itself as a generic something' rather than 'a particular kind or instance' of religion (Smith 1978: 45). As a result, Schleiermacher's theology would appear *prima facie* to be a theology built upon the same axiomatic distinction between 'religion' and 'the religions' identified earlier to be at the heart of contemporary definitions of 'religious experience'. Certainly, Schleiermacher seems to point to something common in human experience—specifically, what might now be termed 'spiritual or religious experience—rather than to an interpretation of Christianity or the Christian tradition *per se*. Thus, in his most developed and mature thought, Schleiermacher describes religion as 'the feeling of absolute dependence' (1999: 16), which is universal and finds expression in all religions. The experience constitutes the primary source material for religious belief and practice and thus also for the theologian. As one commentator has noted, 'Schleiermacher's approach was from experience: from a felt experience of God which he held to be above reason, suprarational, to the rational expression of the experience, which was theology' (Gunton 2002: 175). George Lindbeck has characterized this kind of argument as the 'experiential-expressive' approach to theology, which 'interprets doctrines as noninformative and nondiscursive symbols of wider feelings, attitudes or existential orientations', including 'those deep experiences of the divine (or the self, or the world) which most of us are accustomed to thinking of as peculiarly religious' (1984: 16, 30). Schleiermacher's scheme, then, offers the potential for including religious experience in theological discussion.

Schleiermacher's thought was, and remains, influential. As one example, it is possible to cite the only systematic theology published in the Welsh language during the twentieth century, *Bannau'r Ffydd* (The Pinnacles of the Faith), written by the Welsh Congregational theologian D. Miall Edwards (1873–1941). Steeped in a theological tradition traced back through Harnack and Ritschl to Hegel and Schleiermacher, Edwards's work also demonstrated the deep influence of Otto's *Idea of the Holy*. Edwards asserted the primacy of experience over doctrine and the secondary nature of doctrine as the attempt to 'give a reasonable or intelligent account of the truths which are implicit in human experiences' (1929: 35). Like Schleiermacher, Edwards understood 'religion' to represent the connection between human beings and 'the real', namely the love that is at the heart of the universe, with 'Christian experience' as seen in the New Testament comprising 'the richest expression of it' (1929: 35). Thus all religions were simply human expressions of the same religious experience (Edwards 1921: 81-171, 1923), but Christianity surpassed the other religions because it contained Christ's own experience, which 'reveals the inclination of mind of absolute dependence on God and of filial fellowship with God' (both of which he learnt from Schleiermacher) and in turn enabled others to experience Christ as 'the object of the creature's love and praise and worship' (Edwards 1929: 40, 44). For Edwards, this could be summarized (in the gender-exclusive terms of the time) as the experience of the Fatherhood of God and its corollary, the brotherhood of man. The purpose of the Christian gospel was to promote the experience of God as 'Father', while doctrine should be the 'expression of a relevant and living experience' rather than the expression of timeless truth expressed in propositions.

Much of Edwards's work has not lasted the passage of time: the view that the Christian religion surpasses other religions despite their all sharing a common experience is generally considered *passé*. For others, his dismissal of Christ's ontological sonship in favour of his perceived but highly evolved relationship with God the Father does perhaps run close to the dynamic Monarchianism of Paul of Samosata, a 'heresy' into which Edwards was accused of descending, even if playfully (1926: 184). Nevertheless, in his work Edwards certainly attempted to construct a systematic theology on the basis of religious experience. However, this is not strictly the religious or spiritual experiences that people might have but the assertion that to experience the divine or the 'real' is to experience God as 'Father' and to recognize the common 'brotherhood of man' that emerges as a result.

There are two potential weaknesses associated with Edwards's scheme as well as that of Schleiermacher. First, there is what could be seen as the Kantian objection. While Kant argued that knowledge derives from experience, he maintained that there is no unmediated experience because all our experiences are categorized and understood according to forms that exist in our minds. Thus, as one commentator describes it:

> We have no access to any uninterpreted given. All the data to which we appeal are informed and categorized by antecedent judgments and interpretations. There are no data unshaped by the forms of sense and the categories of judgments, and those forms and categories cannot be legitimately employed to yield knowledge that transcends our experience. (Proudfoot 1985: 3)

In other words, there can be no appeal to a pure experience—religious or other—because all our experiences are perceived, understood, and articulated according to categories that might already exist in the mind or might have been acquired over time as a paradigmatic understanding of the universe is developed and that exist beyond the experience itself. Those categories might include exposure to general or to specific religious concepts, beliefs, and practices. Thus, someone exposed to Christian religion will interpret whatever experience he or she might have in light of Christian teaching and practice. Take, for example, Edwards's assertion that the 'real' at the heart of the universe can be understood to be 'love'. Why should he (and we) conclude that this is the case? Does it come through experience alone or are we taught to believe this because that is part of Christian doctrine? From a theological perspective, then, religious experience itself is not authoritative; experience is understood according to particular paradigms, which have been constructed over time and are articulated through doctrinal statements but which are based on the prior commitment to the Christ event as God's self-disclosure. But unlike the study of religious experience, as outlined above, which places importance on the subject who experiences and attempts to understand it, theology, in such a definition, is predicated on the notion that both revelation and mediation of that revelation are required and have occurred, rendering unnecessary any dependence on immediate sensation and experience. According to the Christian tradition, that mediation comes through the history of Israel and the incarnation of Jesus Christ as recorded in the scriptures and interpreted by the Church. Such a conclusion is supported by the following famous account, written by John Wesley (1703–91), of his conversion:

> In the evening, I went very unwillingly to a society in Aldersgate Street, where one was reading Luther's preface to the Epistle to the Romans. About a quarter before nine, while he was describing the change which God works in the heart through faith in Christ, I felt my heart strangely warmed. I felt I did trust Christ, Christ alone, for salvation; and an assurance was given me that he had taken away *my* sins, even *mine*, and saved *me* from the law of sin and death. (Wesley 1988: 245-50)

For Wesley, the experience was one of real conversion, through which he truly believed that he was 'saved in Christ' rather than that he merely acknowledged the inner logic of the Christian redemptive scheme. Nevertheless, while his 'heart was strangely warmed', he clearly interpreted this as confirming the doctrinal details of which he was already aware. This might be the result of doctrinal and cultural conditioning, which insists that experience is understood according to previously adopted paradigms, but it demonstrates the difficulty encountered when attempts are made to divorce an *experience* from any *interpretation* of it. More technically, it acknowledges both the reality that experience is never wholly unmediated and that *experience* is a more difficult concept to understand than a *specific experience of something*—a point to which I will return below. In the Christian tradition, then, religious experience must have a place, but interpreting it apart from the categories developed by Christian theology appears to place personal experience over divine revelation leading to the charge that to give too much emphasis to the former results in speaking about the self rather than God.

At one level, this might appear to be a rather strange assertion. The theology of the early Church ultimately contained in statements made by the Ecumenical Councils certainly arose from what the Christians of the first four or five centuries perceived to be their *experience* of the risen and ascended Christ mediated by the Holy Spirit and to some extent based on what were considered to be authoritative documents, many of which were finally incorporated into the canon of the New Testament. Alongside this, many of the great thinkers of the Christian tradition have had their *own* experiences, which fall into the category of 'spiritual' or religious experience. Three such examples will suffice and follow.

Christian Experiences

Aquinas

The medieval scholastic, Thomas Aquinas (1225–1274) continues to influence Catholic thinking in particular and Christian thought more broadly, based primarily on his ruminations as contained in the voluminous *Summa Theologica*. However, it appears that he experienced an immediate revelation while attending Mass on 6 December 1273. While reticent about what exactly happened, he did note, 'All that I have written seems like straw to me…compared to what has now been revealed to me' (Weisheipl 1974: 321-22). It is doubtful that Aquinas's words were intended to dismiss completely his speculations in the *Summa*. Instead, his experience confirmed that even after a lifetime's speculation and devotion, God remained elusive, known only in part (see, e.g., 1 Cor. 13:12) and ultimately *knowable* only through revelation. Thus it is unlikely that Aquinas's words were intended to suggest that there was no relationship between his speculation and his epiphany. Nevertheless, this revelation occurred as an *experience* rather than as a direct result of philosophical speculation, although it is impossible to know precisely what (if any) contribution his work had on his response to and processing of his experience. At the very least, Aquinas was almost certainly highlighting the importance for the Christian of devotion and of celebrating Mass, because this is one place in Catholic thought that God's presence in the world is assured. He might well have reflected on this had he not died just over three months later.

Calvin

A further example might be the sixteenth-century Reformer, John Calvin (1509–1564). We know that, sometime between 1528 and 1533, he experienced a 'sudden conversion' when he left behind the Catholicism of his upbringing and embraced Protestantism. But despite his numerous writings, he made very little reference to this experience apart from saying in his commentary on the Psalms that 'God by a sudden conversion subdued and brought my mind to a teachable frame, which was more hardened in such matters than might have been expected from one at my early period in life' (Calvin 1979: xl-xli). The lack of reference to his experience is almost certainly the result of his understanding that the gospel is *doctrina*. Thus it was in receiving Christian teaching that Calvin's salvation was effected. Calvin saw his conversion in terms of rescue from a devotion 'to the superstitions of Popery' to being capable of hearing and understanding true doctrine (Van't Spijker 2009: 18-20; Lee 2004: 108-9). Thus, while Calvin argued in the opening section of his *Institutes of the Christian Religion* that knowledge of God and knowledge of ourselves are bound together, in effect opening the possibility for reflection on personal experience as being a path towards God, he insisted that 'the order of right teaching requires that we discuss of the former first, then proceed afterward to treat the latter' (1960: 39). As one scholar has explained, 'Calvin chooses the path from knowledge of God to knowledge of man, as more convenient to teaching' (Parker 1995: 14), which in effect leaves religious experience as at best occupying a secondary role to sound doctrine gained through an exposition of scripture. It is the particularity of scripture, rather than the vagaries of personal experience, which provide the core material for teaching the Christian faith. Alongside this, there remains the danger that placing the self and personal experience as a primary concern displaces God from his sovereign place in the Universe. If the one, true, sovereign God is displaced, then the replacement is nothing but an idol; placing the self and its experience in the centre simply usurps God's sovereignty. Consequently, to emphasize religious experience as in some way more than a personal matter and as possessing sufficient insight to be authoritative becomes the basest of idolatries.

Augustine

While Calvin was 'not one for writing his "confessions"' (Van't Spijker 2009: 20), one of his revered predecessors, Augustine (354-430), recorded a number of spiritual experiences. In Book VIII of his classic work *The Confessions*, he recounts his agony of spirit, tormented by the urge for physical and, especially, sensual and sexual pleasures (Augustine 1991: 134, 141, 145) when he hears a voice saying '*tolle, lege*' (take up and read) and is led to consider Romans 13:14: '[P]ut on the Lord Jesus Christ, and make no provision for the flesh, to gratify its desires'. He records that 'at once… it was as if a light of relief from all anxiety flooded into my heart. All the shadows of doubt were dispelled' (Augustine 1991: 152-53). But while experiencing the voice was significant, comfort and transformation came in reading the commands of scripture. This response is echoed in his account found in Book IX of an apparently more mystical experience when, with his devout mother, Monica, he was discussing the mysteries of eternal life, in whose light 'the pleasures of the bodily senses' are seen 'to be not even worth considering'. At that point, Augustine records that they both had the following experience:

> Our minds were lifted up by an ardent affection towards eternal being itself. Step by step we climbed beyond all corporeal objects and the heaven itself, where sun, moon, and stars shed light on the earth. We ascended even further by internal reflection and dialogue and wonder at your works, and we entered into our own minds. We moved up beyond them so as to attain to the region of inexhaustible abundance where you feed Israel eternally with truth for food. There life is the wisdom by which all creatures come into being, both things which were and which will be. But wisdom itself is not brought into being but is as it was and always will be. Furthermore, in this wisdom there is no past and future, but only being, since it is eternal. For to exist in the past or in the future is no property of the eternal. And while we talked and panted after it, we touched it in some small degree by a moment of total concentration of the heart. And we sighed and left behind us 'the first fruits of the Spirit' (Rom. 8.23) bound to that higher world, as we returned to the noise of our human speech where a sentence has both a beginning and an ending. But what is to be compared with your word, Lord of our lives? It dwells in you without growing old and gives renewal to all things. (Augustine 1991: 171)

While the language is evocative, the description is ambiguous; its precise meaning remains elusive. The similarities with the more modern examples quoted earlier are striking, although as one commentator has pointed out, there is something anachronistic in interpreting Augustine's words as an 'interest in supersensible experience'; it is the modern rather than ancient world that is fascinated with 'the feel of an experience and its promise of an altered state of awareness' (Wetzel 2007). Augustine's description seeks to convey something of the ineffable, appropriately (if paradoxically) succeeding and simultaneously failing to do so. For him, the ineffable can only be encountered beyond the world of sensory experience in a *regio disimilitudinis* (place of unlikeness). And yet, the ineffable is acknowledged to be the God of the Christians and thus God in his scandalous particularity, while Augustine also confesses that this experience is incomparable with God's 'word'.

As such, the human subject in Augustine's experience recognizes its otherness to God; the experience is rooted in a sense of difference from the non-corporeal reality behind the universe rather than mystical union with it. Furthermore, for Augustine, the true understanding of God is primarily incarnational. It comes to us not through experiences induced through a rejection of the fleshly and the material but as a particular, incarnate being, and this requires the theological axiom that revelation of God comes from beyond our experience in the particular figure of Jesus of Nazareth (Kenney 2005). In this way, mystical experiences are taken at face value and accepted as real experiences, or perhaps even better, as experiences of the Real, but they are understood in terms of God's prior address to human beings in the incarnate Word.

Religious Experience and Revelation

Aquinas's mysterious epiphany, Calvin's 'subita conversio', Augustine's 'mystical experience' as well as Paul's blindness, Luther's thunderstorm, and a host of other experiences are important in the history of Christian thought because they all played a part in the lives of those who made significant, even seminal, contributions to Christian theology. And yet none of these experiences or interpretation of any of them played a direct part in the formation of these theologians' teaching. Furthermore, none of these thinkers advocate similar experiences for others. Their experiences rather confirmed their prior conviction that God is present in the world and therefore can be experienced, but the gospel is to be understood in doctrinal terms and is to be given priority when attempting to understand and convey any particular religious experience. Thus, while there is clearly talk of religious experience in the Christian tradition, its significance in theological reflection is secondary to the revelation of God in Christ.

This leads to a further consideration. Notwithstanding the fact that throughout Christian history some have sought to emphasize God's *immanence* over his *transcendence*, including several infamous attempts to do so during the twentieth century (Campbell 1907; Robinson 1963; see also Clements 1988: 19-48, 178-217), theology has in general concerned itself more with an attempt to understand the revelation of the external referent (i.e., God). This God is seen as the source of any spiritual experiences that people say they have had and is seen to be beyond, although in relation with, his creation and thus made known primarily through revelation rather than 'religious experience'. Lindbeck identified this as the 'linguistic cultural' approach to theology, which 'stresses the ways in which church doctrines function as informative propositions or truth claims about objective reality' (1984: 16). This method, according to Lindbeck, claims that Christianity 'involves learning the story of Israel and of Jesus well enough to interpret and experience oneself and one's world in its terms' (1984: 34). The Christian gospel is 'a *verbum externum* (external word)', which then 'shapes understanding of the self and the world' (Lindbeck 1984: 34). Theology, then, *shapes*, rather than *is shaped by*, human experiences, including those termed religious or spiritual. As a result, psychologists, anthropologists, sociologists, and others are interested in exploring religious experience while what is strictly speaking the Christian *theological* tradition has tended not to give too much attention to religious experience in its deliberations.

Theology as Teaching

Part of the issue for the theologian is the logical difficulty that emerges from positing some kind of pure, unmediated 'experience'. Rather than using Kantian categories to criticize the place given to experience by Schleiermacher and others, the English Reformed theologian Colin Gunton (1941–2003) saw Kant's thought as the *cause* of the problem. He wrote: 'The pit into which Schleiermacher fell was to accept the dogma canonized by Immanuel Kant that we do not experience things; rather, we shape the appearances of things into rational patterns which may or may not be true to reality' (2002: 176). Instead of a general conception of experience, then, Gunton posits the 'experience of things in their particularity' (2002: 176). He continues: 'That is to say, there is not experience *simpliciter*, or even that indefinable oddity called religious experience, but experience of—let us say—the song of a bird, the pain of an injury or the love of another human being' (Gunton 2002: 176). As a result, Schleiermacher developed a concept of experience that 'was internal rather than external, a kind of inward human dynamic through which God was given, rather than the objective self-giving of God to and within the world' (Gunton 2002: 176). Ironically, then, 'religious experience', according to Gunton, can be dismissed theologically because it stresses an ambiguous and generalized divine presence without acknowledging the particularity of God's presence in the world in Jesus Christ through the Holy Spirit. Essential to this scheme is the fundamental distinction between the creation and its Creator, between human beings and God. For Schleiermacher, to be truly human was to be truly religious, with religion representing the claim to an immediate, inherent, or immanent connection between human beings and God. Such access to immediate experience and perception is also fundamental for the study of religious experience.

The truth is that throughout Christian history, this sense of an immediate experience, especially one that possesses a rival authority to that of the scriptures, has proved problematic (see, e.g., Milne 2009). According to Gunton, if there is a fundamental, 'immediate' connection as Schleiermacher supposed, then the whole redemptive scheme apparently outlined in the New Testament becomes redundant. There is no need for reconciliation because the human and divine are in some senses already reconciled. He concludes that this simply denies the very heart of the Christian gospel. For, 'If God is immediately perceivable by all people of all religions then you do not need Christ' (Gunton 2007: 20). Gunton bases his argument on a different axiom, namely that 'in Christ God was reconciling the world to himself' (2 Cor. 5:19) with the concomitant assertion that the interpretation of scripture enables people to come to know God.

The alternative argument that all people can directly perceive the real, the divine, or God results in the definition of 'religion' as the human attempt to seek God and to find him somehow in the depths of human being. But to adopt such a view is to stand precariously at the top of a slippery slope—one that inevitably led to Feuerbach's atheistic projectionism that God is *merely* the projection of our highest thoughts and values—and ultimately to the conclusion that 'the true sense of theology is anthropology' (Feuerbach 1957: xvii). Liberal theologians of the early twentieth century appeared to give credence to this when they quoted the couplet from Alexander Pope's *An Essay on Man*:

> Know then thyself, Presume not God to scan;
> The proper study of Mankind is Man. (Pope 1950: 53)

Despite initial appearances, however, Pope was not particularly interested in the kind of introspection apparently supported by more recent appeals to religious experience, and if the social gospel movements of the period are anything to go by, nor were the liberal theologians of the early twentieth-century, including those, such as Edwards noted above, who gave prominence to 'experience' in their thought. A. D. Nuttall notes that Pope's words, although 'loaded with a weight of history', wherein the reader is invited 'to turn away from the world and look within' (1984: 77), in fact contrast 'futile and unverifiable theology', the word 'scan' possessing the force of 'minute scrupulous attention' (1984: 79) on the one hand and 'finding out about one's own kind' on the other. This perspective does not constitute an abandonment of theology, it simply asserts that the God who is the object of theological investigation always remains elusive, always remains beyond our thoughts, beliefs, creeds, propositions, and even beyond our apparent experience of him. And yet, something of this elusive God is made known to us in a variety of different ways, including how we relate to other people who, despite the so-called 'Fall', still carry the 'image of God' in them. Thus 'know thyself' refers not to the individual looking within, but to the human race or species and can also be interpreted as meaning 'know others' (Nuttall 1984: 77-79). The search into the recesses of the soul or any other form of religious experience is not being implied here, but instead living in relationship with other human beings. In Calvin's terms, this would be the recognition of our common humanity as created in *imago Dei* as justifying the command to love our neighbour (e.g., Calvin 1960: 695, 697, 186-9ff).

For Calvin, love of God and neighbour meant commitment to self-denial (1960: 690-96). Thus the command to 'love your neighbour as yourself' (e.g., Mk. 12:31) has the same force as the so-called 'Golden Rule': 'Do to others as you would have them do to you' (Mt. 7:12; Lk. 6:31), while the parable of the Good Samaritan demonstrates that neighbourliness is not restricted to those who are closest to us but requires the nurture of a disposition that is far more inclusive and wide-ranging (Lk. 10:29-37). Love of self and neighbour are therefore synchronous duties according to this teaching; the one does not precede the other (see, e.g., Francis 2005: xii). Rather, self-love is a *part* of love of the other and *vice versa*, in recognition that all share in God's image. 'Know thyself', then, is not a call to introspection or to the prioritizing of individual experience, understanding, and welfare, but the quest to live together in recognition of common humanity.

While this might reflect some insight into Jesus' teaching, it does not affirm the idea that God is immediately present in these relationships. Instead, as Gunton suggests, the New Testament demonstrates not a continuity between God and humanity, but the 'fundamental ontological difference between God and the world' (1995: 3), a difference that demands divine action in order to draw creation and its Creator into fellowship. As Gunton said, 'If God is God, and not the world, and if we are still to know him, then some form of mediation, some way of getting from here to there, is required' (2003: 164). In other words, in the absence of direct, immediate knowledge, or a revelation, the 'personal relation of God to the world conveyed by forms of words' is needed (Gunton 1995: 106). For Gunton, revelation was God's historical activity in Christ, which does not come directly to human beings but is mediated by the power of the Spirit through creeds, confessions, and proclamation (1995: 18). But revelation is not merely the bearer of information but of *saving knowledge*. 'The unique character and authority of scripture as *revelation*', he wrote, 'is that it claims to be more than the provider of unique information...but also to be the bearer of saving knowledge' (Gunton 1995: 73). For Gunton, the Christian gospel was an event during which God incarnate effects redemption for the created universe. And this communication of necessity had to come from beyond the creation because of the latter's servitude to corruption. To deny the ontological difference between humankind and God, which apparently lies at the heart of the modern claims to religious experience, was for Gunton simply to deny the gospel.

In Gunton's work, we see a basis for theology, which means that theology *informs* religious experience rather than *vice versa*. For him, Christianity was not the sum total of human striving for meaning but the redemptive activity of God in history. Theology was not the sum total of human thought about the meaning of life, but the attempt to deal knowledgeably with the Christian good news. Christ was not a teacher of good deeds, the highest example of the moral man, but the incarnate Word whose death and resurrection proved, and will prove (the eschatological note is significant), to be redemptive for human beings and the creation at large. All this constituted a communication from God to human beings—a revelation of the divine will that is seen once and for all to be love. The gospel was God's self-revealing good news to the world. The theologian's task was to proclaim and expound it and to demonstrate its fundamental credibility despite modern agnosticism and scepticism. Theology, then, is concerned with *teaching*, and Christian theology is concerned with proclaiming and understanding *Christian* teaching. Religious experience *per se* simply does not contribute to theology understood in this way.

Tacit Knowledge

From this discussion it is possible to suggest that the theologian's task does involve acknowledging that the experience of God or the divine is a *genuine* experience, but it is to be understood in light of Christian teaching. Even Schleiermacher and Edwards interpreted 'experience' in Christian terms, although they avoided traditional doctrinal expression in doing so. This points us again to the claim that it is impossible to explore 'pure experience', because all experiences are mediated in some form or another. The phenomenologist might conclude that the mediations are culturally and contextually bound interpretations of a common experience; the theologian might conclude that the 'experience' is the personal appropriation of the external word of the gospel, the working of the Holy Spirit in the hearts of men and women. But, as seen above, theologians have reported that they have had religious experiences, and although few explicit references to them can be found in their constructive work, can it be the case that their experiences made no contribution to how they understood and articulated their faith? While it appears to be the case that their experiences did not directly inform their theology, it remains true that for theologians such as Augustine, Aquinas, Calvin, and others, their experiences were considered to be real experiences of the God who is present in the world. In one sense, then, their experiences remain part of their make-up, which contributes to their epistemological processes and remains implicit in their theological construction. The work of Michael Polanyi (1891–1976) throws some light upon how this might work.

Polanyi began his academic career as a professor of physical chemistry, but later became a professor of philosophy because of his growing fascination with the way in which we come to *know* things. As a result of his thinking, he found himself in opposition to the tendency in science to be functionalist[6] and the sterility of scientific models that claim that to doubt everything would ultimately enable the identification of all truth. Science, he thought, acts as though it follows a strict set of rules that enable experiments to be formulated and ideas verified. In fact, he argued, a scientist will suddenly 'see' a connection between ideas by pursuing a 'hunch' about it, and then formulate an experiment in order to test the hunch. Thus faith and commitment become significant stepping stones for any discovery. Alongside this, Polanyi argued for the priority of faith in all discovery and for the significance of art, morality, religious worship, and other systems for what he termed 'our mental existence' or our *knowing*. 'Objectivism', he wrote, 'has totally falsified our conception of truth, by exalting what we can know and prove while covering up with ambiguous utterance all that we know and *cannot* prove, even though the latter knowledge underlies and must ultimately set its seal to all that we *can* prove' (Polanyi 1958: 286). Polanyi tells us that we can know more than we can tell.

There is, then, a knowledge that we have, which we cannot put into words. This he calls 'tacit knowledge' and he applies it to all knowing. In science, for example, the first step is the identification of a problem. Polanyi wrote: '[T]o see a problem is to see something that is hidden. It is to have an intuition of the coherence of hitherto not comprehended particulars' (1966: 21). In this way the problem is not seen 'only in itself' but as something that pre-empts a future discovery, while at the same time somehow participating in it. In other words, seeing a problem appears to suggest that there is a solution, which can stem from our current ways of knowing or patterns of knowledge without our yet being able to see it or articulate it. Thus the knowledge of the unknown is to some degree tacit in the knowledge of the known, and commitment to the known anticipates the discovery or even revelation of the unknown, even if the unknown will not be completely accounted for by the apparent 'laws' governing the known. It is because what is as yet unknown is potentially to some degree free from the laws that govern what is currently known, that discovery and transformation become possible.

Polanyi's theory of knowledge, then, argues that it is not simply the empirically demonstrable that can be known. This he dismissed as the basest scientism. There is space for intuition, for example, and he claims that all knowledge is based on this, even scientific knowledge. In this way Polanyi carefully and convincingly challenges the notion that we can only know what we can prove, partly because it demonstrates that what we prove will exist only in preconceived paradigms of knowledge. But recognising that there is a relationship between what is known and what is unknown—a clear tacit knowledge that to some extent remains beyond articulation—opens up the whole path of theological enquiry in the first place.

In applying Polanyi's theories, it is possible to suggest that religious experiences present us with the unknown, even when in some ways it is familiar to us. But *knowing* involves a combination of factors rather than the reliance on that which is demonstrable or provable alone, largely because proof and demonstration rely upon trust in the validity of particular paradigms that enable explanation. For some thinkers, it is the 'imagination' that provides the force to combine these factors (see, e.g., Kant 1934; Coleridge 1949; Warnock 1976; Ricoeur 1995). They posit that the imagination is central to finding meaning, living meaningfully in the world as familiar, and constructing new realities. The imagination draws together all our knowledge—both tacit and explicit—including our sensory and extrasensory experiences, our knowledge, our theological and philosophical understanding, our emotional responses, and so on. The imagination draws them all together and thus, even doctrine based on axioms such as 'God is present in this world, as was revealed in Jesus Christ' (Jones 1999: 11) and on the exposition of scripture is informed by all our knowledge, even that which is tacit and that which is the result of an ineffable experience that eludes description. In this way, religious experience contributes to *knowing*, and by its very contribution to our *knowing* participates in theological construction, even when we do not realize it. This hardly prioritises or highlights religious experience, but it acknowledges that it contributes, even if tacitly, to theological reflection.

Conclusions

In summary, it is possible to note four points. First, despite the fact that the Christian tradition is replete with examples of particular, apparently mystical events often experienced by those who produced significant and influential theological work, on the whole theologians are somewhat ambivalent towards religious experience and rarely make experience itself axiomatic for theological reflection. Nevertheless, there remains a sense among theologians that such experiences are *real*, and that what they experienced relates to what they understand to constitute Christian faith.

Second, although Schleiermacher based his work on 'experience', his was not a theology based on 'religious experience' according to the definitions outlined in this chapter. Schleiermacher had a very particular view of experience that was not without its cognitive elements. The 'feeling of absolute dependence' was to be understood as the clue to the reality of 'religion' in contrast with those who had abandoned it as irrational superstition. His argument posited a logical framework to a part of human character that was not open to philosophical investigation or the subject of external moral debate. While his theological conclusions caused controversy, some accepting and developing them and others rejecting them (as seen above), it is important to acknowledge that while his work opens the path to consider religious experience, it does not affirm *any* or *all* phenomena that might be classified under that heading.

Third, what we *know* is made up not only of what is empirically demonstrable and reasonably articulated but also of a knowledge that is tacit but remains beyond full articulation. In this way, religious and other experiences play a role in our knowing even when at times they are not explicitly acknowledged in any explanation we might provide.

Fourth, this tacit knowing might well relate to religious experiences, which theologically speaking might not lend themselves to systematization but remain not merely *possible* but *probable* because theology seeks to articulate something about an ineffable and elusive God who nonetheless remains real and present in the world. Religious experiences therefore retain a place in helping to form our patterns of knowing, whether tacit or explicit, as an aspect, even if one that is not expressly articulated, of *faith seeking understanding*.

Short Biographical Note

Robert Pope is a Reader in Theology, University of Wales Trinity Saint David. His research focuses on two areas, Nonconformist history and theology in England and Wales and theology's interaction with culture.

Notes

1. There appears to be some debate as to whether it was the novelist, Alexandre Dumas (1802–70), or his son, also called Alexandre (1824–95) and also a novelist and dramatist, who coined the phrase.

2. Marianne Rankin suggests that 'religious experience' should be confined to those 'experiences which either confirm or conform to the tenets of a religious tradition or which take place during religious observance or practice, or are the results of lengthy preparation or devotion, of mental training, prayer or fasting'. 'Spiritual experience' may be preferable for 'experiences which do not reflect any specifically religious beliefs' or beliefs specific to a particular religious tradition; 'transcendental experience' for a power beyond the individual self; 'paranormal experience' for powers not explained by science; 'mystical experience' as an inner experience of unity of things or state of unity with the divine. She also defines Exceptional Human Experiences, Peak Experiences, Limit Experiences, Ecstasy, Cosmic Consciousness, Absolute Unitary Being, Out of Body Experiences, Near Death Experiences (Rankin 2008: 11-17). Limitations on space mean it is not possible to engage with this detailed typology in this chapter. Instead, these 'types' are all conflated into the singular term 'religious experience'.

3. Alister Hardy sought to collect examples of 'spiritual' experiences without their being formally identified as 'religious'. He asked the question, 'Have you ever been aware of or influenced by a presence or power, whether you call it God or not, which is different from your everyday self'?' (in Rankin 2008: 3).

4.   That is, attributed to it, as William James suggests, primarily because the experience could be explained by other means even if the religious experience, in his view, produces happiness. Even James's definition of religion as 'the feelings, acts, and experiences of individual men in their solitude, so far as they apprehend themselves to standing in relation to whatever they consider the divine' (James 1923: 31) reveals this idea of ascription. Ultimately, the self who experiences something has to *consider*, and might thus ascribe her or his experience to 'religion'.

5.   One issue that cannot be pursued here because of lack of space is the fact that commentators acknowledge that not everyone will be able to have these experiences. William James, for example, notes: 'There are moments of sentimental and mystical experience...that carry an enormous sense of inner authority and illumination with them when they come. But they come seldom, and they do not come to everyone; and the rest of life makes either no connection with them, or tends to contradict them more than it confirms them' (1923: 16).

6.   Polanyi noted especially the irony that Soviet Russia, based on a socialism claiming scientific certainty, had under Stalin rejected the idea that science should be pursued for its own sake and put it to the service of the collective needs, especially to the agenda set by the Five Year Plans (1966: 3).

Chapter 7

An Argument from Religious Experience: Origins and Revelations

Tristan Nash

Discussions about the nature of religious experience often focus on the source or origin of those experiences. On one side of the debate are the group of arguments known collectively as the argument from religious experience. These arguments often maintain that religious experiences are proof of or evidence for the existence of God, as God is the source of this experience. This is similar to traditional empirical arguments for the existence of material objects, such as tables and trees, in which our experience of these objects is proof for or evidence of their existence, as these objects are the source of the experience.

It is, of course, the case that an experience does not always relate to the existence of an objective reality, as the source of the experience can be internal to the subject's own physiology or psychology. Thus, we may label an experience as a 'hallucination' or a 'projection' if we do not believe the source of the experience to be external to the subject, and as a result we do not believe that the experience provides any evidence for the objective existence of what is being experienced. By seeking to find the source of religious experiences not within an objective religious reality, but within the subject's internal state, these naturalistic explanations can be applied to religious experiences to counter the argument from religious experience.

Any argument that rests upon the source of an experience as evidence for, or proof of, the objective existence of the object of that experience will be open to criticism grounded in alternative explanations as to the origin of that experience. However, arguments from religious experience need not rely upon the source, or origin, of the religious experience in order to support claims about God's existence. Instead the argument from religious experience can focus upon what is revealed by the experience.

William James in *The Varieties of Religious Experience* draws a distinction between two different types of enquiry: the first relates to the nature, constitution, origin, and history of the object of the investigation, and the second relates to the object's importance, meaning or significance. He labels the result of the first of these enquires as an *'existential judgement* or proposition' and the result of the second as a *'proposition of value'* (James 1982: 4). The discussions and arguments that I have mentioned thus far would fall into the first category, as their focus is upon the study of the origin of the religious experience, in order to determine whether the experience is evidence for, or proof of, God's existence.

James explores the naturalistic explanations for religious experience, noting how what he describes as 'medical materialism' would reduce St Paul's vision on the road to Damascus to 'a discharging lesion of the optical cortex', would account for St Teresa's religious experiences as the result of her hysteria, and would label St Francis of Assisi as a 'hereditary degenerate' (James 1982: 13). James casts doubt on the approach of medical materialism by highlighting that it is not only religious experiences that can be accounted for in terms of their physiological or psychological origins, but also scientific theories and arguments held by the atheist:

> [T]here is not a single one of our states of mind, high or low, healthy or morbid, that has not some organic process as its condition. Scientific theories are organically conditioned just as much as religious emotions are; and if we only knew the facts intimately enough, we should doubtless see 'the liver' determining the dicta of the sturdy atheist as decisively as it does those of the Methodist under conviction anxious about his soul. When it alters in one way the blood that percolates it, we get the methodist, when another way, we get the atheist form of mind. So of all our raptures and our drynesses, our longings and pantings, our questions and beliefs. They are equally organically founded, be they of religious or of non-religious content. (James 1982: 14)

James argues that if we are to draw a distinction between religious states of mind, which do not have as their origin sources external to the subject of the experience, and other varieties of thoughts and feelings, which we do think relate to a reality beyond the subject, then we need a psychological theory that accounts for this difference. Otherwise the distinction is simply dogma. However, it is not this argument of James's that I wish to focus on in this work, but rather I wish to explore the way in which he thinks that religious experiences can have a revelational quality independent of their source or origin and how the value of the religious experience can be assessed regarding the quality of its revelation.

James additionally argues that it is not concerns about the origin of a particular state of mind that set it apart as being superior to other thoughts and feelings, but rather the quality of the experience itself or the positive impact the experience has on the subject's life. He maintains that we value such experiences because 'we take an immediate delight in them; or else it is because we believe them to bring us good consequential fruits for life' (James 1982: 15). He further defines this distinction as a difference between 'inner happiness and serviceability' (James 1982: 15). He warns, however, that inner happiness alone should not serve as the test of the value of an experience, otherwise 'drunkenness would be the supremely valid human experience' (James 1982: 16). James further warns that individual religious experiences, perhaps best characterised by the mystical experience, may fail the test of serviceability, as they may not find a place within the subject's broader experiences, or the lessons revealed by the experience may not be borne out over time. As a result, it is the test of serviceability that ultimately establishes the value of a religious experience.

What is revealed by the religious experience is tested against the broader context of life in order to establish whether it is philosophically reasonable and brings about moral good. For example, James argues how St Teresa's nervous disposition—whether it is, as he fears medical materialists might describe it, hysterical, or whether she has the nervous system of the 'placidest cow'—is not relevant in our assessment of the revelations that she experiences (James 1982: 18). These revelations rather need to be tested for their theological merits and stand or fall on the strength of these, rather than on an assessment of her nervous disposition and the possible origins of the experience. James's position is, therefore, one in which the initial sensation of the experience is what makes the experience significant and highlights its religious nature; however, the philosophical reflection upon the experience, in which the revelation is assessed for coherence and the merits that it brings to one's life, is what defines the true worth of the revelation conveyed by the experience.

An example to which this sort of assessment can be applied is the experiences of Ebenezer Scrooge in Charles Dickens's *A Christmas Carol*. In this tale Ebenezer Scrooge is visited by four apparitions: the ghost of his former business partner, Jacob Marley; the ghost of Christmas past; the ghost of Christmas present; and the ghost of Christmas yet to come. Although perhaps not strictly speaking a 'religious' experience, the definition of which can be notoriously difficult, because of the supernatural and profound nature of this experience it shares many of the characteristics of accounts of events categorised as religious experiences. The spirits reveal to Scrooge that his current mean-spirited life is bringing hardship and suffering to others, misery to himself and will result in no one missing him when he dies. Yet, despite the startling and unusual nature of these visitations, it is not the source of the experience that is important in assessing the worth of the revelation brought about by the experience. Indeed, even Scrooge, perhaps to quell his own fears rather than in genuine doubt, questions whether these ghostly manifestations have any reality beyond that of his own senses. When confronted by the ghost of Jacob Marley, Scrooge claims that he has good reason to doubt his senses, as they can be easily affected by even the smallest of things. In protesting to the ghost that he does not believe in him—a claim perhaps undermined by the fact he is engaging the ghost in debate—Scrooge notes that his senses are easily fooled and that the vision may be of organic origin, rather than the spirit of his dead partner:

> 'A slight disorder of the stomach makes them cheats. You may be an undi-gested bit of beef, a blot of mustard, a crumb of cheese, a fragment of an underdone potato. There's more of gravy than of grave about you, what-ever you are!' (Dickens 2009: 21)

Scrooge's protests are similar to the arguments presented by those in support of the naturalistic explanations for religious experiences, in that he is seeking a biological explanation for experiences that at first seem supernatural in origin. However, it is not the origin of the experi-ence that is important to Scrooge, but rather what the experience reveals to him about the way in which he has been living his life. We can apply James's twofold assessment of religious experiences to Dickens's account of Scrooge's experience. It would not be appropriate to describe Scrooge's experience as one of immediate delight or happiness, the first stage of James's assessment of the value of a religious experience, as it is clear that his initial response is one of fear. However, it is worth noting that although Scrooge's experience may not be considered a religious experience in the strict sense, an initial response of fear can be present even in paradig-matic cases of religious experiences. After all, when the Angel of the Lord appeared to the shepherds in the field, he reassured them not to be afraid. It is also the case that although Scrooge is initially fearful of the appari-tions, the overall experience leaves Scrooge in a state of joy and delight. The second part of James's assessment—the serviceability of the experi-ence or the degree to which it can be assessed within the broader frame-work of Scrooge's life—reveals the experience to be of value, for Scrooge's life is transformed by the experience and so are the lives of those whom he affects. Therefore we can conclude, as James does, that the value of an experience can be assessed by the worth to the person's life of the revela-tion produced by the experience.

Such an assessment may also be applied to accounts of religious expe-rience. It is not uncommon for people who have reported having religious experiences also to credit those experiences as providing the impetus for them to change their lives for the better. However, it may be that the impetus for this change in life is grounded in a belief about the origins of that experience. If those having these experiences believe they are expe-riencing God, then this realisation may give their lives new value in their eyes, as they may come to see their lives within a particular religious framework. The nature of the revelation, therefore, and the impact this revelation has upon their life, may be dependent upon the belief in the divine origin of their experience.

In the case of Scrooge, the origin of the revelation, be it 'grave' or 'gravy', is not what matters. What is revealed to Scrooge was already present to him; his attention simply needed to be drawn to it. It just so happens that his attention is aroused by those ghostly apparitions, and it may be that his stubbornness requires just such a shock to bring certain truths about his life to his attention. However, the spirits did not need to force him to change his values; on seeing the harm he was doing to others and to himself, the error of his ways became immediately obvious to him. Ultimately, although it was a supernatural experience that brought him to this realisation, it could also have been the case that the realisation came from an earthlier source, such as seeing the suffering of another caused by his selfishness. If Scrooge were to find out that the ghostly apparitions were nothing but a clever trick or had a physiological or psychological origin, then there is no reason to suspect that this understanding would in any way undermine the revelation, for the revelation was not dependent upon the origin of the experience.

A disconnect between the value and the source of the experience also results in the experience itself not acting as proof of or evidence for the truth of what is revealed by the experience. As we have seen, James ultimately judges the value of the experience on its philosophical coherence and the moral value it has to the subject. The religious experience is reduced to being a delivery mechanism for a revelation, rather than the means by which the truth of the revelation is established. The experience is, therefore, no longer necessary for judging the value of the revelation, and what is revealed by the experience could be established by other means. The impact that Scrooge's character and actions were having on his own quality of life and the lives of those around him was plain to see; his attention just needed to be brought to it. However, it need not have been the supernatural experience that delivered this revelation about his life, and the experience does not act as proof for the truth of what is revealed. The truth of what is revealed is judged by ethical standards and the improvement in the quality of his own life and those affected by him. This approach seems to undermine the value of the experience in itself, especially when compared to the standard argument from religious experience; in which the experience itself is necessary to support the truth claim of the argument.

As we have seen when the religious experience is presented as proof of, or evidence for, the existence of God the focus of the debate is usually on whether God is the source of the experience, or whether the source of the experience is internal to the subject of the experience. Alternatively, there is the assessment offered by James, in which the religious experience is ultimately judged by the philosophical coherence and moral value of what is revealed by the experience. There is, however, a form that the argument from religious experience could take in which the experience acts as a proof for the existence of God, but the experience is not of God.

In order to demonstrate the nature of the religious experience I have in mind, I shall draw parallels with the account of an experience presented by the philosopher Raimond Gaita, which revealed a moral truth to him. Gaita describes how as a student he worked as a ward assistant in a psychiatric hospital. He recalls how some of the patients in this institution had lost many of the faculties that are often considered important for a valued or meaningful life. As a result, the patients were often treated very badly by the staff at the hospital. Gaita recalls how when the patients soiled themselves they were mopped down as if they were animals in the zoo. Gaita writes of how he was initially impressed by small number of psychiatrists who tried to improve the conditions for the patients and who spoke about their 'inalienable *dignity*' (Gaita 2002: 18). However, what left a lasting impression on him was the behaviour of a nun who visited the patients:

> One day a nun came to the ward. In her middle years, only her vivacity made an impression on me until she talked to the patients. Then everything in her demeanour towards them—the way she spoke to them, her facial expressions, the inflexions of her body—contrasted with and showed up the behaviour of those noble psychiatrists. She showed that they were, despite their best efforts, condescending, as I too had been. She thereby revealed that even such patients were, as the psychiatrists and I had sincerely and generously professed, the equals of those who wanted to help them; but she also revealed that in our hearts we did not believe this. (Gaita 2002: 18-19)

The nun's behaviour revealed to Gaita the truth of the patient's full humanity. Unlike James's method for assessing the value of religious experiences, in which what is revealed by the experience is judged by its philosophical coherence and its consequential value, the value of Gaita's experience is not judged against such criteria; it is rather valued for the truth that the experience reveals:

> In the nun's case, her behaviour was striking not for the virtues it expressed, or even for the good it achieved, but for its power to reveal the full humanity of those whose affliction had made their humanity invisible. Love is the name we give to such behaviour. (Gaita 2002: 20)

Gaita's experience was essential for the revelation; unlike the example of Scrooge, in which the experience does not shed any new light on the situation, but rather brings Scrooge's attention to features of his life. For

Gaita, the full-humanity of the patients can only be seen in light of the nun's love. The experience revealed to Gaita what had previously been hidden.

The truth is also not dependent upon the source of the experience, unlike the traditional accounts of the argument from religious experience, in which the experience is empirical proof for the existence of God. In Gaita's example, the source of the experience is not the object that is being demonstrated by the experience. It is not the nun's love that is being revealed by the experience; rather it is the nun's *love* that reveals the truth of the patients' full humanity. This example provides a model for how religious experiences may reveal a truth, the proof of which is not dependent upon the source of that experience. The subject of the experience may make the claim that 'the experience of x proved to me the existence of God', without x being God. In this form of the argument, the experience reveals the truth of God's existence, rather than the experience being of God.

It is the nature of testimony that reports of a person's experience may not be sufficient grounds to convince others of the validity of their claims. However, an experience can act as a proof to the subject of that experience, in the same way that Gaita's experience of the nun was proof to him of the patients' full humanity:

> [A]s someone who was witness to the nun's love and is claimed in fidelity to it, I have no understanding of what it revealed independently of the quality of her love. If I am asked what I mean when I say that even such people as were patients in that ward are fully our equals, I can only say that the quality of her love proved that they are rightly the objects of our non-condescending treatment, that we should do all in our power to respond in that way. But if someone were to now ask me what informs my sense that they are *rightly* the objects of such treatment, I can appeal only to the purity of her love. For me, the purity of the love proved the reality of what it revealed. I have to say 'for me', because one must speak personally about such matters. That after all is the nature of witness. From the point of view of the speculative intelligence, however, I am going around in ever darkening circles, because I allow for no independent justification of her attitude. (Gaita 2002: 21-22)

This form of the argument from religious experience, therefore, is no different from the traditional argument from religious experience, in which the experience of God may act as a proof to the person who is the subject of the experience, but for others it can only act as evidence for the existence of God by virtue of the fact that people have such experiences.

A religious experience that followed the form of Gaita's experience of the nun could be the basis for a form of the argument from religious experience that does not seek proof of or evidence for the existence of God in the *source* of an experience, but rather finds proof of God's existence in what the experience *reveals*.

Short Biographical Note

Tristan Nash is Senior Lecturer in philosophy at the University of Wales Trinity Saint David and Programme Director (MA and BA) for Philosophy at UWTSD.

Section Four:
Reflections on Types of Religious Experience

Chapter 8

Text and Experience:
Reflections on 'Seeing' in the Gospel of John

Catrin H. Williams

Even a cursory glance through the writings of the New Testament reveals that many of the beliefs and practices of the earliest Christian communities described in these texts are underpinned by a wide array of religious experiences. Whether one focuses on the gospel accounts of Jesus' baptism (Mark 1:9-11; Matthew 3:13-17; Luke 3:21-22; see also John 1:31-34), on Luke's dramatic depiction of Paul's call-conversion on the road to Damascus (Acts 9:1-19, 22:6-16, 26:12-18), or on the numerous heavenly visions and ascents attributed to John the seer in the Book of Revelation, it is evident that experiential factors have contributed significantly to the accounts of the origins and development of the early Christian movement. However, despite the prominence of references to, and (albeit brief) descriptions of what can be termed examples of religious experience in the New Testament texts, only in recent decades has biblical scholarship sought to engage with 'religious experience' as a valid analytical category. There are many reasons for this interpretative shift, not least—as I will seek to demonstrate—because of an increasingly fluid understanding of what belongs to the category of 'religious experience' and of the role of texts in the articulation and discernment of experience within early Christianity. In this study I will examine some of the causes of these shifts with reference to the most influential scholarship on the subject before considering the implications of these developments for interpreting the way(s) in which the sensory language of sight relates 'experience' to 'text' within the narratives and discourses of the Gospel of John.

Mapping Out Religious Experience in the Study of the New Testament

It is certainly not an overstatement to claim that New Testament scholarship over the past century has been more preoccupied with the origins and development of the earliest Christian beliefs and doctrinal concepts than with actual religious experiences (see, e.g., Hurtado 2000: 184). One clear exception to this trend were the attempts made by several proponents of the History of Religions School at the end of the nineteenth and early twentieth centuries to reconstruct a more horizontally focused and historical-experiential trajectory for early Christian beliefs and practices; these reconstructions were also firmly set within the context of other religions of antiquity. Much of the work associated with the History of Religions School during this period, including the landmark studies of Hermann Gunkel (1888) and Adolf Deissmann (1911), involved how the early Christians attributed their religious experiences to the effects of the Holy Spirit. Gunkel's examination of early Christian pneumatology focused largely on possible links with Second Temple Judaism, particularly Jewish apocalyptic texts (see, e.g., Frey and Levison 2014: 4-9). However, in response to the growing scholarly emphasis on the religio-historical rootedness of the biblical texts, German Protestantism in the aftermath of the First World War shifted from a liberal to a more dialectical or neo-orthodox form of theology, thus turning its attention to the need 'for a message vertically from above' (Räisänen 2000: 41) and to *theological* interpretations of the New Testament texts (see, e.g., Johnson 1998: 12-14; Frey and Levison 2014: 18-33).

Several decades passed before the origins and nature of religious experience in early Christianity began to emerge once again as a topic for critical analysis. This is, in large part, because of the dominance of the historical-critical method of interpretation within biblical studies during the twentieth century, but also because of the challenges posed by the fact that biblical scholars are reliant on a cluster of ancient texts belonging to past cultures that provide little more than faint traces of genuine religious experiences. Given the lack of detailed information within the New Testament about the scope and contours of possible cases of religious experience, it is difficult—and many would say impossible—to pinpoint and reconstruct the experiences themselves. Nevertheless, in two highly significant studies (1970, 1975) James D. G. Dunn expressed confidence that the New Testament sources could cast some light on the distinctive religious experiences of the early Christians and that, despite significant cultural and historical gaps, one's knowledge and understanding of human experience generally allows some degree of access to religious experiences, even those deriving from the ancient past. In *Baptism in the Holy Spirit* Dunn claims that baptism in the Spirit was 'part of the event (or process) of becoming a Christian... The reception of the Spirit was a very definite and often dramatic *experience*, the decisive and climactic experience in conversion-initiation' (1970: 4). Five years later, in *Jesus and the Spirit*, he again argues from the premise that 'religious experience is the core of religion' (Dunn 1975: 1) and stresses the importance of attempting to uncover Jesus' own religious experiences and those of his first-generation followers through detailed exegetical analysis of the key texts.

And yet, while Dunn's two volumes have generated much interest and discussion, particularly in Pentecostal circles, he continues to represent a minority voice in the investigation of what Luke Timothy Johnson has subsequently described in the subtitle of his own monograph (1998) as the ongoing 'missing dimension' in New Testament studies. Johnson, like Dunn, argues for the centrality of religious experience within the early Christian communities, and by adopting a phenomenological approach drawing on insights from the work of Rudolf Otto and Mircea Eliade, he selects three case studies for closer inspection: baptism, speaking in tongues (glossolalia), and ritual meals. With the aid of cross-cultural comparisons, Johnson proposes that the New Testament bears witness to profound experiences of power; the early Christian believers 'considered themselves caught up by, defined by, a power not in their control but rather controlling them, a power that derived from the crucified and raised Messiah Jesus' (1998: 184).

A substantial proportion of the work on religious experience in early Christianity during the past two and a half decades responds either explicitly or indirectly to some of the methodological issues raised by Johnson's study, particularly his emphasis on individual rather than communal experiences. Because human experience is somatic and psychosomatic, he maintains that it is 'irreducibly individual' (Johnson 1998: 47). Attempts have been made to move away from analysing experience purely through a subjective, internal-individualistic lens in order to be able to take account of the 'social facilitation of experiential moments' (Tite 2013: 10), that is, how religious experiences may have been shaped by social realities and were evaluated within communal settings. The experiential dimension, it is argued, need not be limited to private, numinous encounters with divine power but can also embrace everyday episodes and events experienced by groups as well as individuals. It therefore comes as no surprise that Johnson's definition of 'religious experience', which is a modified version of the definition proposed by Joachim Wach, has come under critical scrutiny from a variety of New Testament scholars. 'Religious experience', he suggests, 'is a response to that which is perceived as ultimate, involving the whole person, characterized by a peculiar intensity, and issuing in action' (Johnson 1998: 60). However, this definition does in fact exclude many forms of religious experience as described in the New Testament, particularly those that cannot be categorized as startling, all-embracing, and distinctively supernatural events (see Meggitt 2000: 687; Batluck 2011: 340; Czachesz 2013: 569). Furthermore, the 'dialectical interaction' that exists in religious thought between tradition, experience, and interpretation must also be acknowledged; in the same way that tradition (and/or interpretative frameworks) can be reinterpreted in the light of (new) experiences, the experiences are themselves shaped by existing traditions (Räisänen 2000: 190). It is important 'to underline the "process" and its dynamics—to call attention to change, reinterpretation, contemporization and reapplication of traditions' (Räisänen 2000: 190) in recognition that 'experience' is often 'that "something" which stands "between" a tradition and its reinterpretation' (Räisänen 2000: 192).

The notion of dialectical interaction between tradition, experience, and interpretation provides a helpful grid with which to assess key features of a recently established programme unit of the Society of Biblical Literature (SBL). The unit in question investigates various aspects of religious experience in ancient Judaism and early Christianity, and many of its papers have been published in the two *Experientia* volumes that have appeared to date (Flannery et al. 2008; Shantz et al. 2012). Contributors to the project work with broad yet clearly defined categories of 'religious experience', and four significant aspects of their methodological approach are worthy of closer comment here and also in the second part of this essay.

First, the editors of the *Experientia* project contend that 'the [textual] articulation of ancient authors' experiences of the divine' (Flannery et al. 2008: 10) inevitably involves engagement with the social and cultural matrix from which early Jewish and Christian texts emerged. In other words, the textual representation of religious experiences cannot be separated from the historical, social, and cultural aspects of the traditions and/or interpretative frameworks that were used to give expression to those experiences. It cannot, moreover, be claimed that 'experience' is only later shaped by 'interpretation' through 'tradition', because there is simultaneous cross-fertilization between all three from the very outset (Flannery et al. 2008: 5 n. 23; see also Rowland 2006: 44-46). In full awareness of some of the criticisms brought against the early History of Religions School, the essays in the first *Experientia* volume—and indeed in the second—contextualise their analyses 'in *texts*' arising in particular *contexts* and communities (Flannery et al. 2008: 6).

Secondly, and the inevitable consequence of recent scholarly attention to the social and cultural *context* of early Christian religious experiences, there is renewed interest in mysticism, that is, in interpreting many of the cases of religious experience in the New Testament writings as profoundly influenced by ancient Jewish mystical traditions. In line with current interpretative approaches, 'mystical' language and experience is understood with reference to themes and motifs embedded in the Jewish (and early Christian) apocalypses. In particular, human seers or visionaries are said to gain access to the revelation of God—to the disclosure of divine mysteries—by means of dreams, visions, and heavenly ascents. Tapping into the extensive debate in late Second Temple Judaism on the impossibility of seeing God, the Jewish apocalypses do nevertheless give varied expression to how human seers encounter God. Some traditions reject the possibility that visionaries can catch anything more than a glimpse of the face of God; the seer, for example, encounters angels and the fiery throne in the seventh heaven, but the 'invisible glory' remains hidden from human view (Apocalypse of Abraham 19:4). Other apocalypses include visions of God, but choose to elaborate on what surrounds, rather than the precise contours of, the divine glory (Hebrew: *kabod*). Thus, 1 Enoch 14, the earliest such apocalyptic vision (second century BCE), speaks of the enthroned Great Glory whose luminous garment is surrounded by blazing fire (14:20) and then adds that no angel is able to come and look at his face and that no flesh can see him (14:21). In some Jewish apocalypses, like 2 Enoch, a more explicitly anthropomorphic description of God's appearance is given; the seer declares that he has seen the face of the Lord 'like iron made burning hot by a fire' (22:1) and has even gazed into his eyes (39:4), but that there is no way of communicating the indescribable face of God (22:2) and that to stand before the face of the divine King is both terrifying and dangerous (39:8). As this selection of apocalyptic traditions demonstrates, visionaries are said to experience extraordinary divine and heavenly sights that can lead to profound personal transformation, but these encounters are also described as causing much physical and emotional upheaval to the seers: not only fear and trembling but, in some cases, a loss of consciousness (e.g., 1 Enoch 71:11; 4 Ezra 10:29-30). What has been argued—but warrants further exploration—is that visionary experiences as recounted in the Jewish and early Christian apocalypses (Stone 1991: 419-28; Rowland 1982, 2006: 41-56), though heavily influenced by existing traditional motifs, are often derived from actual experiences on the part of individual visionaries.

Thirdly, to enquire whether the visionary encounters depicted in the apocalypses reflect direct experiences belongs to the wider question, which is also explored at length in the *Experientia* project, of how one seeks to move from 'text' to 'experience'. While many scholars argue that original experiences of the early Christians are no longer accessible, either because of the private and subjective quality of those experiences or because of how they are narrated in the ancient texts, others seek to pursue the (frequently scant) textual details 'that can be probed' (Flannery et al. 2008: 2). In this respect, the letters of Paul often serve as a valuable starting-point for such endeavours. Though brief and clearly the product of later reflection on original 'events', the personal and bodily nature of Paul's references to his own experiences (e.g., Galatians 1:12, 16, 2:19-20; Philippians 3:7-10; 2 Corinthians 12:1-4) suggest that 'something happened (whether in Paul's brain, mind, psyche, or body), which he then interprets and uses' for the benefit of the readers and hearers of his letters (Engberg-Pedersen 2008: 150; see also Peerbolte 2008: 159-76). Scholarly analyses of this kind propose that it may well be possible in some cases, and with the aid of certain interpretative tools, to uncover features of real religious experiences that were then recounted, often for rhetorical purposes, for the early Christian communities.

Attempting to proceed from text to experience can, finally, be approached from a very different perspective—one that does not so much try to reconstruct elements of real experiences from a text but rather enquires how a text has the capacity to *generate* religious experience. Given that contributors to the *Experientia* project are open to expanding the types of experience that can be labelled 'religious' to include such phenomena as scribal activity, exegesis, and reflection (Flannery et al. 2008: 7), the notion of texts inducing religious experience receives considerable attention in contributions to the first (Deutsch 2008: 83-103; Griffith-Jones 2008: 105-23) and second volumes (Newsom 2012: 205-21; Harkins 2012: 223-42). Again, although reconstructing actual experiences is a difficult enterprise, early Jewish and Christian texts may provide valuable clues about the linguistic and literary strategies devised by ancient authors in order to generate religious experiences. Such strategies can include elements of sensory perception, such as focusing on what is seen or heard or touched (see, e.g., Harkins 2012: 232), and this because they can draw readers/hearers emotionally as well as cognitively to participate in the story in a way that brings about movement from text to experience. Furthermore, in view of the symbiotic relationship between orality and textuality in the first centuries BCE and CE, the performative character of texts like the Qumran *Hodayot* (Newsom 2012: 208-10) or the canonical gospels (see, e.g., Williams 2011: 205-22) meant that they served as significant agents for the construction of common experiences within a community, indeed for the 'normative shaping of religious experience' (Newsom 2012: 208). The active participants in this kind of performative scenario are not envisaged as standing apart from the narrated events but as being experientially transformed in and through the text.

Sight and Faith as Experience in the Gospel of John

This brief outline of recent trends in the critical study of religious experience in early Christianity brings to light a number of issues and emphases that warrant further investigation with reference to John's Gospel, a New Testament text whose experiential character, however defined, still remains largely untapped (although see now the potentially significant discussion in Ashton 2014: 181-99). The reasons for this neglect relate closely to the situation outlined in the initial part of this essay, not least because the Gospel of John, since the earliest stages of its reception, has been regarded as the most *theological* of the four canonical gospels. The author is not interested in religious experiences *per se* but in communicating a distinctively theological (or rather Christological) message. And so, while it is virtually impossible to miss the prominence of experiential language and ideas within the Gospel of John, these—it is claimed—are no more than vehicles for its theological propositions. A change in direction can nevertheless be detected in some scholarly circles, particularly as a consequence of the (re)discovery of possible links between major Johannine motifs and Jewish mystical-apocalyptic thought (see especially Ashton 1991: 383-406; Kanagaraj 1998; Rowland and Morray-Jones 2009: 123-35; Williams and Rowland 2013).

Although little attempt has so far been made to determine whether elements within the Johannine text provide a window into the actual (visionary) experiences of the author and his original readers/hearers, significant clues can be identified suggesting that John's Gospel was intended as an experience-inducing text. I will not explore the proposal that John's Gospel was designed to generate an experiential process leading the reader/hearer sequentially and progressively through a transformation from new birth, like Nicodemus in John 3, to new life, like Lazarus in John 11 (Griffith-Jones 2008: 105-23). Rather, the less ambitious aim of my study is to investigate the nature and function of the language of 'seeing' within the Gospel narrative, in order to determine whether it yields any clues regarding the relationship between 'text' and 'experience' as envisaged by the fourth evangelist. The language of 'seeing' lends itself to such an investigation not only because of the centrality of 'sight' in the mystical-apocalyptic understanding of divine revelation, but because of the prominent use of such language—no less than five different verbs of sight—within the Gospel narrative. Consequently, despite earlier scholarly emphasis under the influence of Rudolf Bultmann on the importance of 'hearing' rather than 'seeing' in the Gospel of John (see Thompson 2001: 105-7, 2007: 215; Ashton 2014: 204), the significance attached to 'seeing' as a vehicle for and expression of faith becomes apparent at various points of the text. An additional factor worthy of consideration is the experience-generating potential of the language of 'seeing' in the Johannine *textual* context, for, as noted by Angela Harkins: 'Sensory perceptions relating to visualization, even when they are stimulated through textualized descriptions, can arouse the emotions and intensify the experience of reenactment' (2012: 232).

In the second part of this essay I will therefore examine four elements or aspects of visuality within the Gospel of John with reference to the prologue (1:1-18), the account that follows of Jesus' words and deeds during his earthly mission, the paradigmatic role ascribed to figures from Israel's past in relation to 'seeing' Jesus, and the relationship between text and experience when a physical seeing of Jesus is no longer an option.

'Seeing' and 'Not Seeing' in the Johannine Prologue

Whatever the composition history of John's Gospel, with many regarding its prologue (1:1-18) as having been added at a later stage in the text's formation, there is no doubt that these 18 verses provide the interpretative lens through which to read the narrative in its present form. The high point of the prologue is its announcement of the coming of the Word made flesh (1:14) and then its elaboration, through a chain of connective statements, on the recognition of Jesus as the definitive revelation of God in the world. This section of the prologue also marks a significant point of transition because, for the first time, the statements unexpectedly shift from the third person to the first person plural to claim that the Word dwelt '*among us*' (1:14a) and '*We have seen* his glory, the glory as of a father's only son, full of grace and truth' (1:14b). These pronouncements are clearly intended to serve as the spoken confession of the author and the community of believers who, in stark contrast to the world (1:10-11), recognize Jesus as the embodiment of God's presence and glory and are 'children of God' (1:12-13). Despite some scholars' claims that the words 'we have seen his glory' represent a proclamation of literal 'seeing' derived from collective (eye)witness testimony to Jesus, the emphasis falls on the faith perception of those who have 'seen' Jesus and recognized his glory after his exaltation/glorification (Lincoln 2002: 8; see also Hurtado 2003: 402). For while the Greek verb for 'seeing' in 1:14 (*theaomai*) can be used to convey physical sight (e.g., John 1:38, 4:35, 6:5), it also denotes seeing with the eyes of faith (see, e.g., 1 John 4:14), as further suggested in the prologue by its combination with 'glory' (*doxa*). This statement is the first indicator of what will become a major motif in the Gospel narrative, namely, the interplay of physical/sensory observation and spiritual/metaphorical sight. Even those who have not seen Jesus physically during his earthly life can perceive, with the eyes of faith, the divine glory that Jesus has manifested during his life, death, and resurrection.

The words, 'we have seen his glory', are not intended primarily as a theological formulation, but—as strongly suggested by the use of 'we' language—as an expression of believers' *revelatory experience* of Jesus, indeed as an articulation of their self-understanding as a community of believers. The question, then, is the extent to which this shared experience of 'seeing Jesus' is already presented in the prologue as a normative religious experience, one that should shape the collective identity of all Johannine Christians. This is certainly suggested by the explicit contrast between those who 'see the glory' and the world's lack of recognition of Jesus, but also because the words 'we have seen his glory' represent a shared worldview and established summary of 'the speaking subject's own experience' (Newsom 2012: 208). In other words, as the centrepoint of the Gospel's introduction, this confession encapsulates the type of definitive 'experiential moment' that should serve as an invitation and template for the identity formation and faith-experience of all new believers or new community members. How this experiential paradigm is appropriated in what follows—the Gospel's central narratives and discourses—will be considered later in this essay.

The final verses of the prologue (1:17-18) provide a rationale for the claims that the incarnate Word manifests God's glory, is full of grace and truth, and dwells among those who receive of his fullness (1:14-16). The close connection between verses 17-18 and their immediate context is suggested by the continued concentration on visual images and related vocabulary appealing to the senses. Both verse 14 and verse 18 maintain a clear focus on visuality, on that which has (or has not) been seen: the statement 'no one has ever seen God' (1:18) certainly recalls the earlier declaration 'we have seen his glory' (1:14). What is also clear is that the phrasing of the first part of verse 18 ('no one has ever seen God') encourages the reader/hearer to interpret the central thrust of the second part as stating that God is 'seen' in Jesus: 'the only-begotten, God, who is close to the Father's heart, he has made him known' (1:18b). In virtue of his unique identity and relationship with God, Jesus has brought the revelation that is tantamount to seeing God in Jesus. In other words, the final statements of the prologue explicate the earlier claim of the believing community (1:14) that they have experienced the theophanic manifestation of Jesus as the embodiment of God's glory on earth. Once again, even if 1:14-18 centres more on the perception and confession of faith than on physical sight (although the latter is suggested by the words 'no one has ever seen God'), this is not to deny the prologue's overarching emphasis on the *visible* manifestation of God's glory in Jesus' earthly form and that seeing, as a result, is presented as a crucial medium for perceiving God's revelation (see, e.g., 11:40, 12:41, 17:24; Thompson 2007: 218). It is the multivalent significance of 'seeing'—to convey physical sight as well as spiritual insight—that underpins the final statements about 'vision' contained in the prologue.

Two further features of the prologue's statements about 'seeing' call for comment. First, the uncompromising character of the opening words of verse 18—'no one has ever seen God'—suggests that they form a response to claims that some chosen individuals have indeed seen God, either in theophanies or through visionary experiences. However, the response is such that it overtly sets Jesus in a completely different category from all other possible contenders. It is likely that the author is responding here to claims made about Moses, who is the topic of comparison and contrast in verse 17, that is, between Moses as the mediator of God's law and Jesus as the source of grace and truth (see also Exodus 34:6). In fact, the final lines of the prologue tap into an extensive debate on the impossibility of seeing God, one that is not limited to the biblical sources (Exodus 33:20-23, see also 19:21; Judges 13:22; 1 Kings 19:11-13; Isaiah 6:5) but extends into many Jewish traditions of the late Second Temple period and beyond. In various Jewish apocalyptic and early mystical circles, the tradition endured that Moses' ascent of Sinai was none other than an ascent to heaven to receive knowledge of the divine mysteries and a direct vision of God (see, e.g., 2 Baruch 4:1-7, 59:3; 4 Ezra 14:3-6; Carter 1990: 43-46). There is evidence elsewhere of the deliberate refutation of such claims to heavenly ascents and visions (see, e.g., John 3:13: 'no one [*oudeis*] has ascended to heaven'), refutations whose structural resemblance to the emphatic 'no one (*oudeis*) has seen God' may yield additional support that Jewish claims about the visionary experiences of Moses are in view, and rejected, in the final verse of the prologue.

Secondly, and as already indicated above, the prologue ends with the assertion that the experience of 'seeing God' is channelled exclusively through Jesus. The *visio Dei* that lies at the heart—and is the goal—of apocalyptic visions and heavenly ascents is centred, according to John, on Jesus as the manifestation of God. In that it refutes and radically reworks the mystical-apocalyptic tradition (Kanagaraj 1998: 215; DeConick 2001: 110; Rowland and Morray-Jones 2009: 125), John's Gospel presents itself as what John Ashton has memorably described as 'an apocalypse in reverse'—a new revelation set on earth, not in heaven (2014: 118). Contrary to what many commentators claim, the last verse of the prologue does not take the opportunity to assert that *Jesus himself has seen God* (which is emphasized in 6:46, see also 5:19, 8:38) but claims that Jesus alone reveals the God who cannot otherwise be seen; thus, those with faith 'see' God because they have seen Jesus (see, e.g., 12:45, 14:7, 9). At this point the fourth evangelist is not so much interested in whether Jesus has seen God, but in his unique identity as 'the only-begotten, God', the one whom *others see* as the incarnation of God's Word, the manifestation of his glory, grace, and truth. Although cursorily attributing to himself the role of seer later in the narrative (6:46), Jesus' experience of seeing God does not—in contrast to that of his believers (1:14)—become the template in the prologue for the religious experience of others, but legitimates his own authority as the exclusive representative of God (see, e.g., 3:12-13, 31-32). The emphasis in John 1:18 is on what Jesus reveals in his capacity as the incarnate Word, on what he makes available to those who 'see' him. The expectation that the prologue places on readers/hearers of the Gospel, however, is that they will respond in a similar manner to the community of believers (1:14) by 'seeing' the divine glory in Jesus, his words, and his deeds.

'Come and See': Seeing and Believing Jesus during his Earthly Ministry

The prologue's retrospective reflections on the importance of 'seeing' Jesus are carried forward into the various scenes of the 'second introduction' to the Gospel, which gives an account within the story line of the testimony of John the Baptist and of the chain of testimony by Jesus' first disciples brought about as a result of John's witness (1:19-51). When Jesus makes his first appearance in the narrative (1:29-34), it is remarked that John sees Jesus coming towards him (1:29). This description of actions, as I have argued elsewhere (2013: 53), is an example of the narrator providing the lens through which events or characters are seen. The focus swiftly turns to John's testimony to Jesus, which again possesses a strongly visual dimension: 'Behold (*ide;* or 'See') the Lamb of God who takes away the sin of the world' (1:29, 36). This divinely commissioned witness (1:6, 33), through an act of speech, points to and encourages others—including the readers/hearers of the text—to look at the one who has so far remained hidden. And what undergirds John's witnessing gaze is his own earlier experience, particularly what he himself *saw* when the Spirit descended on Jesus, presumably on the occasion of his baptism (1:32-34). The enduring significance of this experience is emphasized at the end of this scene, when John the Baptist states: 'And I myself have seen and testified that this is the Chosen One (or Son) of God (1:34).

The importance of seeing, believing, and bearing testimony continues in the calling of Jesus' disciples (1:35-51). Jesus' call to Andrew and an unnamed disciple, 'Come and see' (1:39), is repeated in the next call scene, this time by Philip to Nathanael (1:46, see also 4:29). The play on the literal and metaphorical connotations of 'seeing', which has already been encountered in the prologue, is evident in these scenes as well; whereas the immediate focus at this point is on the visual experience of Jesus, it also anticipates the deeper level of meaning, linked to the experiential dimension of faith, that begins to feature more prominently later in the Gospel account (see, e.g., 6:40, 9:37-39, 14:7).

This series of scenes ends, nevertheless, with a pronouncement by Jesus that is addressed not only to Nathanael, his immediate conversation partner, but to all his disciples: 'You [plural] will see heaven opened and the angels of God ascending and descending upon the Son of Man' (1:51). The use of mystical-apocalyptic language is clear in this allusion to the account of Jacob's dream (Genesis 28:12), but it is also re-envisioned to depict Jesus, the Son of Man, as the link between heaven and earth (see, e.g., 3:13, 6:62): the angels ascend and descend not on the ladder but on the Son of Man, the vision of God on earth (Rowland 2009: 123). But to what does this vision-experience refer? Given that there is no description later in the narrative of angels descending/ascending on Jesus, is the promise 'left unfulfilled' (Ashton 2014: 115)? Rather, as seems more likely, it refers not to a future event as such, but to the whole of Jesus' earthly mission as recounted in the rest of the Gospel: by coming to and seeing Jesus (1:39, 46), the disciples will at the same time experience the heavenly vision of the Son of Man (see, e.g., Reynolds 2008: 102). This promise is not necessarily limited to Jesus' first disciples; the apparent openness of the address ('you') can also include readers/hearers who, by 'seeing' in and through the text, will also encounter the 'greater things' that are promised by Jesus (see, e.g., Lincoln 2005: 122-23). As in the prologue's confessional 'we' statements (1:14), yet another marker or interpretative key is offered (1:51) on how to relate experience to text and text to experience.

Emphasis on genuine 'seeing' continues in the following chapters, particularly in Jesus' encounter with Nicodemus, who is told that no one can 'see the kingdom of God' without being born from above (3:2, see also 1:12-13). These words come immediately after the narrator's remarks about seeing Jesus' miraculous signs without real understanding (2:23-25, see also 4:48, 6:2, 30), that is, not being able to see beyond the powerful signs to their function as 'signifiers' of Jesus' true identity (see, e.g., 2:11, 11:40, 20:30-31). He later emphasizes that being born from above in fact provides believers with the capacity to see 'heavenly things' (3:12), because: 'We speak of what we know and testify to what we have seen' (3:11). Jesus' voice is here fused ('we') with that of the later community of believers. And by virtue of his role as the unique representative of God, he claims the authority to communicate heavenly realities (see, e.g., 3:31-32) to those who, unlike Nicodemus, can move from physical sight to spiritual insight.

The encounters of certain individuals with Jesus are clearly intended to exemplify this movement from one level of seeing to a deeper understanding of his true identity. The Samaritan woman, for example, gradually comes to 'see' that Jesus is a prophet (4:19) and possibly the Messiah (4:29), while challenging her own people to share her vision with the invitation, 'Come and see' (4:29). Undoubtedly the most paradigmatic example of an individual progressively moving from physical to spiritual sight is recorded in the ninth chapter, in which Jesus gives sight to a man blind from birth. The narration of this sign through a series of seven scenes highlights the motif of *transformation*: the healed man first acknowledges Jesus as a prophet (9:17) and then as one who comes from God (9:33) before making a confession of faith in Jesus as 'Lord' (9:38). This transformation is succinctly encapsulated in his response to 'the Jews', 'Though I was blind, now I see' (9:25). The healed man also acts as a model for readers/hearers of the text, as suggested by the fact that he is the central character in most of the scenes (9:8-34), the longest period for Jesus to be absent from the narrative.[1] His transformation from physical blindness to spiritual sight embodies Jesus' claims that it is through new birth that people can 'see' the kingdom of God (3:3) and that faith is necessary to move from darkness to light (12:46). The sign also becomes the occasion for judgement, because while the healed man makes the journey towards spiritual sight and faith in Jesus, the Jewish leaders—because of the clash of their opposing claims—move increasingly towards spiritual blindness (9:39).

Paradigms of Faith from Israel's Past

'Seeing' is afforded prominence in relation to those who encounter Jesus during his earthly life—his disciples, the Samaritan woman, the healed blind man, even the Greeks who wish to 'see' Jesus (12:21)—but also with reference to well-known figures from the past who, in this Gospel, are presented as pivotal witnesses to Jesus and his mission. Thus, the patriarch Abraham is said to have rejoiced at *seeing* Jesus' day (8:56), whereas Isaiah's testimony came about because he *saw* Jesus' glory and spoke about him (12:41).

Abraham becomes the focus of Johannine interest in the eighth chapter, where Jesus engages in an extended dialogue with those described as 'the Jews who had believed in him' (8:31-59). Jesus acknowledges their physical descent from Abraham (8:37) but highlights its incompatibility with their behaviour towards him. To warrant the designation 'children of Abraham', they need to imitate their ancestral father by acting like him and doing 'the works of Abraham' (8:39). From the perspective of John's readers/hearers, the language and structure of this encounter is undoubtedly moulded to evoke a response from them. A stark either/ or scenario is outlined in this bitter dialogue about origins—are they children of Abraham, children of the devil, or children of God?—and the fact that Jesus' opponents fail to respond to his warning about the need for proper actions is designed to encourage readers/hearers to place themselves firmly on the side of 'true disciples' (8:31).

But where does Abraham fit in this scheme? Some clarification emerges as the encounter draws to an end, when Jesus tells his Jewish interlocutors: 'Abraham, your father, rejoiced that he would see my day; he saw [it] and was glad' (8:56). The motifs of the patriarch's rejoicing at the blessings promised by God and the seeing of the future are well documented in Jewish traditions (see, e.g., Jubilees 14-15; 4 Ezra 3:14), but in the hands of the fourth evangelist, Abraham's vision is reconfigured into his 'seeing' of Jesus' day; that is, he 'sees' the earthly mission of the Son. Up to this point in the dialogue, Abraham's role has not been clearly defined, and Jesus' earlier call to do 'the works of Abraham' (8:39), with its capacity to evoke a variety of the patriarch's deeds and attributes, creates a sense of anticipation within the text. Nevertheless, as the extended dialogue draws to its conclusion, Jesus explains that the paramount 'work' to be reproduced by all 'true disciples' (8:31) is to accept his true identity and mission; they—like Abraham—should rejoice that they are seeing Jesus' day. For that reason, Abraham's joyful response upon *seeing* Jesus becomes a model to be emulated by all Johannine believers.

The prophet Isaiah may not receive as much focussed attention as Abraham in the Gospel narrative, but he also acts as an important scriptural witness who has 'seen' Jesus. Indeed, the close Johannine association between seeing and testifying undergirds the second—and final—appearance of Isaiah in the text (12:38-41, see also 1:23), whose testimony is recalled through two quotations (Isaiah 53:1, 6:10) as part of a summary assessment of the unbelief encountered by Jesus during his ministry. To explain how these quotations are subjected to Christological interpretation, John remarks: 'Isaiah said these things because he saw his glory and spoke about him' (12:41). The scriptural setting for this remark is undoubtedly Isaiah's call-vision (Isaiah 6:1-13)—the most well-known prophetic vision in the Hebrew Bible—and it forms the wider context of the immediately preceding quotation from Isaiah 6:10 (John 12:40). Moreover, the reference to the prophet having 'seen his glory' relates specifically to Jewish interpretative renderings of his encounter with the enthroned 'Lord' as a vision of the divine *doxa* (LXX Isaiah 6:1, see also Targum of Isaiah 6:1).

The primary focus of this reference to Isaiah in John 12, as I have argued in some detail elsewhere (2010: 245-72), is the prophet's vision of Jesus' *earthly* life: Isaiah's testimony results from his having seen Jesus' future glory ('he saw his glory'), which is what enabled him to speak about Jesus' mission in the world ('he spoke about him'). Isaiah's vision of Jesus as the glorious figure in the temple becomes the occasion for the prophet to see, ahead of time, the glory manifested by Jesus during his earthly life, and whose rejection ultimately leads to his glorification on the cross. The comment that Isaiah 'saw his glory' (12:41) relates closely in this respect to the preceding remarks on the relationship between signs and faith, blindness and unbelief (12:37-40). Because the signs act as the vehicle for the disclosure of Jesus' glory (2:11, 11:40), the fourth evangelist establishes a contrast between Isaiah, who truly 'saw' the glory of Jesus, and those who, despite seeing the signs with their eyes, lacked the capacity to do so at a deeper level (12:37-38) because of the blinding of their eyes and the hardening of their hearts (12:39-40). The closest Johannine counterpart to the assertion that Isaiah 'saw his glory' is the confession, in the prologue, of those who bear witness to the manifestation of God's glory in human form (1:14). Isaiah's vision is closely aligned to the present revelation of Jesus as the embodiment of God's glory; as a result, the prophet acts as a source of encouragement and paradigmatic example of how truly to 'see' Jesus.

The Gospel of John discloses some valuable clues as to the intended effect of this explicit signalling of Abraham and Isaiah. They may be foundational figures belonging to the past, but they are also made to embody normative values and experiences that should distinguish the community of believers. They are depicted in a way that accords with what should bind together all Johannine Christians: belief in Jesus as the exclusive source of God's revelation and salvation. They are model witnesses to be emulated by others, whether in joyful response upon 'seeing' Jesus (8:56, see also 20:20) or through recognition of Jesus as the manifestation of God's glory (12:41, see also 1:14).

'Seeing' and then 'Not Seeing'

Considerable evidence has been adduced so far in this essay regarding the status of the experience of 'seeing' in relation to the distinctively Johannine form of belief set out in the Gospel, particularly in the first half of the narrative (John 1-12). The second half deals primarily with a different yet related issue, namely how Jesus' disciples will be able to 'see' him following his departure from the world. One of the recurring motifs in the Farewell Discourse (John 13-17), which yields significant glimpses into the values and concerns of the post-Easter community, is the reassurance that the disciples will indeed see Jesus again (14:18-19, 16:22), while, in the final prayer, he offers assurances about their future (eschatological) destiny by looking forward to the time when they will be with him to see his glory (17:24). The earlier promises, nevertheless, find their immediate fulfilment in the resurrection narratives, when Jesus—albeit for a short time—appears to the disciples as the risen Christ. Mary Magdalene, following her own encounter with Jesus, accordingly pronounces, 'I have seen the Lord' (20:18), and the disciples, who 'rejoiced when they saw the Lord' (20:20), declare to Thomas, 'We have seen the Lord' (20:25).

After Thomas' own request to see Jesus is granted, prompting the disciple to make the most exalted of Johannine confessions (20:28: 'My Lord and my God'), Jesus' last words to him make it clear that direct sight is not the only form of access to him: 'Blessed are those who have not seen and yet believe' (20:29). This declaration is not necessarily a rebuke or negative response to Thomas' request to see Jesus' hands and side (see, e.g., O'Brien 2005: 295-96, nor does it denigrate faith derived from sight. However, as suggested by Andrew Lincoln, it does implicitly indicate the importance of accepting the testimony of others rather than seeking a direct, face-to-face encounter with Jesus (2005: 503). 'Although seeing is not believing, there is no believing without seeing, that is, without *somebody's having seen*' (Smith 1999: 384, emphasis added).

Future believers—including the readers/hearers of the Gospel—are assured of another form of testimony that can lead to new ways of experiencing Jesus: the written testimony contained within the narrative itself. 'Seeing' the glory of Jesus, which was manifested during his earthly life, subsequently becomes available through the Johannine text. That 'the path to faith is his [the fourth evangelist's] own book' (Ashton 2014: 179) becomes apparent from the fact that the reflections on 'seeing' and 'not seeing' in John 20:28-29 are immediately followed by what was the

Gospel's originally concluding statement of purpose (as John 21 is a later addition) addressed directly to its readers/hearers: 'These [signs] are written so that you may believe that Jesus is the Messiah, the Son of God, and that through believing you may have life in his name' (20:30-31). For the readers/hearers of the text, and in stark contrast to the characters within it, spiritual insight is ultimately separable from physical sight.

Conclusion

I have highlighted the interpretative challenges as well as opportunities presented by current scholarly approaches to the study of religious experience in relation to the writings of the New Testament. That the issues under consideration are complex—and yet worth pursuing—has been confirmed by an analysis of one particular text whose polyvalent use of the sensory language of sight thoroughly permeates the medium and content of its message. It may not have been possible to make much headway in recovering the kind of religious, possibly visionary, experiences that prompted the fourth evangelist to depict Jesus so distinctively as the embodiment of God's glory, nor indeed in delineating the kind of settings in which such experiences could have originated. What remains, of course, is the text—a narrative that ultimately claims to encode the revelation of Jesus in its written word and, through first-hand engagement with that word, can lead to new experience.

Short Biographical Note
Catrin H. Williams is Reader in New Testament Studies at the School of Theology, Religious Studies and Islamic Studies, University of Wales Trinity Saint David. Her research specialism within New Testament studies is Johannine literature, particularly the Gospel of John. Since 2012 she has been the editor of the *Journal for the Study of the New Testament*.

Notes
1.   For literary strategies encouraging reader/hearer identification with Johannine characters, see O'Brien (2005: 292-93).

Chapter 9

Music as Spiritual Experience

June Boyce-Tillman

Praise the Trinity
Our life-giving music.
She is creating all things.
Life itself is giving birth.
And she is an angel chorus praising
And the splendour of arcane mysteries,
Which are too difficult to understand.
Also from her true life springs for all.

(Hildegard in Boyce-Tillman 2000b: 132)

Music in Western Culture

My concern in this chapter is to explore the potential link between the aesthetic with the spiritual. I have chosen the word 'spiritual' because the word 'aesthetic' has come to be associated with the Western classical tradition, and I wish to be inclusive of non-Western traditions as well. From the ancient goddess traditions (Drinker1995 [1948]), through Plato (Godwin 1987: 3-8) and Hildegard von Bingen (Boyce-Tillman 2000b), spirituality and music have been associated with Western culture. The ancient Greek philosophers developed the relationship between music and spirituality philosophically. Pythagoras, in his notion of three types of music, saw a resolution of the perceived division between body, mind, and spirit (James 1993: 31):

> The words of a hymn represent the body, while the melody represents the soul. Words represent humanity, and melody represents divinity. Thus in a beautiful hymn, in which words and melody are perfectly matched, body and soul, humanity and divinity, are brought into unity. (Van der Weyer 1997: 79)

The opening poem—Hildegard's antiphon to the Trinity—suggests that God *is* actually music. This is reflected in her vision of the choirs of angels. Dionysius in *The Celestial Hierarchy* (2014 [ca. 5th century CE]) describes angels participating in the nature and activity of the Godhead. I suggest that he uses the word 'participation' to reflect the divine life immanent in all things: the inanimate, living, and rational creatures. Such divine immanence 'implies not only a movement from the divine into us, but also that we are part of the life of the divine being' (Fox and Sheldrake 1996: 47). The universe is singing, but we can pick up only part of it because some of it is beyond our hearing. Hildegard envisions God plucking us like a lyre or lute. This feeling is reflected in an account from a woman in 1972:

> As the months went by, there developed within me an ability to hear the voices and music of an inner world... I felt the voice of eternal love communicating with me through music. It seemed to me I was a seven stringed lyre, and when God played on the tautened strings I heard the music with an inner ear. (RERC)

In the hands of the philosophers of the Enlightenment, the link between music and the spiritual became weakened, and the search for the spiritual which had characterized the musical tradition of Europe for hundreds of years, became an essentially secular search. The notion of the connection with the Divine now reappeared in the human sphere, and music and the aesthetic came to be virtually the highest expression of human achievement. The spirits of the outer world could now be identified as human personality traits and emotions (see, e.g., Vitz 1979). In composers' accounts, the location of inspiration became the unconscious (Harvey 1999: 71); the realm of the imagination became devalued (Robinson 2001: 141-42). This change is important for the valuing of the spiritual domain, because the imaginal is an intermediate realm between the purely sensory and the purely spiritual (Corbin 1998 in Leloup 2002: 14-15). The spiritual became associated with notions of self-actualisation (hooks 1994) and self-fulfilment in Abraham Maslow's (1967) hierarchy of human needs, in which he included the aesthetic—the need for beauty, order, and symmetry. As Western culture edged towards an aggressive individualism, a sense of finding some place in a larger whole—that is, the cosmos—became a priority in the human search.

The Re-emergence of Spiritual Intention

This process of objectifying the cosmos associated with the advance of science had not happened in the same way in Eastern cultures, and it was on these cultures that New Age music (Boyce-Tillman 2000a: 155-66) and some areas of rock and jazz traditions (Hamel, 1978/1976: 134-35) drew, in order to offer the desired sense of relationality. This included a more holistic view of the mind/body/spirit relationship, with transcendence approached through physical practices such as chanting (Gass and Brehony 2000) or dancing.

There are increasing numbers of music-making groups with spiritual intentions. For example, groups of overtone chanters meet regularly with spiritual and healing intentions. This form of chanting splits a single note into its component overtones and gives the sense of the sound moving through the body. Jill Purce runs regular workshops helping people to develop this technique for their own healing. Her workshops include group overtone chanting as well as a range of vocal techniques designed to connect with oneself, with others, and with the cosmos, which she sees as re-enchanting Western society by creating an enchanted singing community.[1]

Many New Age traditions pursue their spiritual intentions through linking dance and movement with music. Gabrielle Roth does this in a way that echoes the sense of being played by something beyond oneself that is understood in Hildegard: 'I wasn't controlling the dance—I was being danced... The dancer disappeared inside the dance and I'd find that divine part, divine spirit, the spark of infinite beat... This was my prayer. I was sweating my prayer' (Roth 1992: 2).

In Alf Gabrielsson's descriptions of strong experiences in music, one category he identifies is experiences of the transcendental and existential (Gabrielsson and Lindstrom 1993: 118-39). These experiences demonstrate the synergy between the aesthetic and the spiritual; for example, one person following a deep experience of a Sibelius symphony went to the woods to thank God. Words like 'magical', 'mysterious', 'supernatural', and 'extraterrestrial' appear: 'The narrator feels as if he/she is put in a trance or ecstasy, there may be a feeling or totally merging with something bigger and of glimpsing other worlds or existences' (Gabrielsson 2011: 159)

Some of these musical works have a visionary quality, as in this experience of the Adagietto movement of Gustav Mahler's Symphony No. 5 (1904):

> You lose grasp of time and to a certain extent of space too, in the sense that the whole room I am lying in starts to revolve. In the *fortissimo* on the dominant in the last bars, it is like a light passes over my closed eyes, fading out more and more in the following *diminuendo*. (Gabrielsson 2011: 175)

Sometimes there is a direct message from God, such as 'It was as if his voice was there in the prayer of God' during a performance of Zoltán Kodály's (1923) *Psalmus Hungaricus* (Gabrielsson 2011: 180). Gabrielsson (2011: 402) also identifies a category entitled Music and Existence, which is a state of 'just being' often described as 'holy' (Gabrielsson 2011: 149). These are sometimes transformative: a pop ballad 'meant an end to years of battling with myself and all the others and everyone around me... Ah! I found my way home' (Gabrielsson 2011: 157).

Peter Hills and Michael Argyle (1998) concluded that 'religious' and 'musical' were very similar terms that included such characteristics as 'glimpsing another world' and 'loss of sense of self'. This account from a 65-year-old woman draws similar parallels:

> Countless are the times great music has brought me spellbound to the 'gates of Heaven'—the hush during a Beethoven symphony, a sermon in itself. I've often said that to me, a good concert was far more full of awe— God, if you like, than many a church service. (RERC archives)

Gabrielsson also identifies similarities between music and religious experiences:

> In experiences of God I often feel completely broken-hearted and at the same time eternally grateful to God who wants to come so close to me. So it was shocking to experience the same feelings but from a totally different cause, namely music. The music was not sacral bit it gave me the same feeling as in the meeting with God. (Gabrielsson 2011: 454)

Thus, Gabrielsson began to develop a typology for musical experiences that included those of a spiritual or religious character.

In the 21st century an atheist spirituality has developed that looks to the arts for the role religion has traditionally played. First of all, Alain de Botton acknowledges the two important functions for religion—both extrapersonal in creating community and intrapersonal in enabling people to survive the difficulties of life (de Botton 2012: 5-6). De Botton's hope is that that the arts might be as effective as religion in their ability to guide, humanize, and console, and views them potentially as 'secular society's sacraments' (de Botton 2012: 32).

The Musical Experience

> My approach fits broadly in the area of phenomenology, drawing on Martin Heidegger's insights. According to Kai Nielsen, Heidegger understood art as having the potential to open our eyes to see the world we live in more clearly. He redefined 'truth' as 'what we human beings sense', rather than locating it in some sense of reality or correctness. (Nielsen in Beyer 1996: 174)

The musical experience, therefore, is essentially the human relationship with the music. This relationship is one of encounter, drawing on Martin Buber's concept of the power of the I/Thou relationship (1997: 57). These ideas are based on those of the philosopher, Emanuel Levinas (1969: 33), who described the power of the encounter with someone different from us with whom we can form a relationship. This relationship for Levinas represented an encounter with infinity and a way of being in which the spiritual resides in the flow between the two 'others' who retain their differences in the meeting. This notion links with John Dewey's idea of experience, which is an 'interaction of organism and environment which, when it is carried to the full, is a transformation of interaction into participation and communication' (1994 [1980]: 22).

I view the musical experience as an encounter with different aspects of the cosmos, including:

- anOther self (who created the music);
- anOther culture (that is separate from us historically or geographically);
- a world of abstract ideas (illustrated by the way in which all the sounds fit together); and
- the environment (in that instruments are made of wood, plastic, metal and so on). (Boyce-Tillman 2004)

I suggest that when these encounters are achieved for the musicker, a spiritual domain is entered.

The Liminal/Spiritual Space

Music has the possibility of creating a liminal space, and the perceived effectiveness of a musical experience is often closely related to this. Insofar as a musical experience takes us out of 'everyday' consciousness with its concerns for food, clothing, and practical issues and moves us into another dimension, we regard the musical experience as successful, whether we are composers, performers, or listeners. In this way, 'Art uproots us into virtual reality' (Galtung 2008: 54). Rowan Williams describes the 'aesthetic sense of inaccessibility' as 'unrestricted time' (Williams 2012: 18). Victor Turner (1969), drawing on an analysis of ritual, described this liminality as a character of being or dwelling for extended periods of time in a spatial, social, and spiritual threshold, like pilgrims. Arnold Van Gennep (1960 [1909]) saw a parallel, transitional stage in rituals that are transpersonal and consciousness-changing.

The notion that at the heart of this liminal experience is *relationship* is supported by Katya Mandoki, who describes humans' relation to art as a 'latching-on to the nipple': 'Adhesion is the essential aesthetic operation both at an individual and at a collective level' (2007: 67). Here we can see the linkage between the aesthetic and the spiritual. We understand this connection in the engagement of a small child in this account from Panos Kanellopoulos:

> An eight-year-old child immerses herself in a piano improvisation, exploring with particular care and concentration aspects of musical ideas that emerge and develop in the moment of their occurrence... There is an

overwhelming sense of fragility in this music-making process, as well as a
density of attention, a care for maintaining fluency, and a prevalent sense
of adventure. (Kanellopoulos 2013)

The child's experience could be regarded as a good example of 'flow'
(Csikszentmihalyi and Csikszentmihalyi 1988; Csikszentmihalyi 1993; Custodero 2002, 2005). This experience (sometimes called 'the zone') is one
in which a person is fully engaged mentally in an activity so that there
is a feeling of total immersion in a process often accompanied by joy,
excitement and energy. Lori Custodero might call the child's experience
'aesthetic': 'I propose that "being with" *music* generates a sense of the aesthetic as we both transform musical materials—timbres, pitches, rhythms,
phrases, harmonies—and are transformed by our experiences with them'
(Custodero 2005: 36, emphasis original).

In describing the liminal experience in music, I have drawn from a
number of sources. Isabel Clarke's (2005: 93) notion of the transliminal
way of knowing draws on cognitive psychology (Thalbourne et al. 1997)
and has to do with our 'porous' relation to other beings and our ability to
tolerate paradox. She distinguishes this from the propositional knowing
of the everyday. To access the other way of knowing we cross an internal
'limen' or threshold. Other areas that I have drawn on in examining the
experience are:

- *ecstasy*, which is often associated with the idea of 'the holy' coming
  from the religious/spiritual literature (Otto 1923; Laski 1961)—
  that is, a sense of these experiences being 'given' and coming from
  beyond in some way;
- *trance*, which comes from anthropological (Rouget 1987), New Age
  (Collin 1997; Goldman 1992; Stewart 1987), and psychotherapeutic
  literature (Inglis 1990)—that is, entering a different form of consciousness from everyday living for the purposes of healing;
- *mysticism*, which comes from religious traditions, especially Christianity (Underhill in Rankin 2005), and goes beyond creedal statements and moral codes to the 'heart of the matter' embracing
  'unknowing';
- *peak experiences* (Maslow 1967), which are necessary to human
  beings just as food and shelter are;
- *the religious experience* (Rankin 2005), which is variously defined and
  treated by a variety of writers who often link it with religious faith;
- *the spiritual experience of children* (Hay and Nye 1998; Erricker et al.
  1997; Hay 1982; Robinson 1977), in which identity construction and
  meaning making is stressed;
- *intuition* (Noddings and Shore 1984);
- *the Greek agora* (Yeorgouli-Bourzoucos 2004);

- *studies in consciousness* (Lancaster 2004);
- *symmetric logic* (Matte Blanco in Bomford 2005); and
- *liminality or liminoid* (Turner 1969, 1974), which means rooted in religious ritual but found in religionless contexts.

Although they can be defined distinctively, the above terms may be understood as representing staging points along what is actually a continuum describing a state that is more or less differentiated from everyday knowing.

Spirituality, Religion and Culture

Does this mean that *all* music is potentially spiritual? Is there not then a *secular* music? Does not music's impact on us depend on our previous experiences and the context in which the music is placed? If the experience is essentially related to context and experiencer (Boyce-Tillman 2016), then the idea of a universal spiritual music is challenged. This is an idea regularly found in the literature but not compatible with my thinking about the spiritual as formed between the nature of the music and the person either making or listening to it. Gilbert Rouget understands music as simply one component in the ritual but varying in relation to the ritual in which it is embedded (1997: 31). In our Western culture, the importance of the religious origins of particular music may simply be the result of the increasing dependence of our society on words for entering the musical experience (Blake 1997: 7). If we know that the origins of the music are religious, we are more likely to have an experience that we would define as 'religious'.

Spirituality and Christianity

Many accounts of the religious experience associated with music are associated with Christian contexts. In 1970, one man wrote: 'At the age of 88 years I am practically religionless except that most days I am obsessed with Moody and Sankey hymns' (RERC). And a woman recounted a healing experience during a hymn:

> After the address came the hymn 'All hail the power of Jesus' name'. During the singing of it I felt the power of God falling upon me. My sister felt it too, and said 'Floie, you're going to walk'. The Lord gave me faith then. (RERC)

These quotations indicate that Christian theology has long viewed music as a spiritual experience (see, e.g., Ingalls et al. 2013). Music has been regarded as iconic, but Terence Thomas and Elizabeth Manning understand the iconic effect as being in the relationship between music and personal taste; these authors, although acknowledging the dominance of Western classical music in the literature, open up the power of the sacred in a variety of musics (1995).

Christian theology would place all the strands identified above in the context of a world that is a manifestation of God (Begbie 2000: 271). Other theologians have used music as a metaphor in theological reflection. For example, David Ford (1999) uses music's transformative quality in *Self and Salvation, Being Transformed*; Richard Holloway (2000) in *Godless Morality: Keeping Religion out of Ethics* uses musical improvisation as a metaphor for moral choice—ascribing a capacity for improvisation to God. The musical tastes of many leading European theologians and the tight interface between the Western classical European tradition and the Church in terms of employment for so much of its history demonstrate a linkage with Christianity and for much of European history:

> I gratefully confess that thirty-five years ago...the Clarinet Concerto KV 622, this last orchestral work of Mozart's completed precisely two months before his death, of unsurpassable beauty, intensity and inwardness, completely without traces of gloom or resignation, delighted, strengthened, consoled, and in short, brought a touch of 'bliss' to a doctoral student in theology almost every day. (Kung 1992: 27-28)

It is arguably through this type of thinking that the idea emerges that certain pieces will generate a spiritual experience, whatever the context. But this experience depends on a person's enculturation and training. Such thinking is often supported by considering intention as an important part in the 'sacredness' of the experience. This line of thought that might be understood as limiting spiritual experience to Western classical masterpieces is now challenged by the popularity of folk and jazz traditions and is being tempered by the embracing of a greater variety of styles in the approach to the transcendence of God (Saliers 2007).

Hymnody is another example of implicit and explicit theology and is sometimes called 'lyrical theology' because it can cause theological understanding to penetrate deeper into the believer's psyche. Indeed, the theology of the Church—especially in the Protestant traditions—was taught primarily by its hymnody because of the power of linking theology and singing. However, the issue of the conservatism of texts and their lack of inclusion or social protest means that even some believers fail to have any sort of spiritual experience from the musicking (Boyce-Tillman 2014).

Nevertheless, the cultural place of religious music—whether sung or listened to—means that some people who no longer subscribe to the doctrinal tenets of Christianity may still be transported by religious music. I remember a self-declared atheist singing with great joy 'How Great Thou Art' because of its relationship to his Welsh roots. For many older people, hymns learned in childhood have reminiscence power regardless of contemporary personal belief; thus, a hymn like 'Praise My Soul the King of Heaven' was used for many services such as weddings and funerals for much of the twentieth century.

In liturgy—such as that in the elaborate rituals associated with Easter—the combination of movement, music, speech, costume, and theatre contributes to the mood of uplift that many seek in Christian worship. However, the effectiveness of the music depends entirely on a particular context, and when transplanted, it may lack sacred power. James Lancelot (1995), in declaring music as a sacrament and linking it with divine generosity, concludes that secular music can act in a sacred way, although he does go on to limit this to 'the mainstream of Western music as millions of people understand it' (Lancelot 1995: 183), probably because of his own cultural background. In summary, there are many claims for the essential relationship between music, spirituality and religion. Although Lancelot is writing from a Christian perspective, similar claims could be made in Judaism, Hinduism, and Sikhism, to name just three possible examples.

Conclusion

I have explored the varied relationships made between music and spirituality by tracing them through the history of Western thought—from the mystical thinking of the medieval church to its place in contemporary post-secular culture. In so doing, I have set up a phenomenographic map of the experience of music, which relates to analyses of the spiritual experience. By challenging the notion of a universal sacred music in favour of the sacredness being generated by the music and musicker (Small 1998), I have opened up the possibility of deriving spiritual experience from most musical traditions. Following theorists of atheist spirituality, I have offered the possibility of music functioning in a way that was once regarded as the domain of religion, which has revealed the use of music as a medium for spiritual transformation in a variety of contexts.

Short Biographical Note

June Boyce-Tillman is Professor of Applied Music at the University of Winchester and composer and international performer, especially in the work of Hildegard of Bingen and healing with a research focus on the possibilities of intercultural sharing through composing/improvising/singing; she was awarded a MBE for her services to Music and Education.

Notes

1. See 'Jill Purce—The Healing Workshop', at http://www.jillpurce.com/.

Chapter 10

Is It Possible to Have a 'Religious Experience' in Cyberspace?

Gary Bunt

Whether it is possible to attain a religious experience online is perhaps in the eye of the beholder and dependent on the individual definition of 'religious experience'. If that definition includes access to 'the sacred' in some form or participation in a ritual that brings the individual closer to a deity, then it might be possible to attain a religious experience online. With increases in digital literacy and improvements in internet access, the possibilities of a religious experience in cyberspace may be enhanced. However, we are not necessarily talking about a separation between online and offline space any more. The methods in which people use mobile devices such as tablets and mobile phones as part of their everyday dialogues and transactions means that increasingly there is an integration between the analogue and digital, the online and the offline. This means there has been an assimilation of technology into daily life, and that can include the ways in which religions are mediated. The focus of this chapter is on the World Wide Web and mobile technology, with a particular emphasis on apps (applications). However, it is recognised that there are other zones of cyberspace with sacred resonance, such are virtual worlds and online gaming, which are beyond the scope of this work.

In the early days of the internet during the 1990s, it was necessary to turn on a desk-bound computer and then switch on an internet modem, which would slowly dial up an Internet Service Provider to enable a person to go online. Once online, the options for interaction and digital religious experiences were relatively limited compared with contemporary opportunities. Mediation initially was text bound, through chat rooms and emails primarily, until the emergence of browsers such as Mosaic and Netscape in the mid-1990s. The exponential growth of the internet focused on the World Wide Web and included religious content generated by adherents, enthusiasts, and organisations. This growth has evolved in line with innovations in technology.

In some circles, especially within less digitally literate generations, there was a reluctance to develop internet content, which reflected in some cases a lack of awareness of the potential of the medium or concerns that somehow the digital media would have a corrupting or negative influence on readers and users. This meant that in some religious contexts, key organisations and platforms did not develop useful and regularly updated internet sites, and there were some significant gaps in the religious marketplace. Into this vacuum alternative religious voices emerged and acquired growing audiences and levels of influence for their worldviews. Representative bodies of many religious organisations, perhaps more traditionally rooted in print-based delivery media, had to play 'catch up' once they realised that the internet was not a fad, but increasingly part of everyday lives. There has since been a contestation for online influence, which is still being played out within contemporary contexts (Cowan and Dawson 2004).

Increasingly, this integrated approach to religion and online media has included the use of digital devices utilised in different ways within places of worship. In the Sheikh Zayed Grand Mosque in Abu Dhabi, for example, a computer screen is fitted on the *minbar* (prayer lectern), in order for the imam to read the Friday sermon, which may be relayed live and also recorded for digital streaming. The same imam may be updating activities online via the #grandmosque hashtag. In Saudi Arabia, religious leaders have gathered millions of followers for their daily tweets, which incorporate ideas about 'the sacred' and religious experiences. Within pilgrimage, mobile phone technology is utilised at every stage of the Hajj in order to advise the pilgrim on religious ritual, organise parties of pilgrims, provide recitation appropriate to stages of pilgrimage, and even record the experience in order to convey it to others outside of Mecca, although the use of digital technology is not officially sanctioned (Bunt 2016).

The phenomenon of integrating technology with ritual practice is not limited to Islam. In 2013, some churches in the UK started to encourage people to bring their mobile devices into church, where they could be used to access religious texts and encourage a level of participation within worship (*Daily Mail* 2013). Such developments may suggest that there is an integrated approach to the application of technology as part of the facilitation of some forms of religious experience (Campbell 2013).

Given the saturation of digital media, however, one might also question whether religious space should be a sanctuary from computer-mediated technology in its multifarious forms. For some, religious reflection does not require a digital interface, and in fact, going offline may provide a greater focus. However, in places where access to religious figures or sacred spaces is limited, it may be a necessity to go online in order that some form of religious experience can be facilitated. The technology itself can offer a level of liminality or transition from one religious state to another. It can also inform one's perception of a religious location through information provision, images, sounds, and advice. For some, there may be may be increased opportunities for religious reflection through the use of digital media, especially given that mobile phones and tablets can access a plethora of religious material wherever it is possible to obtain a digital signal. One significant question is how, given that the internet is always on, can this impact the religious lives of adherents? The separation between spiritual and secular, divine and mundane can be problematic if one is constantly receiving updates and information about religious issues through social media. Would switching devices off constitute a religious act or inhibit access to religious knowledge through loss of connectivity?

Some of us live in a digitally saturated context for work, home life, and points in between; we are constantly 'connected', and manufacturers continue to provide new interfaces through which the internet can be accessed. The 'internet of things' is a phenomenon in which everyday devices can be linked into the internet, from household appliances—and indeed the whole house—to cars and everyday objects; attempts by Google to introduce wearable Google Glasses may have stalled in 2015, but this was an experiment to integrate digital devices into users' lives at every stage of their waking hours. Even the most devout, technologically literate person may be challenged by constant streaming of religious content, and indeed there may be spaces where the presence of 'the sacred' is inappropriate or demeaning, even if delivered by a digital device.

When exploring ideas about religious experiences online, one has to consider that content is generated for different types of audiences. Religious content forms one strand in a much wider pattern of digital consumption, including shopping, newsgathering, information exchange, conversation, and even some of the more disreputable areas of the internet (for some) in which ideas of 'the sacred' are somewhat lacking, such as within parts of the Dark Web. A range of digital interfaces has emerged to present opportunities for participation and interaction on religious matters. A generation of digital natives operating in religious contexts have developed apps and made use of social media in all its forms in order to create platforms for expressing ideas of religiosity. Whereas, in the early days of the internet, chat rooms and websites had the greatest significance, now consideration is given to Twitter, Facebook, Instagram, Vines, and even SnapChat and other forms of instant messaging.

Within a variety of religious perspectives, there have been processes of acknowledgement, transition, and net literacy that have been relevant in moving forward the integration of digital media into religious process. These may be through a variety of entry points and interfaces. Knowledge about sacred texts, which can form an element of a religious experience, has been facilitated through the extensive efforts to place texts, translations, and commentaries online. The Long Tail associated with digital demand, in which the internet has facilitated markets for even the most obscure products, might be an appropriate analogy for the ways in which different religious perspectives have been created and developed online (Anderson 2004). The internet can provide access to obscure perspectives and minority views, which may be difficult, dangerous, or impossible to present within analogue contexts. So-called 'cults', New Religious Movements, and more obscure branches of mainstream faith have found audiences and momentum through generating online presence.

In some cases, specific forms of religious expression have emerged online, as distinct from the offline forms, including platforms that have no resonance in analogue contexts. For example, rituals and forms of participation have emerged that are articulated in cyberspace in ways that may be impossible offline, especially considering how these activities bring together participants and actors from diverse global contexts and backgrounds, often utilising identities that feature avatars and forms of anonymity (Dawson 2005). In another example, Second Life, forms of religious expression play out to provide a 'religious experience' in a virtual world (Wagner 2011).

Critical issues have emerged in relation to content creation, including understanding the motivation behind the creators of content and the ways in which interfaces are developed in order that they become 'sticky' online experiences for users and participants.[1] This means that online interfaces have gone beyond simply providing text to providing more immersive experiences. There might also be issues as to the veracity of any information provided about religion and the way in which it is presented online; a website that has high degrees of usability, searchability, and an infrastructure that is easy to navigate is likely to attain a greater audience than an equivalent site with design faults, no matter the veracity of the content (Bunt 2009). There have been cases of sites constructed purporting to present particular religious perspectives, which were later determined to be fraudulent. A prominent case in this regard is that of SuraLikeIt, a website that presented verses purporting to be from the Qur'an, but were fabrications that had negative connotations about Islam (Bunt 200: 123-30).

The veracity of data is particularly important when sacred texts are being presented online. It is possible for errors to creep in, and a lack of editorial input can mean that these are published and indeed utilised inadvertently or otherwise within religious contexts. Deliberate changes of emphasis, particularly in translations, can also have an impact on the meaning of a text. Sacred texts have become searchable objects, which can be studied and drawn upon in ways that are very different in terms of mediation to traditional print texts or indeed manuscripts. This may aid people in terms of their personal study, and such resources are very popular among students studying different religions—although attention has been drawn by some to the veracity of sources that have been presented as authentic. The acceptance of online content as accurate can be problematic, especially in an era in which publication can be immediate and lacking a sustained editorial process.

Shifts in technology have meant that the ways in which religious materials are accessed and experienced have also changed over time. This can include a shift from the traditional printed word: people may still read books, but they access them and absorb the information in different ways through online media. There can also be ways in which sources can be accessed through multimedia, and the overwhelming choice of content in various forms can be a challenge.

The role of internet gatekeepers to mediate materials and guide interested readers has grown in importance, particularly in the context of religion. Simply going online and using a search engine may be insufficient, given the overwhelming choice of sources that are available to facilitate a religious experience or develop religious knowledge. There is also a transformation in terms of access to authority: some religious perspectives now encourage people to email them or send questions via online forms, which will be responded to by specific religious authorities. This grants a new form of access—consultation of experts—to the mediation of religious knowledge, but it can also challenge traditional, real-world authorities in localised contexts. Authority can be subverted through the use of such fora, and there is evidence that people will shop around for a religious opinion that suits their requirements and expectations, even if this involves consulting several different perspectives (Bunt 2003: 124-34). The potential levels of anonymity mean that consultations can be undertaken even in locations where challenges to tradition are dangerous or problematic, although this does not negate the potential for censorship and even prosecution in some contexts. Internet users have an expectation that their questions will be answered quickly online, but some scholars and authorities have been overwhelmed with questions, some of which are less serious than others, and there is a phenomenon of seeking of religious answers online that has now entered the realm of entertainment.

Such developments mean that academics seeking to explore ideas about contemporary religion have to include reference to the internet as a potential-change agent and source of authority. New questions have emerged about how to interpret such information, and some academics are focusing on these issues from diverse perspectives, linking into other disciplinary fields as well as referring back to studies associated with media, religion, and culture (Hadden and Cowan 2000; Institute for Religious Studies 2005). Among the questions that one might ask over those associated with a phenomenology of religion on the internet: does a hyperlink have value as a religious object? Is computer-mediated religion legitimate in the eyes of its practitioners? Is liminality the equivalent to (or supplementary to) more traditional forms of mediation? (Bunt 2008: 705-20).

In order to approach these issues one has to establish the aims of online religious content in its various forms: it may be to provide a window into religion for outsiders, reinforcement of followers, conversion, networking between and within religious perspectives, or a closed site limited to a specific group of followers or members. Nuanced models apply and one cannot stereotype about this; similarly, there are diverse reader profiles for the forms of content associated with religious expression. We live in a world where even the most obscure and reluctant forms of religious belief and expression in diverse cultures have found a place online, and the expansion of digital interfaces into numerous languages and scripts helped facilitate this, along with the reduction in the digital divide, which has resulted in a growth of access to internet content through a variety of devices.

Perhaps one of the most personal forms of digital media interaction will be via cell phone or tablet, especially given the always-on nature of such devices. It seems relevant, therefore, to take a brief look at some of the apps that have been designed especially for facilitating proximity to religious knowledge, values, and potentially even experiences. For example, the Vatican has developed multilingual platforms over time to promote the papacy and Roman Catholic values. These have evolved from static webpages to high-functioning apps (Vatican 2015). This technological transition can be seen in the different ways pontiffs have publically accessed online devices. For example, Pope John Paul II was photographed using a laptop with a papal seal in order to send an email containing an apology 'for a string of injustices, including sexual abuse, committed by Roman Catholic clergy in the Pacific nations' (BBC News 2001); Pope Benedict XVI was filmed using an iPad with appropriate technological assistance from adjacent clergy to deliver an early papal tweet; and Pope Francis was filmed posing for selfies with young tourists to the Vatican.

Pope Francis features on the Pope App, which has the papal seal on it and is linked to the newspaper *Vatican Today*. The free app is available for Apple and Android devices and is available in English, French, Italian, Portuguese, and Spanish (Pontificium Consilium de Communicationibus Socialibus). It contains a direct link to the official Vatican Twitter feed, *@Pontifex*, with links to news, web cams, video, photos, and live feeds of papal activities. The extent to which this app allows a form of experiential connection with the papacy is open to question; clearly, the Pope is not personally posting all of his tweets, but he must have some input or influence over their content. The *@Pontifex* Twitter page in English indicated

6.39 million followers in June 2015, while the account only followed eight other Twitter accounts representing the eight other languages used for papal tweets. This included an Arabic feed with over 203,000 followers; a Latin feed with over 359,000 followers; and the Spanish feed with 9.1 1 million followers (Pontifex 2015). All told, 'More than 14 million people follow the Pope at @*Pontifex* in nine languages and each tweet made by the Pontiff is on average retweeted nearly 17,000 times, Twiplomacy revealed' (*Daily Mail* 2014).

In terms of numbers of followers, the Pope was the second-most popular world leader on Twitter (after Barack Obama) in 2015, with the highest number of retweets (Twitlomacy 2015). The header on @*Pontifex* shows the Pope waving to a crowd, many of whom are holding cameras, mobile phones, and tablets. The app itself is publicised on the main Vatican site, along with other apps providing access to Vatican documentation, prayer, and an 'augmented reality' experience, which provides on-site information to visitors as they tour religious sites. Feedback from some users of these latter apps and my personal use suggest that there is further developmental work to be done in order to make them a smooth user-experience. In the Vatican, there were other concerns relating to offensive responses posted on social media, and this was one reason that there was no official Papal Facebook page:

> [T]he head of the Vatican's pontifical council for social communications, Archbishop Claudio Maria Celli, said during a speech in New York that the offensive replies @*Pontifex* was getting on Twitter were creating a 'crisis' in the Vatican.
>
> Mr Celli said that although abusive comments on Twitter were easier to ignore, those on Facebook would be 'more prominent'. (Independent 2014)

One of the most popular apps in numerical terms associated with religion is the Bible App, produced for Android and Apple by YouVersion. The company's publicity suggests that it has been 'installed on more than 170 million unique devices, all over the world [and] offers more than 1,000 Bible versions, in more than 770 languages' (YouVersion 2015). The app itself has a searchable interface and the ability to share, email, and customise passages from the different translations of the Bible via social media or SMS. The app was also offering a version for Apple Watch, meaning that sacred texts have a potential to be wearable. Again, there may be issues of how the sacred text is used within appropriate places; with digital media, issues associated with the sanctity and cleanliness of an environment in which a text is mediated do not necessarily apply. But its availability indicates that wearable technology may contribute to some form of 'religious experience'.

There are several examples of key religious texts that have been integrated into apps, offering access to and immersion with core values associated with the sacred origins of religions. The Qur'an is available in numerous translations and versions via apps. A good example of this is Muslim Pro, which can incorporate GPS-linked prayer reminder times based on individual location, recitations of the Qur'an in a variety of styles, prayer direction information, and other localised data (MuslimPro). The production of such apps has become a competitive market, appearing in different translated languages and versions, including phonetic transcription for non-Arabic speakers (Islam: the Quran). Some versions are free, and others offer bonus levels for payment.

Apps were also relevant for enhancing levels of religious knowledge within diverse contexts. For example, diverse perspectives associated with Judaism introduced interactive materials to improve Jewish knowledge throughout the Diaspora. This included a variety of packages developed by G-dcast for educators, children, families, and adult learners. Promotional material for apps was backed up with YouTube clips of children playing various games; the Exodus app encouraged children to solve problems whilst developing Jewish values; the Leviticus app focused on the types of sacrifice that are appropriate (or not). One user described it as 'kind of like Bible Fruit Ninja!', reflecting a popular game for mobile phones (iTunes 2013; Kurivilla 2013). G-dcast also developed Radical Rabbis: The Adventures of Hillel and Shammai, which had a 'retro' aesthetic from early computer game platforms, including computer-generated klezmer music. The extent to which these apps develop a form of religious experience might be open to question, but they can stimulate discussions and form a useful educational basis on which to build (G-dcast 2014).

There are several examples of religious texts that have been integrated into apps. For example, the *Bhagavad-Gita* has been developed as an app with translations (iTunes 2010); a seven-language Android version integrates with social media, whilst a variety of apps in different languages offer further exposure to developing an understanding of the *Bhagavad-Gita* (Appolicious). Different forms of Buddhism are also reflected online, including information on meditation and the thoughts of the Buddha (iTunes 2014). Given the exiled status of the Dalai Lama, it is not surprising that over the years Tibetan Buddhism has developed a substantial online presence (Helland 2014). There are a number of apps associated with the Dalai Lama, although these are not necessarily officially endorsed. To an extent, the religious messages regarding the Dalai Lama have fused with other messages associated with Tibet. The Dalai Lama has over 11.3 million followers on Twitter, with content drawing primarily on quotations and also summaries of activities (Dalai Lama 2015).

Sikhism also has a significant online presence with aspects of spirituality presented through diverse media, which are understood as a way of developing religious lives (Singh 2014). Apps can be accessed that explain many details about Sikhism, including the key holy scripture Guru Granth Sahib, rendered in multimedia form and copiously illustrated, along with information about prayer and the necessary hymns utilised to meditate (Google Play 2015). As such, within a single resource there are many aspects of Sikh religious practice and experience that can be facilitated via a digital device. The Android App Store indicates numerous apps available for many aspects of Sikhism, with an equivalent available in the Apple Store.

A quick survey of these apps demonstrates that digital media are an area in which significant investment has been undertaken as a means of facilitating forms of religious expression, knowledge development, and perhaps even a sense of the numinous. Such media forms have gone past the gimmick stage, especially with digital natives, to become a core part of religious identity and knowledge in the contemporary world. In an always-on society saturated with digital media, one might feel that the sense of 'the sacred' has been diminished; however, depending on individual definitions and perspectives, one might still seek out and locate a 'religious experience' online. While there are still sages, saints, gurus, and adepts in the real world, increasingly one might use a search engine in order to seek out a digital idea of 'the sacred'. Consequently, it is anticipated that religious interests will continue to invest time, money, and even faith in further developing digital media output to reflect their place within the contemporary cyber landscape and to further enhance the possibilities for 'religious experience' online.

Short Biographical Note

Gary R. Bunt is Reader in Islamic Studies and Religious Studies at the University of Wales Trinity Saint David with a research focus on Islam, Muslims, and the internet.

Notes

1.   The term 'sticky' refers to online content that encourages readers to return on a regular basis—for example, for updates or new material, and/or to content designed to encourage readers to stay on a page for a sustained period.

Bibliography

Alexander, C., P. Robinson, D. Orme-Johnson, R. Schneider, and K. Walton. 'The Effects of Transcendental Meditation Compared to Other Methods of Relaxation and Meditation in Reducing Risk Factors, Morbidity, and Mortality'. *Homeostasis* 35.4/5 (1994): 243-64.

Alexander, C., J. Davies, C. Dixon, M. Dillbeck, S. Drucker, R. Oetzel, J. Muehlman, and D. Orme-Johnson. 'Growth of Higher Stages of Consciousness: The Vedic Psychology of Human Development'. In *Higher Stages of Human Development: Perspectives on Adult Growth*, ed. C. Alexander and E. Langer, 286-340. New York: Oxford University Press, 1990.

Anderson, Chris. 'The Long Tail'. *Wired* 12.10 (2004), at http://www.wired.com/2004/10/tail/ (accessed 18 April 2015).

Appolicious. '*Shrimad Bhagavad Gita* in Hindi by Prateek Arora' (2014), at http://www.androidapps.com/book-news/apps/473697-shrimad-bhagavad-gita-in-hindi-prateek-arora-naraincom (accessed 24 June 2015).

Ashton, John. *Understanding the Fourth Gospel.* Oxford, UK: Clarendon Press, 1991.

—*The Gospel of John and Christian Origins.* Minneapolis, MN: Fortress Press, 2014.

Auerbach, Loyd. *ESP, Hauntings and Poltergeists.* New York: Warner Books, 1986.

Augustine. *Confessions,* trans. H. Chadwick. Oxford, UK: Oxford University Press, 1991.

Baars, Bernard. *In the Theater of Consciousness.* New York: Oxford University Press, 1997.

Badham, Paul. 'Religious and Near-death Experience in Relation to Belief in a Future Life'. *Mortality* 2.1 (1997): 7-21.

Barnard, G. William. 'Explaining the Unexplainable: Wayne Proudfoot's "Religious Experience"'. *Journal of the American Academy of Religion* 60.2 (1992): 231-56.

Batluck, Mark. 'Religious Experience in New Testament Research', *Currents in Biblical Research* 9 (2011): 339-63.

BBC News. 'Pope Sends First E-mail Apology' (2001), at http://ews.bbc.co.uk/1/hi/world/europe/1671540.stm (accessed 23 November 2001).

Begbie, Jeremy. *Theology, Music and Time.* Cambridge, UK: Cambridge University Press, 2000.

Belanti, John, Mahendra Perera, and Karuppiah Jagadheesan. 'Phenomenology of Near-death Experiences: A Cross-cultural Perspective'. *Transcultural Psychiatry* 45.1 (2008): 121-33.

Bessant, Annie. *The Ancient Wisdom.* Adyar, IN: The Theosophical Publishing House, 1939.

Beyer, Anders (ed.). *The Music of Per Norgard: Fourteen Interpretative Essays.* Aldershot, UK: Scolar Press, 1996.

Blake, Andrew. *The Land without Music: Music Culture and Society in Twentieth Century Britain.* Manchester, UK: Manchester University Press, 1997.

Blanke, Olaf, Theodor Landis, Laurent Spinelli, and Margitta Seeck. 'Out-of-body Experience and Autoscopy of Neurological Origin'. *Brain* 127.2 (2003): 243-58.

Blanes, Ruy and Espirito Santo, Diana (eds.). *The Social Life of Spirits*. Chicago, IL: Chicago University Press, 2014.

Bocking, Brian. 'Mysticism: No Experience Necessary?' *DISKUS* 7 (2006), at http://basr.ac.uk/diskus_old/diskus7/bocking.htm (accessed 16 April 2016).

Boddy, Janice. 'Spirits and Selves in Northern Sudan: the Cultural Therapeutics of Possession and Trance'. *American Ethnologist* 15.1 (1988): 4-27.

Bomford, Rodney. 'Ignacio Matte Blanco and the Logic of God'. In *Ways of Knowing: Science and Mysticism today*, ed. Chris Clarke, 127-42. Exeter, UK: Imprint Academic, 2005.

Bourguignon, Erika. 'World Distribution and Patterns of Possession States'. In *Trance and Possession States*, ed. R. Prince, 3-34. Montreal: R. M. Bucke Memorial Society, 1967.

—*Cross-cultural Study of Dissociational States*. Columbus: Ohio State University Press, 1968.

—*Possession*. San Francisco: Chandler and Sharpe, 1976a.

—'Spirit Possession Beliefs and Social Structure'. In *The Realm of the Extra-human Ideas and Actions*, ed. A. Bhardati, 17-26. The Hague, NL: Mouton, 1976b.

—*Psychological Anthropology: An Introduction to Human Nature and Cultural Difference*. New York: Holt, Rinehart and Winston, 1979.

—(ed.). *Religion, Altered States of Consciousness and Social Change*. Columbus: Ohio State University Press, 1973.

Bourguignon, Erika and Tom Evascu. 'Altered States of Consciousness within a General Evolutionary Perspective: A Holocultural Analysis'. *Behavior Science Research* 12.3 (1977): 197-216.

Bowie, Fiona. 'Devising Methods for the Study of the Afterlife: Cognition, Empathy and Engagement'. In *Paranthropology: Anthropological Approaches to the Paranormal*, ed. Jack Hunter, 99-106. Bristol, UK: Paranthropology, 2012.

—'Building Bridges, Dissolving Boundaries: Toward a Methodology for the Ethnographic Study of the Afterlife, Mediumship, and Spiritual Beings'. *Journal of the American Academy of Religion* 81.3 (2013): 698-733.

—'Believing Impossible Things: Scepticism and Ethnographic Enquiry'. In *Talking with the Spirits: Ethnographies from Between the Worlds*, ed. Jack Hunter and David Luke, 19-56. Brisbane, AU: Daily Grail Publishing, 2014.

Boyce-Tillman, June. *Constructing Musical Healing: The Wounds That Sing*. London: Jessica Kingsley, 2000a.

—*The Creative Spirit—Harmonious Living with Hildegard of Bingen*. Norwich, UK: Canterbury Press, 2000b.

—'Towards an Ecology of Music Education'. *Philosophy of Music Education Review* 12.2 (2004): 102-25.

—'Music as Spiritual Experience'. *Modern Believing: Church and Society* 47.3 (2006): 20-31.

—*In Tune with Heaven or Not: Women in Christian Liturgical Music*. Oxford, UK: Peter Lang, 2014.

—*Experiencing Music—Restoring the Spiritual: Music as Wellbeing*. Oxford, UK: Peter Lang, 2016.

Bremmer, Jan. *The Early Greek Concept of the Soul*. Princeton, NJ: Princeton University Press, 1983.

Bubandt, Nils. 'Interview with an Ancestor: Spirits as Informants and the Politics of Possession in North Maluku'. *Ethnography*. 10.3 (2009): 291-316.

Buber, Martin. *I and Thou*, trans. Walter Kaufmann. New York: Charles Scribner's Sons, 1970.

Buhrman, Sarasvati. 'Trance Types and Amnesia Revisited: Using Detailed Interviews to Fill in the Gaps'. *Anthropology of Consciousness* 8.1 (1997): 10-21.

Bunt, Gary R. *Virtually Islamic: Computer-Mediated Communication and Cyber Islamic Environments*. Cardiff, UK: University of Wales Press, 2000.

—*Islam in the Digital Age: E-jihad, Online Fatwas and Cyber Islamic Environments*, London: Pluto Press, 2003.

—'Religion and the Internet'. In *The Oxford Handbook of the Sociology of Religion*, ed. Peter B. Clarke, 705-22. Oxford, UK: Oxford University Press, 2008.

—*iMuslims: Rewiring the House of Islam*. Chapel Hill: University of North Carolina Press/ C. Hurst, 2009.

—'Decoding the Hajj in Cyberspace'. In *The Hajj: Pilgrimage in Islam*, ed. Eric Taliacozzo and Shawkat M. Toorawa, 231-48. Cambridge, UK: Cambridge University Press, 2016.

Calvin, John. *Institutes of the Christian Religion*, vol. 1, ed. John T. McNeill, trans. Ford Lewis Battles. London: SCM, 1960.

—*Commentary on the Book of Psalms*, vol. 1, trans. James Anderson. Grand Rapids, MI: Baker Book House, 1979.

Campbell, Heidi. *Digital Religion: Understanding Religious Practice in New Media Worlds*. London: Routledge, 2013.

Campbell, Reginald John. *The New Theology*. London: Chapman and Hall, 1907.

Carter, Chris. *Science and the Near-Death Experience: How Consciousness Survives Death*. Rochester, NY: Inner Traditions, 2010.

Carter, Warren. 'The Prologue and John's Gospel: Function, Symbol and the Definitive Word', *Journal for the Study of the New Testament* 39 (1990): 35-58.

Castillo, Richard. 'Divided Consciousness and Enlightenment in Hindu Yogis'. *The Anthropology of Consciousness* 2.304 (1991): 1-6.

Clarke, Isabel. 'There is a Crack in Everything—That's How the Light Gets In. In *Ways of Knowing*, ed. Chris Clarke, 20-102. Exeter, UK: Imprint Academic, 2005.

Claus, Peter Jay. 'Spirit Possession and Spirit Mediumship from the Perspective of Tulu Oral Traditions'. *Culture, Medicine and Psychiatry* 3 (1979): 29-52.

Clements, Keith W. *Lovers of Discord: Twentieth Century Theological Controversies in England*. London: SPCK, 1988.

Cohen, Emma. *The Mind Possessed: the Cognition of Spirit Possession in an Afro-Brazilian Religious Tradition*. Oxford, UK: Oxford University Press, 2007.

—'What is Spirit Possession? Defining, Comparing, and Explaining Two Possession Forms'. *Ethnos* 73.1 (2008): 101-26.

Cole, Peter. *Religious Experience*. London: Hodder Murray, 2005.

Coleridge, Samuel Taylor. *Biographia Literaia*, vol. I, ed. J. Shawcross. London: Oxford University Press, 1949.

Collin, Matthew. *Altered State: The Story of Ecstasy Culture and Acid House*. London: Serpent's Tail, 1997.

Couliano, Ioan P. *Out of this World: Otherworldly Journeys from Gilgamesh to Albert Einstein*. Boston, MA: Shambhala, 1991.

Cowan, Douglas E. and Dawson, Lorne L. (eds). *Religion Online: Finding Faith on the Internet*. New York: Routledge, 2004.

Crapanzano, Vincent. 'Introduction'. In *Case Studies in Spirit Possession*, ed. Vincent Crapanzano and Vivian Garrison, 1-40. New York: Wiley, 1977.

Crookall, Robert. *The Study and Practice of Astral Projection: The Definitive Survey on Out-of-Body Experiences.* Secaucus, NJ: Citadel Press, 1960.

Csikszentmihalyi, Mihaly. *The Evolving Self.* New York: Harper and Row, 1993.

Csikszentmihalyi, Mihaly and Isabella Selega Csikszentmihalyi. *Psychological Studies of Flow in Consciousness.* Cambridge, UK: Cambridge University Press, 1988.

Csordas, Thomas J. 'Embodiment as a Paradigm for Anthropology'. *Ethos* 18.1 (1990): 5-47.

—'Somatic Modes of Attention'. *Cultural Anthropology* 8.2 (1993): 135-56.

Cupitt, Don. *Mysticism After Modernity.* Oxford, UK: Blackwell, 1998.

Custodero, Lori. 'Seeking Challenge, Finding Skill: Flow Experience in Music Education'. *Arts Education and Policy Review* 103.3 (2002): 3-9.

—'Observable Indicators of Flow Experience: A Developmental Perspective of Musical Engagement in Young Children from Infancy to School Age'. *Music Education Research* 7.2 (2005): 185-209.

Czachesz, Istvan. 'Jesus' Religious Experience in the Gospels: Toward a Cognitive Neuroscience Approach'. In *Jesus—Gestalt und Gestaltungen: Rezeptionen des Galiläers in Wissenschaft, Kirche und Gesellschaft. Festschrift für Gerd Theißen zum 70. Geburtstag,* ed. Petra von Gemünden, David G. Horrell and Max Küchler, 569-95. Göttingen, SW: Vandenhoeck & Ruprecht, 2013.

Daily Mail. 'And lo, the Word of God Was Spread by Tablet... Church Uses WiFi and Computers to Stream Prayers and Hymns' (2013), at http://www.dailymail.co.uk/news/article-2305298/iWorship-Church-uses-WiFi-tablet-computers-stream-prayers-hymns-congregation-UKs-digital-service.html (accessed 7 April 2013).

—'Tweet Success for the Pope: Francis Beats Obama into Second Place as He is Named the Most Influential User on the Planet' (2014), at http://www.dailymail.co.uk/news/article-2675915/Tweet-success-Pope-Francis-beats-Obama-second-place-named-influential-user-planet.html (accessed 1 July 2014).

Dalai Lama. 'Dalai Lama' (2015), at https://twitter.com/dalailama (accessed 24 June 2015).

Dalenberg, Constance J., Bethany L. Brand, David H. Gleaves et al. 'Evaluation of the Evidence for the Trauma and Fantasy Models of Dissociation'. *Psychological Bulletin* 138.3 (2012): 550-88.

d'Aquili, Eugene. 'Senses of Reality in Science and Religion: A Neuroepistemological Perspective'. *Zygon* 17.4 (1982): 361-83.

d'Aquili, Eugene, and Andrew Newberg. 'Religious and Mystical States: A Neuropsychological Model. *Zygon* 28.2 (1993): 177-200.

—*The Mystical Mind: Probing the Biology of Religious Experience.* Minneapolis, MN: Fortress Press, 1999.

Davis, Caroline Franks. *The Evidential Force of Religious Experience.* Oxford, UK: Oxford University Press, 1989.

Dawson, Lorne L. 'The Mediation of Religious Experience in Cyberspace'. In *Religion and Cyberspace,* ed. Morten Hojsgaard and Margit Warburg, 15-37. London: Routledge, 2005.

Day, Abby. *Believing in Belonging: Belief and Social Identity in the Modern World.* Oxford, UK: Oxford University Press, 2011.

De Brébeuf, Jean. *Relation of What Occurred in the Country of the Hurons in the Year 1636. Travels and Explorations of the Jesuit Missionaries in New France,* vol. X, ed. Rueben Gold Thwaites, trans. James McFie Hunter. Cleveland, OH: Burrows Brothers, 1897 [1636].

De Botton, Alain. *Religion for Atheists; A Non-believer's Guide to the Uses of Religion*. London: Hamish Hamilton, 2012.

DeConick, April D. *Voices of the Mystics: Early Christian Discourse in the Gospels of John and Thomas and Other Ancient Christian Literature* (JSNTSS 157). Sheffield, UK: Sheffield Academic Press, 2001.

De Groot, Jan Jakob Maria. *The Religious System of China*, vol. I. Leyden, NL: Brill, 1892.

Deissmann, Adolf. *Paulus: Eine kultur- und religionsgeschichtliche Skizze*. Tübingen, DE: Mohr Siebeck, 1911.

De Sahagún, Bernardino. *The Florentine Codex*, trans. Arthur J. O. Anderson and Charles E. Desjarlais, Robert. *Body and Emotion: the Aesthetic of Illness and Healing in Nepal Himalayas*. Philadelphia: University of Pennsylvania Press, 1992.

Deutsch, Celia. 'Visions, Mysteries, and the Interpretive Task: Text Work and Religious Experience in Philo and Clement'. In *Experientia Volume 1: Inquiry into Religious Experience in Early Judaism and Early Christianity*, ed. Frances Flannery, Colleen Shantz and Rodney A. Werline, 83-102. Atlanta, GA: SBL, 2008.

Devereux, George. 'Shamans as Neurotics'. *American Anthropologist* 63.5 (1961): 1088-90.

Dewey, John. *Art as Experience*. New York: Capricorn Books, 1934.

Dibble. Santa Fe, NM: Monographs of the School of American Research, 1547-69 [trans. 1973–78].

Dickens, Charles. *A Christmas Carol*. London: Vintage, 2009.

Dickie, Maria Amelia Schmidt. *Religious Experience and Culture—Testing Possibilities*. Antropologia em Primeira Mão, 1. Florianópolis, BR: Universidade Federal de Santa Catarina, 2007.

Dillistone, Frederick William. *Religious Experience and Christian Faith*. London: SCM, 1983.

Dimach, Cassiope. 'Islam: The Quran' (2015), at https://play.google.com/store/apps/details?id=com.chaks.quran&hl=en (accessed 23 June 2015).

Dionysius the Areopagite. *The Celestial Hierarchy*. Whitefish, MT: Kessinger Publishing, 2004.

Douglas, Mary. *Purity and Danger*. London: Routledge & Kegan Paul, 1966.

—*Natural Symbols*. Harmondsworth, UK: Penguin, 1973.

Drinker, Sophie. *Music and Women, The Story of Women in their Relation to Music*. New York: City University of New York/The Feminist Press, 1995 [1948].

Dunn, James D. G. *Baptism in the Holy Spirit: A Re-examination of the New Testament Teaching on the Gift of the Spirit in Relation to Pentecostalism Today*. Studies in Biblical Theology. London: SCM, 1970.

—*Jesus and the Spirit: A Study of the Religious and Charismatic Experience of Jesus and the First Christians as Reflected in the New Testament*. London: SCM, 1975.

Durkheim, Émile. *The Elementary Forms of the Religious Life*, trans. Karen Fields. New York: Free Press, 1995 [1912].

Edwards, David Miall. *Crist a Gwareiddiad: Sef Traethodau ar Faterion Diwinyddol a Chymdeithasol* [Christ and Civilization: Namely Essays on Theological and Social Matters]. Dolgellau, UK: Hughes Bros, 1921.

—*Cristnogaeth a Chrefyddau Eraill* (*Christianity and Other Religions*). Dolgellau, UK: Hughes Bros, 1923.

—'Dr Thomas Rees of Bangor'. *The Welsh Outlook* 13.7 (1926): 182-85.

—*Bannau'r Ffydd: Dehongliad Beirniadol o Brif Athrawiaethau'r Grefydd Gristnogol* (The Pinnacles of Faith: A Critical Interpretation of the Primary Doctrines of Christian Religion). Wrexham, UK: Hughes a'i Fab, 1929.

Eliade, Mircea. *Shamanism: Archaic Techniques of Ecstasy*. New York: Pantheon Books,

1964. [Originally published as *Le Chamanisme et les Techniques Archaïques de l'Extase*, Paris: Librairie Payot, 1951].

Emmons, Charles F. 'Spirit Mediums in Hong Kong and the United States'. In *Talking with the Spirits: Ethnographies from Between the Worlds*, ed. Jack Hunter and David Luke, 301-23. Brisbane, AU: Daily Grail Publishing, 2014.

Engberg-Pedersen, Troels. 'The Construction of Religious Experience in Paul, In *Experientia Volume 1: Inquiry into Religious Experience in Early Judaism and Early Christianity*, ed. Frances Flannery, Colleen Shantz and Rodney A. Werline, 147-57. Atlanta, GA: SBL, 2008.

Engler, Steven. 'Ritual Theory and Attitudes to Agency in Brazilian Spirit Possession', *Method and Theory in the Study of Religions* 21 (2009): 460-92.

Erricker, Clive, Jane Erricker, Cathy Ota, Danny Sullivan, and Mandy Fletcher. *The Education of the Whole Child*. London: Cassell, 1997.

Espirito Santo, Diana, Arnaud Halloy, Pierre Liénard and Emma Cohen. 'Around The Mind Possessed: The Cognition of Spirit Possession in an Afro-Brazilian Religious Tradition by Emma Cohen'. *Religion and Society: Advances in Research* 1 (2010): 164-76.

Evans, Donald. 'Can Philosophers Limit What Mystics Can Do?'. *Religious Studies* 25 (1988): 53-60.

Evans-Pritchard, Edward E. *The Nuer*. Oxford, UK: Oxford University Press, 1940.

—*Witchcraft, Oracles and Magic among the Azande*. Abridged edn. Oxford, UK: Clarendon Press, 1976 [1937].

Fabian, Johannes. *Time and the Other*. New York: Colombia University Press, 1983.

Favret-Saada, Jeanne. *Deadly Words: Witchcraft in the Bocage*. Cambridge, UK: Cambridge University Press, 1980.

—'Unwitching as Therapy'. *American Ethnologist* 16.1 (1989): 40-56.

—'About Participation'. *Culture, Medicine and Psychiatry* 14 (1990): 189-99.

—*The Anti-Witch*. Chicago, IL: Hau Books, 2015.

Fenwick, Peter and Elizabeth Fenwick. *The Truth in the Light: An Investigation of Over 300 Near-Death Experiences*. London: BCA, 1995.

Feuerbach, Ludwig. *The Essence of Christianity*, trans. George Eliot. New York: Harper, 1957.

Firth, Raymond. *Tikopia Ritual and Belief*. Boston, MA: Beacon, 1967.

Fitzgerald, Timothy. '"Experiences Deemed Religious": Radical Critique or Temporary Fix? Strategic Ambiguity in Ann Taves' *Religious Experience Reconsidered*'. *Religion* 40.4 (2010): 296-99.

Flannery, Frances, Nicolae Roddy, Colleen Shantz and Rodney A. Werline (eds.). 'Introduction: Religious Experience, Past and Present'. In *Experientia*, vol. 1, 1-10. Atlanta, GA: SBL, 2008.

Foges, Peter. 'An Atheist Meets the Masters of the Universe'. *Lapham's Quarterly* (2010), at http://www.laphamsquarterly.org/roundtable/roundtable/an-atheist-meets-the-masters-of-the-universe.php (accessed 06 June 2013).

Ford, David. *Self and Salvation, Being Transformed*. Cambridge, UK: Cambridge University Press, 1999.

Forman, Robert K. C. 'Mysticism, Constructivism, and Forgetting'. In *The Problem of Pure Consciousness*, ed. R. K. C. Forman, 3-49. Oxford, UK: Oxford University Press, 1990.

—*The Innate Capacity*. New York: Oxford University Press, 1998.

Fox, Mark. *Religion, Spirituality and the Near-Death Experience*. London: Routledge, 2002.

Francis, Leslie J. *Faith and Psychology: Personality, Religion and the Individual.* London: Darton, Longman and Todd, 2005.

Fox, Matthew and Rupert Sheldrake. *The Physics of Angels: Exploring the Realm Where Science and Spirit Meet.* New York: Monkfish Book Publishing, 1996.

Franks-Davis, Caroline. *The Evidential Force of Religious Experience.* Oxford, UK: Clarendon Press, 1989.

Frazer, James. *The Golden Bough.* 2 vols. London, 1890.

Frey, Jörg and John R. Levison. 'The Origins of Early Christian Pneumatology: On the Rediscovery and Reshaping of the History of Religions Quest'. In *The Holy Spirit, Inspiration, and the Cultures of Antiquity: Multidisciplinary Perspectives*, 1-37. Berlin: de Gruyter, 2014.

Gabbard, Glen O. and Stuart W. Twemlow. *With the Eyes of the Mind: An Empirical Analysis of Out-of-body States.* New York: Praeger, 1984.

Gabrielsson, Alf. *Strong Experiences with Music: Music is Much More than Just Music*, trans. Rod Bradbury. Oxford: Oxford University Press, 2011.

Gabrielsson, Alf and S. Lindstrom. 'On Strong Experiences of Music'. *Musik, Psychologie, Jahrbuch der Deutschen Gesellschaft fur Musikpsychologie* 10 (1993): 118-39.

Gaita, Raimond. *A Common Humanity; Thinking About Love and Truth and Justice.* London: Routledge, 2002.

Galtung, Johan. 'Peace, Music and the Arts: In Search of Interconnections'. In *Music and Conflict transformation: Harmonies and Dissonances in Geopolitics*, ed. Olivier Urbain, 53-62. London: I. B. Tauris, 2008.

Gardiner, Eileen (ed.). *Visions of Heaven and Hell Before Dante.* New York: Italica, 1989.

Gass, Robert and Kathleen A. Brehony. *Chanting: Discovering Spirit in Sound.* London: Broadway, 2000.

G-dcast. 'G-dcast' (2014), at http://www.g-dcast.com/# (accessed 01 July 2014).

Geertz, Armin W. 'Brain, Body and Culture: A Biocultural Theory of Religion'. *Method and Theory in the Study of Religion* 22 (2010): 304-21.

Glass-Coffin, Bonnie. 'Belief Is Not Experience: Transformation as a Tool for Bridging the Ontological Divide in Anthropological Research and Reporting'. *International Journal of Transpersonal Studies* 32 (2013): 117-26.

Godwin, Jocelyn. *Music, Magic and Mysticism: A Sourcebook.* London: Arkana, 1987.

Goldman, Jonathan. *Healing Sounds—The Power of Harmonics.* Shaftesbury, Dorset, UK: Element Books, 1992.

Goldman, Márcio. 'A Construção Ritual da Pessoa: A Possessão no Candomblé'. *Religião e Sociedade* 12.1 (1985): 22-54.

—'Os Tambores dos Vivos e os Tambores dos Mortos. Etnografia, Antropologia e Política em Ilhéus, Bahia'. *Revista de Antropologia* 46.2 (2003): 446-76.

—'Jeanne Favret-Saada, os Afetos, a Etnografia'. *Cadernos de Campo* 13 (2005): 149-53.

—'Alteridade e Experiência: Antropologia e Teoria Etnográfica'. *Etnográfica* 10.1 (2006): 161-73.

—'How to Learn in an Afro-Brazilian Spirit Possession Religion: Ontology and Multiplicity in Candomblé'. In *Learning Religion: Anthropological Approaches*, ed. David Berliner and Ramon Sarró, 103-19. New York: Berghahn Books, 2007.

Goodman, Felicitas. *How about Demons? Possession and Exorcism in the Modern World.* Bloomington: Indiana University Press, 1988.

Google Play. 'Guru Granth Sahib—Sikhism' (2015), at https://play.google.com/store/apps/details?id=com.hmobile.gurugranthsahib (accessed 24 June 2015).

Goulet, Jean-Guy and Bruce Granville Miller. *Extraordinary Anthropology: Transformations in the Field*. Lincoln: University of Nebraska Press, 2007 [2006].

Graham, Fabian. 'Vessels for the Gods: *Tang-Ki* Spirit Mediumship in Singapore and Taiwan'. In *Talking with the Spirits: Ethnographies from Between the Worlds*, ed. Jack Hunter and David Luke, 325-45. Brisbane, AU: Daily Grail Publishing, 2014.

Greenfield, Sidney M. *Spirits with Scalpels: The Cultural Biology of Religious Healing in Brazil*. Walnut Creek, CA: Left Coast Press, 2008.

Greyson, Bruce. 'The Near-death Experience Scale: Construction, Reliability and Validity'. *Journal of Nervous and Mental Disease* 171.6 (1983): 369-75.

—'The Incidence of Near-death Experiences. *Medicine and Psychiatry* 1 (1998): 92-99.

—'Near-death Experiences'. In *Varieties of Anomalous Experience: Examining the Scientific Evidence*, ed. E. Cardena, S. J. Lynn, and S. Krippner, 315-52. Washington, DC: American Psychological Association, 2000.

Griffith-Jones, Robin. 'Transformation by a Text: The Gospel of John'. In *Experientia Volume 1: Inquiry into Religious Experience in Early Judaism and Early Christianity*, ed. Frances Flannery, Colleen Shantz, and Rodney A. Werline, 105-23. Atlanta, GA: SBL, 2008.

Gunkel, Hermann. *Die Wirkungen des heiligen Geistes nach der populären Anschauung der apostolischen Zeit und der Lehre des Apostels Paulus*. Göttingen, SW: Vandenhoeck & Ruprecht, 1888.

Gunson, Niel. 'An Account of the Mamaia or Visionary Heresy of Tahiti, 1826–1841'. *Journal of the Polynesian Society* 7.2 (1962): 208-43.

Gunton, Colin E. *A Brief Theology of Revelation*. Edinburgh, UK: T & T Clark, 1995.

—*The Christian Faith: An Introduction to Christian Doctrine*. Oxford, UK: Blackwell, 2002.

—*Father, Son and Holy Spirit: Toward a Fully Trinitarian Theology*. London: T & T Clark, 2003.

—*The Barth Lectures*. London: T & T Clark, 2007.

Gustus, Sandie. *Less Incomplete: A Guide to Experiencing the Human Condition Beyond the Physical Body*. Winchester, UK: O-Books, 2011.

Guthrie, Stewart. *Faces in the Clouds*. New edn. New York: Oxford University Press, 1995.

Hadden, Jeffrey K. and Cowan, Douglas E. (eds.). *Religion on the Internet: Research Prospects and Promises*. New York: Elsevier Science, 2000.

Hageman, John et al. 'The Neurobiology of Trance and Mediumship in Brazil'. In *Mysterious Minds: The Neurobiology of Psychic*, ed. Stanley Krippner and Harris Friedman, 85-112. Santa Barbara, CA: Greenwood, 2010.

Halloy, Arnaud. 'Gods in the Flesh: Learning Emotions in the Xangô Possession Cult (Brazil)'. *Ethnos: Journal of Anthropology* 77.2 (2012): 177-202.

Halperin, Daniel. 'Memory and "Consciousness" in an Evolving Brazilian Possession Religion', *Anthropology of Consciousness* 6.4 (1995): 1-17.

Hamel, Peter. *Through Music to the Self—How to Appreciate and Experience Music Anew*, trans. Peter Lemusurier. Tisbury, UK: Compton Press, 1978 [1976].

Hanegraaff, Wouter J. *Esotericism and the Academy: Rejected Knowledge in Western Culture*. Cambridge, UK: Cambridge University Press, 2012.

Haraldsson, Erlendur. 'Spontaneous Psychic Phenomena and Folk-beliefs: National Surveys and National Differences'. *Journal of the Society for Psychical Research* 53 (1985): 145-58.

—*The Departed Among the Living: An Investigative Study of Afterlife Encounters*. Guildford, Surrey, UK: White Crow Books, 2012.

Hardy, Alister. *The Divine Flame: An Essay towards a Natural History of Religion.* Oxford, UK: Religious Experience Research Unit, 1966.

—*The Spiritual Nature of Man: A Study of Contemporary Religious Experience.* Oxford, UK: Oxford University Press, 1979.

Hariot, Thomas. *A Briefe and True Report of the New Found Land of Virginia.* London: n.p., 1588.

Harkins, Angela K. 'Religious Experience through the Lens of Critical Spatiality: A Look at Embodiment Language in Prayers and Hymns'. In *Experientia*, vol. 2, Linking Text and Experience, ed. Colleen Shantz and Rodney A. Werline, 223-42. Atlanta, GA: SBL, 2012.

Harner, Michael. *The Way of the Shaman: A Guide to Power and Healing.* New York: Bantam Books, 1982.

Harvey, Jonathan. *Music and Inspiration.* London: Faber and Faber, 1999.

Hay, David. *Exploring Inner Space: Scientists and Experience.* Harmondsworth, UK: Penguin Books, 1982.

—*Religious Experience Today: Studying the Facts.* London: Mowbray, 1990.

Hay David and Rebecca Nye. *The Spirit of the Child.* London: Fount, 1998.

Hebert, Russel, Dietrich Lehmann, Gabriel Tan, Fred Travis, and Alarik Arenander. 'Enhanced EEG Alpha Time-domain Phase Synchrony During Transcendental Meditation: Implications for Cortical Integration Theory'. *Signal Processing* 85.11 (2005): 2213-32.

Helland, Christopher. 'Virtual Tibet: From Media Spectacle to Co-Located Sacred Space'. In *Buddhism, the Internet, and Digital Media: The Pixel in the Lotus*, ed. Gregory Grieve and Danielle Veidlinger, 155-72. New York: Routledge, 2014.

Hills, Peter, and Michael Argyle. 'Positive Moods Derived from Leisure and Their Relationship to Happiness and Personality'. *Personality and Individual Differences* 25.3 (1998): 523-35.

Hives, Frank, and Gascoigne Lumley. *Glimpses into Infinity.* London: J. Lane, 1931.

Holbraad, Martin. 'Definitive Evidence From Cuban Gods'. *Journal of the Royal Anthropological Institute* (N.S.) (2008): 93-109.

—'Ontography and Alterity: Defining Anthropological Truth'. *Social Analysis* 53.2 (2009): 80-93.

Holloway, Richard. *Godless Morality.* Edinburgh, UK: Canongate, 1999.

hooks, bell. *Teaching to Transgress: Education as the Practice of Freedom.* New York: Routledge, 1994.

Hufford, David J. *The Terror that Comes in the Night: An Experience-Centred Study of Supernatural Assault Traditions.* Philadelphia: University of Pennsylvania Press, 1982.

—'Beings Without Bodies: An Experience-Centred Theory of the Belief in Spirits'. In *Out of the Ordinary: Folklore and the Supernatural*, ed. Barbara Walker, 11-45. Logan: Utah State University Press, 1995.

—'Sleep Paralysis as Spiritual Experience'. *Transcultural Psychiatry* 42.1 (2005): 11-45.

—'Modernity's Defences'. Presentation at a *Symposium on Anthropology of the Paranormal*, Esalen Institute Centre for Theory and Research, Big Sur, California, October 2013.

—'Sleep Paralysis'. In *Ghosts, Spirits, and Psychics*, ed. Matt Cardin, 289-93. Santa Barbara, CA: ABC-Clio, 2015.

Hultkrantz, Åke. *The North American Indian Orpheus Tradition.* Stockholm, SE: Statens Etnografiska, 1957.

Hunt, Harry. *On the Nature of Consciousness.* New Haven, CN: Yale University Press, 1995a.

—'Some Developmental Issues in Transpersonal Experience'. *Journal of Mind and Behavior* 16.2 (1995b): 115-34.

—'The Linguistic Network of Signifiers and Imaginal Polysemy: An Essay in the Co-dependent Origination of Symbolic Forms'. *Journal of Mind and Behavior* 16.4 (1995c): 405-20.

Hunter, Jack (ed.). *Paranthropology: Anthropological Approaches to the Paranormal.* Bristol, UK: Paranthropology, 2012.

—(ed.). *Strange Dimensions: A Paranthropology Anthology.* Llanrhaeadr-ym-Mochnant, UK: Psychoid Books, 2015.

Hunter, Jack and David Luke (eds.). *Talking with the Spirits: Ethnographies from Between the Worlds.* Brisbane, AU Daily Grail Publishing, 2014.

Hurtado, Larry. W. 'Religious Experience and Religious Innovation in the New Testament', *The Journal of Religion* 80 (2000): 183-205.

—*Lord Jesus Christ: Devotion to Jesus in Earliest Christianity.* Grand Rapids, MI: William B. Eerdmans, 2003.

Huskinson, Lucy and Bettina E. Schmidt. 'Introduction'. In *Spirit Possession and Trance: New Interdisciplinary Perspectives*, ed. Lucy Huskinson and Bettina E. Schmidt, 97-116. London: Continuum, 2010.

Independent. 'The Reason Why the Pope Has a Twitter and Not a Facebook Account' (2014), at http://www.independent.co.uk/news/people/the-reason-why-the-pope-has-a-twitter-and-not-a-facebook-account-9426746.html (accessed 23 May 2014).

Ingalls, Monique, Carolyn Landau, and Tom Wagner (eds.). *Christian Congregational Music, Performance, Identity and Experience.* Farnborough, UK: Ashgate, 2013.

Inglis, Brian. *Trance: A Natural History of Altered States of Mind.* London: Paladin, Grafton Books, 1990.

Ingold, Tim. *The Perception of the Environment: Essays on Livelihood, Dwelling and Skill.* London: Routledge, 2000.

Institute for Religious Studies. '*Heidelberg Journal of Religions* on the Internet' (2005), at http://journals.ub.uni-heidelberg/index.php/religions/ (accessed 26 June 2015).

iTunes. '*Bhagavad Gita*' (2010), at https://itunes.apple.com/gb/app/bhagavad-gita-sanskrit-english/id336105959?mt=8 (accessed 24 June 2015).

—'Leviticus app' (2013), at https://itunes.apple.com/us/app/leviticus!/id589546556?mt=8 (accessed 3 July 2014).

—'Buddhist Meditation' (2014), at https://itunes.apple.com/us/app/buddhist-meditation/id544695689 (accessed 24 June 2015).

James, Jamie. *The Music of the Sphere: Music, Science and the Natural Order of the Universe.* London: Abacus, 1993.

James, William. *The Principles of Psychology.* 2 vol. New York: n.p. 1890.

—*The Varieties of Religious Experience: A Study of Human Nature.* Rockwell, MD: Arc Manor, 2008, 1982, 1923 [1902].

—'A Suggestion About Mysticism'. *The Journal of Philosophy* 7.4 (2010): 85-92.

Jansen, Karl. *Ketamine: Dreams and Realities.* Santa Cruz, CA: Multidisciplinary Association for Psychedelic Studies, 2001.

Johnson, Luke Timothy. *Religious Experience in Earliest Christianity: A Missing Dimension in New Testament Studies.* Minneapolis, MN: Fortress Press, 1998.

Johnson, Paul. 'An Atlantic Genealogy of "Spirit Possession"'. *Comparative Studies in Society and History* 53.2 (2011): 393-425.

Jones, Gareth. *Christian Theology: A Brief Introduction.* Cambridge, UK: Polity, 1999.

Jordan, David K. *Gods, Ghosts, and Ancestors: Folk Religion in a Taiwanese Village*. Berkeley: University of California Press, 1972.

Kagan, Annie. *The Afterlife of Billy Fingers: How My Bad-Boy Brother Proved to Me There's Life After Death*. Charlottesville, VA: Hampton Roads, 2013.

Kalweit, Holger. *Dreamtime and Inner Space: The World of the Shaman*. Boston, MA: Shambhala, 1984 [trans. 1988].

Kanagaraj, Jey J. *'Mysticism' in the Gospel of John: An Inquiry into its Background* (JSNTSS 158). Sheffield, UK: Sheffield Academic Press, 1998.

Kanellopoulos, Panos. 'Response to Boyce-Tillman's Paper "Spirited Education—Religionless Spirituality"' at the *Ninth International Symposium on the Philosophy of Music Education* at Teachers College, Columbia University, New York, 05-08 June 2013.

Katz, Stephen T. 'Language, Epistemology, and Mysticism'. In *Mysticism and Philosophical Analysis*, ed. S. T. Katz, 22-74. Oxford, UK: Oxford University Press, 1978.

Kellehear, Allan. *Experiences Near Death: Beyond Medicine and Religion*. Oxford, UK: Oxford University Press, 1996.

Keller, Mary. *The Hammer and the Flute: Women, Power, & Spirit Possession*. Baltimore, MD: John Hopkins University Press, 2002.

Kelly, Edward F. and Emily Williams Kelly et al. (eds.). *Irreducible Mind: Toward a Psychology for the 21st Century*. Lanham, MD: Rowman & Littlefield, 2010.

Kenney, John Peter. *The Mysticism of Saint Augustine: Rereading the Confessions*. London: Routledge, 2005.

King, Sallie B. 'Two Epistemological Models for the Interpretation of Mysticism'. *Journal of the American Academy of Religion* 41.2 (1988): 257-79.

Kodály, Zoltán. *Psalmus Hungaricus*. Musical composition. Vienna, AT: Universal edn., 1923.

Krippner, Stanley. 'The Epistemology and Technologies of Shamanic States of Consciousness. In *Cognitive Models and Spiritual Maps*, ed. J. Andresen and R. K. C. Forman, 93-118. Bowling Green, OH: Imprint Academic, 2000.

—'Learning from the Spirits: Candomblé, Umbanda, and Kardecismo in Recife, Brazil'. *Anthropology of Consciousness* 19.1 (2008): 1-32.

Krippner, Stanley and H. L. Friedman (eds.). *Debating Psychic Experience*. Santa Barbara, CA: Praeger, 2010.

Kroeber, Alfred. 'Psychotic Factors in Shamanism'. *Journal of Personality* 8 (1940): 204-15.

Kung, Hans. *Mozart: Traces of Transcendence*. London: SCM, 1992.

Kuruvilla, Carol. 'Religious Mobile Apps Changing the Faith-based Landscape in America' (2013), at http://www.nydailynews.com/news/national/gutenberg-moment-mobile-apps-changing-america-religious-landscape-article-1.1527004 (accessed 23 November 2013).

Lachman, Gary. *Swedenborg*. New York: Tarcher/Penguin, 2012.

Lambek, Michael. *Human Spirits: A Cultural Account of Trance in Mayotte*. Cambridge, UK: Cambridge University Press, 1981.

—'Provincializing God? Provocations from an Anthropology of Religion'. In *Religion: Beyond a Concept*, ed. Hent de Vries, 120-38. New York: Fordham University Press, 2008.

Lancaster, Brian L. *Approaches to consciousness: The Marriage of Science and Mysticism*, Basingstoke, UK: Palgrave, Macmillan, 2004.

Lancelot, James. 'Music as Sacrament'. In *The Sense of the Sacramental: Movement and Measure in Art and Music, Place and Time*, ed. David Loades and Ann Loades Ann, 179-85. London: SPCK, 1995.

Landes, Ruth. *The City of Women*. New York: Macmillan, 1947.

Lang, Andrew. *Cock Lane and Common Sense*. New York: Longmans, Green, and Co. 1894.

—*The Making of Religion*. New York: Longmans, Green, and Co., 1898.

Laski, Marghanita. *Ecstasy: A Study of Some Secular and Religious Experiences*. London: Cresset Press, 1961.

Laughlin, Charles, John McManus, and Eugene d'Aquili. *Brain, Symbol, and Experience toward a Neurophenomenology of Consciousness*. New York: Columbia University Press, 1992.

Le Clercq, Chrétien. *New Relation of Gaspesia*, ed. and trans. W. F. Ganong. Toronto, CA: The Champlain Society, 1910 [1691].

Lee, Hwan Bong. 'Calvin's Sudden Conversion (*Subita Conversio*) and its Historical Meaning'. *Acta Theologica Supplementum* 5 (2004): 103-16 (at http://www.ajol.info/index.php/actat/article/viewFile/52272/40898, accessed 24 August 2015).

Leloup, Jena-Yves. *The Gospel of Mary Magdalene*, trans. Joseph Rowe. Rochester, VT: Inner Traditions, 2002.

Levinas, Emmanuel. *Totality and Infinity: An Essay on Exteriority*, trans. Alphonso Lingis. Pittsburgh, PA: Duquesne University Press, 1969.

Lévi-Strauss, Claude. *Structural Anthropology*. New York: Basic Books, 1963.

—*Introduction to a Science of Mythology*. 4 vols. London: Jonathan Cape, 1970-82.

Lévy-Bruhl, Lucien. *The Notebooks on Primitive Mentality*. Oxford, UK: Blackwell, 1975 [1949].

Lewis, Ioan M. *Religion in Context*. Cambridge, UK: Cambridge University Press, 1986.

—*Ecstatic Religion: An Anthropological Study of Spirit Possession and Shamanism*. Harmondsworth, UK: Penguin Books, 1989 [1971]. [Reprinted as *Ecstatic Religion: A Study of Shamanism and Spirit Possession*, 3rd edn. New York: Routledge, 2003.]

Lienhardt, Godfrey. *Divinity and Experience: The Religion of the Dinka*. Oxford, UK: Oxford University Press, 1961.

Lincoln, Andrew T. 'The Beloved Disciple as Eyewitness and the Fourth Gospel as Witness'. *Journal for the Study of the New Testament* 85 (2002): 3-26.

—*The Gospel According to St John*. Black's NT Commentaries. London: Continuum, 2005.

Lindbeck, George A. *The Nature of Doctrine: Religion and Theology in a Postliberal Age*. Philadelphia, PA: Westminster Press, 1984.

Lonergan, Bernard. *The Collected Works of Bernard Lonergan*. 5th rev. edn., ed. Frederick E. Crowe and Robert M. Doran. Toronto, CA: University of Toronto Press, 1992.

Lopez, C., P. Halje, O. Blanke. 'Body Ownership and Embodiment: Vestibular and Multisensory Mechanisms'. *Clinical Neurophysiology* 38.3 (2008): 149-61.

Luhrmann, Tanya M. *When God Talks Back*. New York: Knopf, 2012.

—'Hearing the Voice of God'. In *Strange Dimensions*, ed. Jack Hunter, 69-71. Llanrhaeadr-ym-Mochnant, UK: Psychoid Books, 2015.

Lukoff, David, Francis Lu and Robert Tuner. 'Toward a more Culturally Sensitive DSM-IV: Psychoreligious and Psychospiritual Problems'. *Journal of Nervous and Mental Disease* 180 (1992): 673-82.

Mahler, Gustav. *Fifth Symphony*. Musical composition. Leipzig, DE: Peters, 1904.

Malinowski, Bronislaw. *Argonauts of the Western Pacific*. London: Routledge & Kegan Paul, 1922.

—'The Unity of Anthropology'. *Nature* 112 (1923): 314-17.

—*Magic, Science, and Religion, and Other Essays*. Boston, MA: Beacon Press, 1948.

Mandoki, Katya. *Everyday Aesthetics: Prosaics, the Play of Culture and Social Identities*. Farnborough, UK: Ashgate, 2007.

Maslow, Abraham. H. 'The Creative Attitude'. In *Explorations in Creativity*, ed. Ross L. Mooney and Taher A. Razik, 40-55. New York: Harper and Row, 1967.

Mauss, Marcel. 'The Techniques of the Body'. *Economy and Society* 2.1 (1973): 70-88.

Mayer, Gerhard and René Gründer. 'The Importance of Extraordinary Experiences for Adopting Heterodox Beliefs or an Alternative Religious Worldview'. *Journal of the Society for Psychical Research* 75.1 (2011): 14-25.

McClenon, James. *Wondrous Events: Foundations of Religious Belief*. Philadelphia, PA: University of Pennsylvania Press, 1994.

—*Wondrous Healing: Shamanism, Human Evolution, and the Origin of Religion*. DeKalb, IL: Northern Illinois University Press, 2002.

McCutcheon, Russell T. 'Introduction'. In *Religious Experience: A Reader*, ed. Craig Martin and Russell T. McCutcheon, 1-16. Sheffield, UK: Equinox, 2012.

Meggitt, Justin. 'Review of L. T. Johnson, *Religious Experience in Earliest Christianity*'. *Journal of Theological Studies* 51 (2000): 685-88.

Metzinger, Thomas. 'Out-of-body Experiences as the Origin of the Concept of the "Soul"'. *Mind and Matter* 3.1 (2005): 57-84.

—*The Ego Tunnel: The Science of the Mind and the Myth of the Self*. New York: Basic Books, 2009.

Milne, Garnet Howard. *The Westminster Confession of Faith and the Cessation of Special Revelation: The Majority Puritan Viewpoint on whether Extra Biblical Prophecy is Still Possible*. Milton Keynes, UK: Patternoster, 2009.

Mittermaier, Amira. 'How to Do Things with Examples: Sufis, Dreams, and Anthropology'. In *The Power of Example: Anthropological Explorations in Persuasion, Evocation, and Imitation*, ed. Andreas Bandak and Lars Hojer, 129-43. London: Wiley-Blackwell, 2015.

Moen, Bruce. *Voyages into the Unknown*. Exploring the Afterlife Series, vol. 1. Charlottesville, VA: Hampton Roads, 1997.

Moody, Raymond. *Life After Life*. New York: Bantam, 1975.

Mooney, James. *The Ghost-Dance Religion and the Sioux Outbreak of 1890*. Washington, DC: Government Printing Office, 1896.

Monroe, Robert A. *Journeys Out of the Body*. New York: Broadway Books, 1971.

Moreira-Almeida, Alexander. 'Differentiating Spiritual from Psychotic Experiences'. *British Journal of Psychiatry* 195 (2009): 370-71.

Moreira-Almeida, Alexander and Francisco Lotufo Neto. 'Diretrizes Metodológicas para Investigar Estados Alterados de Conciência e Experiências Anômalas'. *Revista Psiquiatria Clínica* 30.1 (2003): 21-28.

Moreira-Almeida, Alexander, Francisco Lotufo Neto and Bruce Greyson. 'Dissociative and Psychotic Experiences in Brazilian Spirit Mediums'. *Psychotherapy and Psychosomatics* 76 (2007): 57-58.

Moreman, Christopher M. (ed.). *The Spiritualist Movement: Speaking with the Dead in America and around the World*, vol. 3, Social and Cultural Responses. Santa Barbara, CA: Praeger, 2013.

Motta, Roverto. 'Body Trance and Word Trance in Brazilian Religion'. *Current Sociology* 53.2 (2005): 293-308.

Münzel, Mark. 'Tanz als Verehrung der Götter oder Verhöhnung der Geister: Ein Vergleich Afrobrasilianischer und Amazonasindianischer Tänze'. *Jahrbuch Tanzforschung* 8 (1997): 150-61.

Murdock, George P. *Ethnographic Atlas*. Pittsburgh, PA: University of Pittsburgh Press, 1967.

Murdock, George and Doug White. 'Standard Cross-cultural Sample'. *Ethnology* 8 (1969): 329-69.

MuslimPro. 'Muslim Pro' (2015), at http://www.muslimpro.com/en/ (accessed 23 June 2015).

Newsom, Carol A. 'Religious Experience in the Dead Sea Scrolls: Two Case Studies'. In *Experientia*, vol. 2, Linking Text and Experience, ed. Colleen Shantz and Rodney A. Werline, 205-21. Atlanta, GA: SBL, 2012.

Newton, N. *Foundations of Understanding*. Philadelphia: John Benjamins, 1996.

Nina Rodrigues, Raimundo. *O Animismo Fetichista dos Negros Bahianos*. Rio de Janeiro: Civilização Brasileira, 1935.

Noddings, Nel, and Paul J. Shore. *Awakening the Inner Eye: Intuition in Education*. New York: Teachers College Press, 1984.

Noll, Richard. 'Shamanism and Schizophrenia: A State-Specific Approach to the "Schizophrenia Metaphor" of Shamanic States'. *American Ethnologist* 10.3 (1983): 443-59.

Noyes, Russell, Peter Fenwick, Janice Miner Holden, and Sandra Rozan Christian. 'Aftereffects of Pleasurable Western Adult Near-death Experiences'. In *The Handbook of Near-Death Experiences*, ed. Janice Miner Holden and Bruce Greyson, 41-62. Santa Barbara, CA: Praeger, 2009.

Nuttall, Anthony David. *Pope's 'Essay on Man'*. London: George Allen and Unwin, 1984.

Odajnyk, V. Walter. *Gathering the Light: A Psychology of Meditation*. Boston, MA: Shambhala Publications, 1993.

O'Brien, Kelli S. 'Written that You May Believe: John 20 and Narrative Rhetoric', *Catholic Biblical Quarterly* 67 (2005): 284-302.

Oesterreich, Traugott K. *Possession, Demoniacal and Other, among Primitive Races, in Antiquity, the Middle Ages, and Modern Times*. New York: R. R. Smith, 1930.

Okely, Judith. 'Fieldwork Embodied'. In *Embodying Sociology: Retrospects, Progress and Prospects*, ed. Chris Shilling, 65-79. Oxford, UK: Blackwell, 2007.

—*Anthropological Practice: Fieldwork and the Ethnographic Method*. London: Berg, 2012.

Oliveros, Pauline. *Deep Listening*. Sound Recording. New Albion Records, San Francisco, 1989.

Osis, Karl. 'Insider's View of the OBE: A Questionnaire Study'. In *Research in Parapsychology*, ed. William G. Roll, 50-51. Methuen, NJ: Scarecrow Press, 1979.

Otto, Rudolf. *The Idea of the Holy: An Inquiry into the Non-rational Factor in the Idea of the Divine and its Relation to the Rational*, trans. John W. Harvey. Oxford, UK: Oxford University Press, 1950, 1936, 1923 [1917].

Parker, Thomas Henry Louis. *Calvin: An Introduction to His Thought*. London: Chapman, 1995.

Parnia, Sam, Ken Spearpoint, Gabrielle de Vos, Peter Fenwick et. al. 'AWARE—AWAreness during REsuscitation—A Prospective Study'. *Resuscitation* 85.12 (2014): 1799-1805.

Peerbolte, Bert Jan Lietaert. 'Paul's Rapture: 2 Corinthians 12:2-4 and the Language of the Mystics'. In *Experientia*, vol. 1, Inquiry into Religious Experience in Early Judaism and Early Christianity, ed. Colleen Shantz and Rodney A. Werline, 159-76. Atlanta, GA: SBL, 2008.

Piaget, Jean. *Biology and Knowledge*. Chicago, IL: University of Chicago Press, 1971.

Pierini, Emily. 'Becoming a Spirit Medium: Initiatory Learning and the Self in the Vale do Amanhecer'. *Ethnos: Journal of Anthropology* 81.2 (2016a): 290-314.

—*Becoming a Jaguar: Spiritual Routes in the Vale do Amanhecer*. In *Handbook of Brazilian Religions*, ed. Bettina E. Schmidt and Steven Engler. Leiden, NL: Brill, forthcoming 2016b.

Pilch, John J. *Flights of the Soul: Visions, Heavenly Journeys, and Peak Experiences in the Biblical World*. Grand Rapids, MI: Eerdmans, 2011.

Pink, Sarah. *Doing Sensory Ethnography*. London: Sage, 2009.

Platthy, Jeno. *Near-Death Experiences in Antiquity*. Santa Claus, IN: Federation of International Poetry Associations of UNESCO, 1992.

Polanyi, Michael. *Personal Knowledge: Towards a Post-Critical Philosophy*, 1958. London: Routledge and K. Paul, 1958.

—*The Tacit Dimension*. Garden City, NY: Doubleday, 1966.

Pontifex. 'Pope Francis' (2012), at https://twitter.com/Pontifex (accessed 24 June 2015).

Pontificium Consilium de Communicationibus Socialibus. 'iTunes: The Pope App' (2015), at https://itunes.apple.com/en/app/the-pope-app/id593468235?mt=8 (accessed 24 June 2015).

Pope, Alexander. *An Essay on Man*, ed. M. Mack. London: Methuen, 1950.

Previc, Fred. 'The Role of the Extrapersonal Brain Systems in Religious Activity. *Consciousness and Cognition* 15 (2006): 500-39.

—*The Dopaminergic Mind in Human Evolution and History*. Cambridge, UK: Cambridge University Press, 2009.

Proudfoot, Wayne. *Religious Experience*. Berkeley: University of California Press, 1985.

—'Response'. *Journal of the American Academy of Religion* 61.4 (1993): 793-803.

Purce, Jill. 'The Healing Voice', at http://www.jillpurce.com/ (accessed 27 April 2016).

Radcliffe-Brown, A. R. *Structure and Function in Primitive Society*. London: Cohen & West, 1952.

Räisänen, Heikki. *Beyond New Testament Theology: A Story and a Programme*. 2nd edn. London: SCM, 2000.

Rankin, Marianne. *An Introduction to Religious and Spiritual Experience*. London: Continuum, 2008 [2005].

Religious Experience Research Centre (RERC). Accounts of Religious Experience. Archives at Lampeter University, UK.

Rennie, Bryan. 'Manufacturing McCutcheon: The Failure of Understanding in the Academic Study of Religion'. *Culture and Religion* 1.1 (2000): 105-12.

Reynolds, Benjamin E. *The Apocalyptic Son of Man in the Gospel of John* (WUNT 2.249). Tübingen, DE: Mohr Siebeck, 2008.

Ricoeur, Paul. 'The Model of the Text: Meaningful Action Considered as a Text'. *Social Research* 38.3 (1971): 529-62.

—*Figuring the Sacred: Religion, Narrative and Imagination*, ed. M. I. Wallace, trans. D. Pellauer. Minneapolis, MN: Fortress Press, 1995.

Robinson, John A. T. *Honest to God*. London: SCM, 1963.

Robinson, Edward. *The Original Vision: A Study of the Religious Experience of Childhood*, Oxford: Religious Experience Research Centre, 1977.

Robinson, Ken. *Out of our Minds: Learning to be Creative*. Oxford: Capstone, 2001.

Rock, Adam and Stanley Krippner. 'Demystifying Shamans and Their World: A Multidisciplinary Study'. Charlottesville, VA: Imprint Academic, 2011.

Rosaldo, Renato. 'Grief and Headhunter's Rage: On the Cultural Force of Emotions'.

In *Text, Play and Story: The Construction and Reconstruction of Self and Society*, ed. Edward Bruner, 178-95. Washington, DC: American Ethnological Society, 1984.

Roth, Gabrielle. *Sweating My Prayers—An interview with Alex Fisher*, 1992.

Rouget, Gilbert. *Music and Trance: A Theory of the Relations between Music and Possession*, trans. Brunhilde Biebuyck. Chicago, IL: University of Chicago Press, 1987.

Rowland, Christopher. *The Open Heaven: A Study of Apocalyptic in Judaism and Early Christianity*. London: SPCK, 1982.

Rowland, Christopher, Patricia Gibbons, and Vicente Dobroruka. 'Visionary Experience in Ancient Judaism and Christianity'. In *Paradise Now: Essays on Early Jewish and Christian Mysticism*, ed. April D. DeConick, 41-56. Atlanta, GA: SBL, 2006.

Rowland, Christopher, and Christopher R. A. Morray-Jones. *The Mystery of God: Early Jewish Mysticism and the New Testament* (CRINT 12). Leiden, NL: Brill, 2009.

Ruby, Robert H. and John A. Brown. *John Slocum and the Indian Shaker Church.* Norman: University of Oklahoma, 1996.

Ryle, Gilbert. *The Concept of Mind*. Chicago, IL: University of Chicago Press, 1949.

Saliers, Don E. *Music and Theology*. Nashville, TN: Abingdon, 2007.

Santori, Penny. *The Near-death Experiences of Hospitalized Intensive Care Patients: A Five-year Clinical Study*. Lampeter, UK: Mellen, 2008.

Schachter, Stanley and Jerome E. Singer. 'Cognitive, Social, and Physiological Determinants of Emotional State'. *Psychological Review* 69 (1962): 379-99.

Schachter, Steven. 'Religion and the Brain: Evidence from Temporal Lobe Epilepsy'. In *Where God and Science Meet: How Brain and Evolutionary Studies Alter our Understanding of Religion*, ed. P. McNamara, 171-88. Westport, CT: Praeger, 2006.

Schleiermacher, Friedrich. *On Religion: Speeches to Its Cultured Despisers*, trans. John Oman. Louisville, KY: Westminster/John Knox Press, 1994 [1799].

—*The Christian Faith*, trans. H. R. Mackintosh and J. S. Stewart. London: T & T Clark, 1999 [1830].

Schmidt, Bettina E. *Von Geistern, Orichas und den Puertoricanern: zur Verbindung von Religion und Ethnizität*. Marburg, DE: Curupira, 1995.

—*Caribbean Diaspora in USA: Diversity of Caribbean Religions in New York City*. Aldershot, UK: Ashgate, 2008.

—*Spirit and Trance in Brazil: Anthropology of Religious Experiences*. London: Bloomsbury, 2016.

Schoun, Frithjof. *The Transcendent Unity of Religions*, trans. P. Townsend. New York: Harper and Row, 1975.

Seligman, Rebecca and Laurence Kirmayer. 'Dissociative Experience and Cultural Neuroscience: Narrative, Metaphor and Mechanism. *Medicine and Psychiatry* 32.1 (2008): 31-64.

Sharf, Robert. 'Experience'. In *Critical Terms in Religious Studies*, ed. M. C. Taylor, 94-115. Chicago, IL: University of Chicago Press, 1998. Repr. as 'The Rhetoric of Experience and the Study of Religion'. *Journal of Consciousness Studies* 7.11/12 (2000): 267-87.

Shiels, Dean. 'A Cross-cultural Study of Beliefs in Out-of-the-body Experiences'. *Journal of the Society for Psychical Research* 49.775 (1978): 697-741.

Short, Larry. 'Mysticism, Mediation, and the Non-lingusitic'. *Journal of the American Academy of Religion* 93.4 (1995): 659-75.

Shushan, Gregory. *Conceptions of the Afterlife in Early Civilizations: Universalism, Constructivism, and Near-Death Experience*. London: Continuum, 2009.

—'Afterlife conceptions in the Vedas'. *Religion Compass* 5.6 (2011): 202-13.

—'Rehabilitating the Neglected "Similar": Confronting the Issue of Cross-cultural Similarities in the Study of Religions'. *Paranthropology: Journal of Anthropological Approaches to the Paranormal* 4.2 (2013): 48-53.

—'Extraordinary Experiences and Religious Beliefs: Deconstructing Some Contemporary Philosophical Axioms.' *Method and Theory in the Study of Religion* 26 (2014): 384-416.

—*Near-Death Experience, Shamanism, and Afterlife Conceptions in Indigenous Societies: An Ethnohistorical Approach*, forthcoming.

Silverman, Julian. 'Shamanism and Acute Schizophrenia'. *American Anthropologist* 69 (1967): 21-31.

Singh, Jasjit. 'Sikh-ing Online: the Role of the Internet in the Religious Lives of Young British Sikhs'. *Contemporary South Asia* 22 (2014): 82-97.

Small, Christopher. *Musicking: The Meanings of Performing and Listening*. Middletown, CT: Wesleyan University Press, 1998.

Smart, Ninian. *The Religious Experience of Mankind*, 3rd edn., 8th edn. New York: Charles Scribner's Sons, 1978, 1984 [1969].

Smith, Dwight Moody. *John*. Abingdon New Testament Commentaries. Nashville, TN: Abingdon Press, 1999.

Smith, Huston. *Forgotten Truth: The Primordial Tradition*. New York: Harper and Row, 1976.

—*Cleansing the Doors of Perception: The Religious Significance of Entheogenic Plants and Chemicals*. Los Angeles, CA: Tarcher, 2000.

Smith, Wilfred Cantwell. *The Meaning and End of Religion*. London: SPCK 1978 [1962].

Stevenson, Ian and Bruce Greyson. 'Near-Death Experiences: Relevance to the Question of Survival after Death'. In *The Near-Death Experience: A Reader*, ed. Lee W. Bailey and Jenny Yates, 199-206. London: Routledge, 1996.

Stewart, Robert John. *Music and the Elemental Psyche: A Practical Guide to Music and Changing Consciousness*. Wellingborough, UK: Aquarian Press, 1987.

Stocking, George W. Jr. *After Tylor: British Social Anthropology 1888-1951*. London: Athlone Press, 1996.

Stoller, Galen. *My Life After Life: A Posthumous Memoir*, ed. K. Paul Stoller. Santa Fe, NM: Dream Treader Press, 2011.

Stoller, Paul. *Fusion of the Worlds: an Ethnography of Possession among the Songhay of Niger*. Chicago, IL: University of Chicago Press, 1989.

—*Sensuous Scholarship*. Philadelphia: University of Pennsylvania Press, 1997.

Stoller, Paul and Cheryl Olkes. *In Sorcery's Shadow*. Chicago, IL: University of Chicago Press, 1987.

Stone, Michael E. 'Apocalyptic—Vision or Hallucination?'. In *Selected Studies in Pseudepigrapha and Apocrypha with Special Reference to the Armenian Tradition* (SVTP 9), 419-28. Leiden, NL: Brill, 1991.

Stroebe, Wolfgang and Margaret S. Stroebe. *Bereavement and Health: The Psychological and Physical Consequences of Partner Loss*. Cambridge, UK: Cambridge University Press, 1987.

Sutcliffe, Steven J. and Ingvild S. Gilhus (eds.). *New Age Spirituality: Rethinking Religion*. Durham, UK: Acumen, 2013.

Swatridge, Colin. *Oxford Guide to Effective Argument and Critical Thinking*. Oxford, UK: Oxford University Press, 2014.

Swedenborg, Emanuel. *The Economy of the Animal Kingdom*. New York: New Church Board of Publication, 1903 [1740-41].

Taimni, I. K. *The Science of Yoga*. Wheaton, IL: Theosophical Publishing House, 1967.

Takahashi, T., T. Murata, T. Hamada, M. Omori, H. Kosaka, M. Kikuchi, H. Yoshida and Y. Wada. 'Changes in EEG and Autonomic Nervous System Activity During Meditation and Their Association with Personality Traits'. *International Journal of Psychophysiology* 55.2 (2005): 199-207.

Taves, Ann. *Fits, Trances, and Visions: Experiencing Religion and Explaining Experience from Wesley to James*. Princeton, NJ: Princeton University Press, 1999.

—*Religious Experience Reconsidered*. Princeton, NJ: Princeton University Press, 2009.

Taylor, Eugene, Michael Murphy, and Steven Donovan. *The Physical and Psychological Effects of Meditation: A Review of Contemporary Research with a Comprehensive Bibliography: 1931-1996*. Sausalito, CA: Institute of Noetic Sciences, 1997.

Thalbourne Michael A., Luke Bartemucci, P. S. Delin, B. Fox, and O. Nofi. 'Transliminality, Its Nature and Correlates'. *The Journal of the American Society for Psychical Research* 91 (1997): 305-31.

Thomas, Terence, and Elizabeth Manning. 'The Iconic Function of Music'. In *The Sense of the Sacramental: Movement and Measure in Art and Music, Place and Time*, ed. David Brown and Ann Loades, 159-71. London: SPCK, 1995.

Thompson, Marianne Meye. *The God of the Gospel of John*. Grand Rapids, MI: William B. Eerdmans, 2001.

—'Jesus: "The One Who Sees God"'. In *Israel's God and Rebecca's Children: Christology and Community in Early Judaism and Christianity. Essays in Honor of Larry W. Hurtado and Alan F. Segal*, ed. David B. Capes, April D. DeConick, Helen K. Bond, and Troy A. Miller, 215-26. Waco, TX: Baylor University Press, 2007.

Tite, Philip L. 'Theoretical Challenges in Studying Religious Experience in Gnosticism: A Prolegomena for Social Analysis', *Bulletin for the Study of Religion* 42 (2013): 8-18.

Tsai, Yi-jia and Ping-yin Kuan. 'Conceptualization and Methodology of the Survey'. In *Religious Experience in Contemporary Taiwan*, ed. Yen-zen Tsai, 19-31. Taipei, TW: Graduate Institute of Religious Studies, National Chengchi University, 2010.

Turner, Edith. *Experiencing Ritual*. Philadelphia: University of Pennsylvania Press, 1992.

—'The Reality of Spirits: A Tabooed or Permitted Field of Study'. *Anthropology of Consciousness* 4.1 (1993): 9-12.

—*Heart of Lightness*. Oxford: Berghahn, 2005.

—'Discussion: Ethnography as a Transformative Experience'. *Anthropology and Humanism* 35.2 (2010): 218-26.

—*Communitas: The Anthropology of Collective Joy*. New York: Palgrave Macmillan, 2012.

Turner, Harold W. and Peter R. Mackenzie. *Commentary on 'The Idea of the Holy'*. Aberdeen, UK: Aberdeen People's Press, 1977.

Turner, Victor. *The Ritual Process: Structure and Anti-structure*. Ithaca, NY: Cornell University Press, 1991 [1969].

—*Dramas, Fields and Metaphors: Symbolic Action in Human Society*. Ithaca, NY: Cornell University Press, 1974.

Twitlomacy. 'How World Leaders Connect on Twitter' (2015), at http://twiplomacy. com/blog/twiplomacy-study-2015/ (accessed 23 June 2015).

Tylor, Edward Burnett. *Primitive Culture*. London: John Murray, 1871.

—'On a Method of Investigating the Development of Institutions, Applied to Laws of Marriage and Descent'. *Journal of the Anthropological Institute* 18 (1888): 288-89.

Tymn, Michael. *Resurrecting Leonora Piper*. Guildford, UK: White Crow Books, 2013.

Tyrrell, George Nugent Merle. *Apparitions*. London: Gerald Duckworth, 1943.

Urry, James. *Before Social Anthropology*. Philadelphia, PA: Harwood Academic, 1973.

Van der Weyer, Robert (ed.). *Hildegard in a Nutshell*. London: Hodder and Stoughton, 1997.

Van Gennep, Arnold. *The Rites of Passage*. London: Routledge & Kegan Paul, 1960 [1909].

Van Lommel, Pim. *Consciousness Beyond Life*. New York: Harper One, 2010.

Van't Spijker, Willem. *Calvin: A Brief Guide to His Life and Thought*, trans. Lyle D. Bierma. Louisville, KY: Westminster/John Knox, 2009.

Vatican. 'La Santa Sede' (2015), at http://w2.vatican.va/content/vatican/it.html (accessed 24 June 2015).

Vieira, Waldo. *Projections of the Conscious: A Diary of Out-of-Body Experiences*. New York: IAC, 2007.

Vitz Paul. *Psychology as Religion: The Cult of Self Worship*. London: Lion, 1979.

Viveiros de Castro, Eduardo. 'Cosmological Deixis and Amerindian Perspectivism'. *Journal of the Royal Anthropological Institute* 4.3 (1998): 469-88.

Wade, Jenny. 'In a Sacred Manner We Died: Native American Near-death Experiences'. *Journal of Near-Death Studies* 22.2 (2003): 83-115.

Wagner, Rachel. 'Our Lady of Persistent Liminality: Virtual Church, Cyberspace and Second Life'. In *God In The Details: American Religion in Popular Culture*, 2nd edn., ed. Eric Michael Mazur and Tara K. Koda, 271-90. Abingdon, UK: Routledge, 2011.

Ward, Colleen. 'The Cross-Cultural Study of Altered States of Consciousness and Mental Health'. In *Altered States of Consciousness and Mental Health*, ed. Colleen Ward, 15-35. Newbury Park, CA: Sage, 1989.

Warnock, Mary. *Imagination*. London: Faber and Faber, 1976.

Weisheipl OP, J. Athanasius. *Friar Thomas D'Aquino: His Life, Thought, and Work*. Garden City, NY: Doubleday, 1974.

Wesley, John. *The Works of John Wesley*, vol. 18, 1735-38, ed. W. R. Ward and R. P. Heitzenrater. Nashville, TN: Abingdon Press, 1988.

Wetzel, James. 'Review of J. P. Kenney, *The Mysticism of Saint Augustine: Rereading the Confessions*'. London: Routledge, 2005; also (2007), at https://ndpr.nd.edu/news/23095-the-mysticism-of-saint-augustine-rereading-the-confessions/ (accessed 24 August 2015).

Wilber, Ken. *The Spectrum of Consciousness*. Wheaton, IL: Theosophical Publishing House, 1977.

—*The Atman Project*. Wheaton, IL: Theosophical Publishing House, 1980.

—'The Spectrum of Development'. In *Transformations of Consciousness*, ed. Ken Wilber, Jack Engler, and Daniel Brown. Boston, MA: Shambhala Publications, 1986.

Williams, Catrin H. 'The Reception of Isaiah's Call-Vision in John 12:41'. In *Judaism, Jewish Identities and the Gospel Tradition: Festschrift for Professor Maurice Casey*, ed. James Crossley, 245-72. London: Equinox Press, 2010.

—'Abraham as a Figure of Memory in John 8.31-59'. In *The Fourth Gospel in First-Century Media Culture* (LNTS 426), ed. Anthony Le Donne and Tom Thatcher, 205-22. London: T & T Clark, 2011.

—'John (the Baptist): The Witness on the Threshold'. In *Character Studies in the Fourth Gospel: Narrative Approaches to Seventy Figures in John* (WUNT 1:314), ed. Steven Hunt, Francois Tolmie, and Ruben Zimmermann, 46-60. Tübingen, DE: Mohr Siebeck, 2013.

Williams, Catrin H. and Christopher Rowland (eds.). *John's Gospel and Intimations of Apocalyptic*. London: Bloomsbury, 2013.

Williams, Rowan. *Faith in the Public Square*. London: Bloomsbury, 2012.

Willoughby, William Charles. *The Soul of the Bantu*. London: Student Christian Movement, 1928.

Winkelman, M. 'Trance States: A Theoretical Model and Cross-cultural Analysis'. *Ethos* 14 (1986): 174-203.

—'Shamans and Other "Magico-religious Healers": A Cross-cultural Study of Their Origins, Nature, and Social Transformation'. *Ethos* 18.3 (1990): 308-52.

—'Shamans, Priests, and Witches. A Cross-cultural Study of Magico-religious Practitioners'. *Anthropological Research Papers* 44 (1992): i-vii, 1-191.

—'The Evolution of Consciousness: Transpersonal Theories in Light of Cultural Relativism'. *Anthropology of Consciousness* 4.3 (1993): 3-9.

—'Neurophenomenology and Genetic Epistemology as a Basis for the Study of Consciousness'. *J Social and Evolutionary Systems* 19.3 (1997): 217-36.

—*Shamanism the Neural Ecology of Consciousness and Healing.* Westport, CN: Bergin and Garvey, 2000.

—'Spirits as Human Nature and the Fundamental Structures of Consciousness'. In *From Shaman to Scientist*, ed. J. Houran, 59-96. Oxford, UK: The Scarecrow Press, 2004.

—*Shamanism: A Biopsychosocial Paradigm of Consciousness and Healing*, 2nd edn. Santa Barbara, CA: ABC-CLIO Praeger, 2010.

—'Afterword: Paradigms and Methods for Anomalous Research'. In *Paranthropology: Anthropological Approaches to the Paranormal*, ed. Jack Hunter, 199-214. Bristol, UK: Paranthropology, 2012.

—'Shamanism and Psychedelics: A Biogenetic Structural Paradigm of Ecopsychology'. *European Journal of Ecopsychology* 4 (2013): 90-115.

—'Shamanism and the Brain'. In *Religion: Mental Religion*, ed. Niki Kasumi Clements. Macmillan Interdisciplinary Handbooks: Religion Series. Farmington Hills, MI: Macmillan Reference USA, forthcoming 2016.

Winkelman, Michael and Doug White. 'A Cross-cultural Study of Magico-religious Practitioners and Trance States: Data Base. In *Human Relations Area Files Research Series in Quantitative Cross-cultural Data*, vol. 3, ed. D. Levinson and R. Wagner. New Haven, CN: HRAF Press, 1987.

Winkelman, Michael and Philip Peek (eds.). *Divination and Healing: Potent Vision.* Tucson: University of Arizona Press, 2004.

Wren-Lewis, John. 'The Dazzling Dark: A Near-death Experience Opens the Door to a Permanent Transformation'. *What is Enlightenment?*, n.d., at http://www.nonduality.com/dazdark.htm (accessed 18 April 2016).

Yao, Xinzhong and Paul Badham. *Religious Experience in Contemporary China.* Cardiff, UK: University of Wales, 2007.

Yeorgouli-Bourzoucos, Styliani. 'Improvisation in the Curriculum of the Special Music Schools in Hellas'. Unpublished PhD thesis. University College, Winchester, UK, 2004.

Young, David E. and Jean-Guy Goulet (eds.). *Being Changed by Cross-Cultural Encounters: The Anthropology of Extraordinary Experience.* Peterborough, ON, CA: Broadview Press, 1994.

YouVersion. 'YouVersion Announces New Bible App' (2015), at http://blog.youversion.com/2015/03/youversion-announces-new-bible-app-feature-verse-images/ (accessed 26 June 2015).

Zaleski, Carol. *Otherworld Journeys: Accounts of Near-Death Experiences in Medieval and Modern Times.* Oxford, UK: Oxford University Press, 1987.

Ziewe, Jurgen. *Multi-Dimensional Man: A Voyage of Discovery into the Heart of Creation* (2008), at http://www.lightandmagic.co.uk; http://www.multidimensionalman.com (accessed 19 May 2015).

Index